The Psychology of Love

Volume 1
The Many Forms and Rewards

Volume 2
Emotion and Romance

Volume 3
Meaning and Culture

Volume 4
Research and Literature

The Psychology of Love

Volume I

The Many Forms and Rewards

Michele A. Paludi, Editor

Women's Psychology

Michele A. Paludi, Series Editor

 PRAEGER

AN IMPRINT OF ABC-CLIO, LLC
Santa Barbara, California • Denver, Colorado • Oxford, England

Library of Congress Cataloging-in-Publication Data

The psychology of love / Michele A. Paludi, editor.
       v. cm. — (Women's psychology.)
   Includes bibliographical references and index.
   Contents: v. 1. The many forms and rewards —
   ISBN 978-0-313-39315-0 (hbk. : alk. paper) — ISBN 978-0-313-39316-7 (ebook)
   1. Love—Psychological aspects.   2. Love—Social aspects.   3. Love—Cross-cultural studies.   4. Interpersonal relations.   I. Paludi, Michele Antoinette.
   BF575.L8P783 2012
   152.4'1—dc23

                                                                    2011051532

ISBN: 978-0-313-39315-0
EISBN: 978-0-313-39316-7

16 15 14 13 12   1 2 3 4 5

This book is also available on the World Wide Web as an eBook.
Visit www.abc-clio.com for details.

Praeger
An Imprint of ABC-CLIO, LLC

ABC-CLIO, LLC
130 Cremona Drive, P.O. Box 1911
Santa Barbara, California 93116-1911

This book is printed on acid-free paper ∞

Manufactured in the United States of America

If someone thinks that love and peace is a cliché that must have been left behind in the Sixties, that's his problem. Love and peace are eternal.
—*John Lennon*

For Antoinette and Michael
With love,
Michele

Contents

Series Foreword   ix
Michele A. Paludi

Foreword   xi
Florence L. Denmark

Foreword   xiii
Joan C. Chrisler

Acknowledgments   xv

Introduction   xvii
Michele A. Paludi

1.   What Is Love?   1
Benita Zahn

2.   Yes, We Do. Even at Our Age   3
Nieli Langer

3.   Psychological Definitions of Love   15
Jennifer F. Hsia and William E. Schweinle

4.   Platonic Couple Love: How Couples View Their Close Couple Friends   19
Geoffrey L. Greif and Kathleen Holtz Deal

5. Sexual and Romantic Interests in Opposite-Sex Friendships 35
April Bleske-Rechek

6. Disinterested Love in Cross-Class Romance Films, 1915–1939 43
Stephen Sharot

7. Sexual Script or Sexual Improv? Nontraditional Sexual Paths 59
Wind Goodfriend

8. Support and Interference from Social Network Members:
A Conceptual Framework 73
Jacki Fitzpatrick

9. Media and Relationships: An Emerging Research Area 89
Kimberly R. Johnson and Bjarne M. Holmes

10. Breaking Up Is Hard to Do: The Impact of Relationship
Dissolution on Psychological Distress 107
Laura J. Hunt and Man Cheung Chung

11. Attachment and Romantic Relationships: The Roles
of Working Models of Self and Other 133
Erica G. Hepper and Katherine B. Carnelley

12. Crossing the Line Online: Racial Preference of Internet Daters 155
Kathryn A. Sweeney and Anne L. Borden

13. Woolf, Le Guin, and Winterson: Androgyny as a Literary
Strategy in Twentieth-Century Women's Writing 175
Cristina Liquori

Appendix: List of Feminist Books Dealing with Relationships for
Young Readers and Teens 197
Michele A. Paludi

About the Editor and Contributors 201

Index 207

Series Foreword

Michele A. Paludi

Because women's work is never done and is underpaid or unpaid or boring or repetitious and we're the first to get fired and what we look like is more important than what we do and if we get raped it's our fault and if we get beaten we must have provoked it and if we raise our voices we're nagging bitches and if we enjoy sex we're nymphos and if we don't we're frigid and if we love women it's because we can't get a "real" man and if we ask our doctor too many questions we're neurotic and/or pushy and if we expect childcare we're selfish and if we stand up for our rights we're aggressive and "unfeminine" and if we don't we're typical weak females and if we want to get married we're out to trap a man and if we don't we're unnatural and because we still can't get an adequate safe contraceptive but men can walk on the moon and if we can't cope or don't want a pregnancy we're made to feel guilty about abortion and . . . for lots of other reasons we are part of the women's liberation movement.

Author unknown, quoted in the *Torch*, September 14, 1987

This sentiment underlies the major goals of Praeger's Women's Psychology book series:

1. *Valuing women.* The books in this series value women by valuing children and affordable child care; by respecting all physiques, not just placing worth on slender women; by acknowledging older women's wisdom, beauty, and aging; by viewing women who have been sexually victimized

as survivors; by respecting women who work inside and outside of the home; and by respecting women's choices of careers, of whom they mentor, of their reproductive rights, their spirituality, and their sexuality.

2. *Treating women as the norm.* The books in this series make up for women's issues typically being omitted, trivialized, or dismissed from other books on psychology.

3. *Taking a non-Eurocentric view of women's experiences.* The books in this series integrate the scholarship on race and ethnicity into women's psychology, thus providing a psychology of *all* women. Women typically have been described collectively, but we are diverse.

4. *Facilitating connections between readers' experiences and psychological theories and empirical research.* The books in this series offer readers opportunities to challenge their views about women, feminism, sexual victimization, gender role socialization, education, and equal rights. These texts thus encourage women readers to value themselves and others. The accounts of women's experiences as reflected through research and personal stories in the texts in this series have been included for readers so they might derive strength from the efforts of others who have worked for social change on the interpersonal, organizational, and societal levels.

A student in one of my courses on the psychology of women once stated, "I learned so much about women. Women face many issues: discrimination, sexism, prejudices . . . by society. Women need to work together to change how society views us. I learned so much and talked about much of the issues brought up in class to my friends and family. My attitudes have changed toward a lot of things. I got to look at myself, my life, and what I see for the future" (Paludi 2002). It is my hope that readers of the books in this series also reflect on the topics and look at themselves, their own lives, and what they see for the future.

The Psychology of Love, a four-volume set, provides readers with the opportunity to accomplish this goal and offers suggestions for all of us who want to know more about romance, friendship, commitment, and attachment as well as how relationships begin, what sustains them, and what contributes to their dissolution.

REFERENCE

Paludi, M. 2002. *The psychology of women.* 2nd ed. Upper Saddle River, NJ: Prentice Hall.

Foreword

Florence L. Denmark

"Love" is a word that is used and heard every day of our lives. It is a thought, a feeling, and an expression that often has different meanings and serves different purposes for different people. For some, it is a feeling of desire to fully surround your life by a person or thing; for others, it serves to protect and preserve. Often people want to feel love so desperately that they are willing to do whatever is necessary to get it. It is love that we all search for in our lives, and it is love that drives us to behave in ways that deviate from our true selves.

The Psychology of Love is a scholarly four-volume set edited by Michele Paludi, an outstanding psychologist. All too often, books on the topic of love spoken about in the popular press are not scholarly or well researched. Yet love is a complex issue that requires the attention of scholars from many disciplines working together, and this book set meets that objective.

This book set brings together professionals from various fields of study who provide their insight, wisdom, and research to create a rich and engaging piece of work. The authors in this book cover the various forms and meanings of love, ranging from the historical development of love to love in relation to peace and violence. Love is explored through its context in poetry, philosophy, mythology, biology, and psychology.

The chapters are innovative and comprehensive, covering all aspects of love. Some of the information will be well known to some, but no matter how well informed, readers will be challenged to think differently about the subjects presented, and they will be rewarded with understanding and insight into the psychology of love.

Foreword

Joan C. Chrisler

How do I love thee?
Let me count the ways.

Elizabeth Barrett Browning, 1850

Ah, love. It is a topic of universal interest, and it has been at least since the time of humankind's earliest written records. The courtly love between squires and their ladies, the fond devotion between parents and children, the affectionate bonds of friendship, the passion between young lovers, and the warm companionship of elderly couples have been celebrated through the millennia, as have people's love and adoration of gods, goddesses, and nature. Love is surely the most common theme in poetry, novels, popular music, operas, and films, and it is among the most common in art. Its central place in cultures around the world illustrates its importance to the human psyche.[1]

Love is so important to us that we use the word loosely to describe our "relationship" to anything or anyone we care about deeply. We love our pets; our country; our most comfortable clothes; treasured gifts; warm, sunny days; our favorite food and drink; and the authors, actors, and musicians we admire. On occasion students have even told me that they love my classes.

A favorite class of many students is Intimate Relationships, a seminar that usually is fully enrolled and has a waiting list. According to Erik Erikson (1963 [1950]), the major task of young adulthood is intimacy versus isolation, and my students are eager to learn anything that might help them to secure and maintain a romantic partnership. I can count on them to scramble for the opportunity to present to the class during the week we discuss love. I always teach the course in the spring so that we can have a St. Valentine's Day party in class. Valentine's Day is the favorite holiday of lovers, a day set aside for romance and warm expressions of caring, often symbolized by handmade cards or expensive gifts. Those without a special someone can always hope for a Valentine card from a secret admirer.

People are preoccupied with love, but can we ever understand it? Is it a spiritual connection, a social construction, or a biochemical reaction? U.S. Senator William Proxmire of Wisconsin thought that love ought to remain in the province of poets and that we should all admit that it is more important to enjoy love than to understand it. He bestowed several of his Golden Fleece Awards (for projects that bilk taxpayers by wasting their money) on social scientists whose work is featured on the syllabus of my Intimate Relationships class. I take issue with his view, and I am pleased to see that the editor and authors of this volume share my stance. I look forward to reading their work and learning more about the importance of love and romance in art and in life.

Despite all the sadness in this world, love brings us happiness. Perhaps it is the only thing that can. Although the Beatles may be incorrect in their assertion that all we need is love, life might not be worth living without it. So here's to love and to *The Psychology of Love*—books for the head and the heart!

NOTE

1. "Psyche" is used variously to refer to the soul or the mind ("psychology," the study of the mind). In Greek mythology, Psyche was a mortal maiden so beautiful that Eros/Cupid himself fell in love with her.

REFERENCES

Browning, E. B. 1956. Sonnet 43 from *Sonnets from the Portuguese*. In *An Oxford anthology of English poetry,* 2nd ed., edited by H. F. Lowry and W. Thorp, 1059. New York: Oxford University Press.
Erikson, E. 1963 [1950]. *Childhood and society*. 2nd ed. New York: Norton.

Acknowledgments

When the power of love overcomes the love of power, the world will know peace.

Jimi Hendrix

For most of my career I have devoted research attention to and worked to combat violence and victimization in educational institutions, workplaces, and relationships. I have addressed power abuses committed by faculty, parents, dating partners, and supervisors/managers. I have seen the impact of such abuses on children, adolescents, and adults in terms of their emotional health, physical well-being, career goals, interpersonal relationships, and self-concept. And I have assisted college campuses and workplaces in preventing as well as dealing with the aftermath of violence, including gun violence.

Those of us who do this type of work need safe havens because the impact of surrounding ourselves with violence takes its toll on our own relationships, work, and sense of contributions to our disciplines, for we challenge the very power structure that fosters violence. It is through relationships I have cultivated over the years that I have found this respite from working on violence. I thank my family, friends, and colleagues for helping me to see Hendrix's lyrics are apt: Rosalie Paludi, Lucille Paludi, Carmen A. Paludi Jr., Paula K. Lundberg-Love, Florence L. Denmark, Darlene C. DeFour, Breena C. Coates, Steven Earle, Tony LoFrumento, Catherine Raycroft, David Raycroft, and Josephine Tan. The safe haven they provide helps me continue to do what many students and employees have requested of me: continue to make their lives safer.

My sincere thanks to Debbie Carvalko and her colleagues at Praeger for providing me this opportunity to take a break from editing another text on discrimination and violence and focus on love and peace.

My parents, Antoinette Rose Peccichio Paludi and Michael Anthony Paludi, deserve my recognition for encouraging me to continue to speak out about discrimination and violence and find peaceful solutions for schools and workplaces. They were first-generation Americans who experienced much discriminatory treatment. Most of the work on this four-volume set had been completed when my sisters and I acknowledged the thirtieth year since our father's passing and the twenty-sixth year since our mother's. Antoinette and Michael were peaceful and loving, which is why I dedicate this book set to them. In so doing, I offer them my praise. They followed this definition of love, one I cherish:

Love is patient, love is kind. It does not envy, it does not boast, it is not proud. It does not dishonor others, it is not self-seeking, it is not easily angered, it keeps no record of wrongs. Love does not delight in evil but rejoices with the truth. It always protects, always trusts, always hopes, always perseveres. (1 Cor. 13)

Introduction

Michele A. Paludi

WHAT IS LOVE? ANSWERS FROM POETRY, PHILOSOPHY, MYTHOLOGY, BIOLOGY AND PSYCHOLOGY

All you need is love.

The Beatles

Even a cursory glance at websites listing love quotations and poems reveals hundreds upon hundreds of definitions of "love" from poets, philosophers, lyricists, psychologists, and educators. For example:

Jean Anouilh: "Love is, above all else, the gift of oneself."
Robert Frost: "Love is an irresistible desire to be irresistibly desired."
E. Joseph Cossman: "Love is a friendship set to music."
Aristotle: "Love is composed of a single soul inhabiting two bodies."
Lao Tzu: "Love is of all passions the strongest, for it attacks simultaneously the head, the heart and the senses."
Zora Neale Hurston: "Love makes your soul crawl out from its hiding place."
Erich Fromm: "Love is union with somebody, or something, outside oneself, under the condition of retaining the separateness and integrity of one's own self."

And love is defined in Elizabeth Barrett Browning's famous sonnet:

How do I love thee? Let me count the ways.
I love thee to the depth and breadth and height
My soul can reach, when feeling out of sight

For the ends of Being and ideal Grace.
I love thee to the level of everyday's
Most quiet need, by sun and candle-light.
I love thee freely, as men strive for Right;
I love thee purely, as they turn from Praise.
I love thee with a passion put to use
In my old griefs, and with my childhood's faith.
I love thee with a love I seemed to lose
With my lost saints, —I love thee with the breath,
Smiles, tears, of all my life! —and, if God choose,
I shall but love thee better after death.

Mythologies have gods and goddesses of love (Stassinopoulos 2004). For example, in Roman mythology, Cupid or Amor is the god of passionate love; Venus is the goddess of passionate love. In Greek mythology, Aphrodite is the goddess of passionate love; Eros is the god of passionate love. Freya is the goddess of love in Norse mythology. Kama is the god of sensual love in Hindu mythology; Rati is the goddess of passionate love. And in Aztec mythology, Xochipilli is the god of love.

In addition, cultural characterizations of love also highlight forms of love for which individuals have the capacity (Graham and Christiansen 2009; Sprecher et al. 1994). For example, *amae* is a Japanese word meaning "indulgent dependence" and is central to child rearing in Japan. It includes mothers hugging and indulging their children. In Turkey, love is defined as love for a person, one's parents, or one's god. *Ask* is the term for being in love and is reserved for loving in a romantic or sexual way.

In Greek, there are five words for love: *agape* means love of the soul; *eros* is equated with passionate love, longing, and sexual desire; *philia* deals with love of family, friends, and community; *storge* refers to parental love for a child; and *xenia* is hospitality extended toward guests. In Japanese Buddhism, *ai* is caring, passionate love and a fundamental desire that develops toward selflessness or selfishness.

Contrast cultural definitions with those from the biological and social sciences. The field of biology views love as a mammalian drive, akin to thirst and hunger (Buss 2008; Kenrick 2008). Psychology views love from a social and cultural perspective (e.g., Hendrick and Hendrick 2008; Schmitt 2008). For example, Sternberg (1988) identified three elements that characterize relationships: passion, intimacy, and commitment. Sternberg's theory includes the following types of love:

1. Nonliking: neither passion, intimacy, nor commitment is present
2. Infatuation: only passion is present
3. Liking: only intimacy is present
4. Empty love: only commitment is present
5. Romantic love: both passion and intimacy are present
6. Fatuous love: both passion and commitment are present

7. Companionate love: both intimacy and commitment are present
8. Consummate love: passion, intimacy, and commitment are present

A theory of love by Hendrick and Hendrick (2008), referred to as Love Styles, identified six theories that individuals use in their interpersonal relationships:

1. Eros: passionate physical love based on physical appearance
2. Ludus: playful love
3. Storge: affectionate love that is based on similarity
4. Pragma: pragmatic love
5. Mania: unstable, highly emotional love
6. Agape: spiritual, altruistic love

In addition, Rubin (1970) measured both love and liking. He asked individuals regarding their attitudes toward their loved one. For example:

If (loved one) were feeling badly, my first duty would be to cheer him/her up.
I find it easy to ignore (loved one's) faults.
I would do almost anything for (loved one).
One of my primary concerns is (loved one's) welfare.
I would forgive (loved one) for practically anything.
I would greatly enjoy being confided in by (loved one).

Rubin (1970) also developed a Like scale. The following statements are from this scale:

I would highly recommend (friend) for a responsible job.
I have great confidence in (friend's) judgment.
(Friend) is one of the most likeable people I know.
(Friend) is the sort of person who I myself would like to be.

Individuals respond to each statement on a nine-point Likert scale from "Not True" to "Definitely True." Rubin identified romantic love as being made up of three elements: attachment (the need to be cared for and be with the other person); caring (valuing the other person's happiness and needs as much as your own), and intimacy (sharing private feelings and thoughts with the other person). Good friends score high on Rubin's Like scale; however, significant others rated high on his Love scale.

Perhaps children's definitions of love provide us with the most elegant answers to the question "What is love?" (amyfabulous 2008, 1):

"Love is when you go out to eat and give somebody most of your French fries without making them give you any of theirs." (Chrissy, six years old)

"Love is when my mommy makes coffee for my daddy and she takes a sip before giving it to him, to make sure the taste is OK." (Danny, seven years old)

"Love is like a little old woman and a little old man who are still friends even after they know each other so well." (Tommy, six years old)

"When you love somebody, your eyelashes go up and down and little stars come out of you." (Karen, seven years old)

"When my grandmother got arthritis, she couldn't bend over and paint her toenails anymore. So my grandfather does it for her all the time, even when his hands got arthritis too. That's love." (Rebecca, eight years old)

"Love is when a girl puts on perfume and a boy puts on shaving cologne and they go out and smell each other." (Karl, five years old)

"You really shouldn't say 'I love you' unless you mean it. But if you mean it, you should say it a lot. People forget." (Jessica, eight years old)

CELEBRATING A DAY OF LOVE

What is love? Just from this brief overview it is clear that love is any number of emotions and meanings, depending on the context. And there are many celebrations or holidays for love. For example, Valentine's Day was established in 500 AD by Pope Gelasius I (*History of Valentine's Day*, 2011). Although Pope Paul VI removed this celebration from the Roman calendar of saints in 1969, the religious observance of Valentine's Day is still allowed. Chaucer's "Parlement of Foules" is the first identified association between Valentine's Day and romantic love (Oruch 1981). Chaucer wrote the poem in honor of the first anniversary of the engagement of King Richard II of England to Anne of Bohemia (Kelly 1986):

For this was on seynt Volantynys day
Whan euery bryd comyth here to chese his make.
(For this was Saint Valentine's Day, when every bird cometh
there to choose his mate).

Today, St. Valentine's Day as a day of celebrating love is practiced throughout the world. Valentine's Day is referred to as Sevgililer Gunu, or "Sweethearts' Day," in Turkey. In Mexico, Costa Rica, and Ecuador, Valentine's Day is known as Dia del Amor y la Amistad, or "Day of Love and Friendship." A proverb in Slovenia states that "St. Valentine brings the keys of roots," therefore, plants and flowers begin to grow. Valentine's Day is the day when the first work in the fields and vineyard begins. In both Finland and Estonia, Valentine's Day is "Friend's Day": Ystavanpaiva in Finland and Sobrapaev in Estonia.

In the United States, Valentine's Day is celebrated on February 14. As I was completing much of the writing and editing of *The Psychology of Love*, Valentine's Day 2011 was being celebrated. As in previous years, advertisements from florists depicted roses as the classic symbol of romance. Restaurants featured Valentine

Day "specials," for example, "dinner and wine for two with chocolate cordials for dessert." Department stores and websites identified "gifts for your Valentine," in categories such as "romantic," "naughty," "personalized," and "unique." Radio stations played "classic love songs" such as "When a Man Loves a Woman," "You're in My Heart," "I Will Always Love You," and "Endless Love." Pictures of cupids with arrows graced mass-produced Valentine greeting cards, cards that historically were handwritten (Schmidt 1993).

In time for Valentine's Day, numerous websites listed the "most romantic movies ever made" to watch with your loved one. *Woman's World* magazine's (2011) Valentine's issue featured a story titled "What Does Your Favorite Movie Couple Say about You?" The article stated that individuals who favor *Gone with the Wind*'s Scarlett and Rhett are "persistent optimists." Fans of *When Harry Met Sally* were described as "down-to-earth brainiacs," people who prefer *Titanic*'s Rose and Jack were characterized as "dynamic romantics," and fans of *The Notebook*'s Allie and Noah were described as being "loyal go-getters." I decided to view some of these films in order to find how they answered the question that prompts considerable debate, speculation, and introspection: What is love?

THEMES IN ROMANTIC MOVIES: WHAT IS LOVE?

Characteristics of interpersonal love (defined as the love between two individuals that is deeper than like and the love found in families, in couples, in volunteer work, and in charity work) (Fehr 1994; Fletcher and Clark 2003; Hendrick and Hendrick 2008) include the following:

1. Affection: the appreciation of another person
2. Attachment: the satisfaction of emotional needs
3. Reciprocation: mutual love
4. Commitment: desire to maintain love
5. Emotional intimacy: exchanging emotions and feelings
6. Kinship: family bonds
7. Passion: sexual desire
8. Physical intimacy: living together
9. Self-interest: desiring rewards from another

As with the various definitions of love I presented at the beginning of this introduction, the films I watched highlight many forms of interpersonal love. Below, I summarize some of the films using the categories of love identified by psychologists.

Love is the word used to label the sexual excitement of the young, the habituation of the middle-aged, and the mutual dependence of the old.
John Ciardi

The movie *Valentine's Day*, for example, portrayed all of these forms of love identified by Sternberg (1988) and Hendrick and Hendrick (2008): the first love experience of adolescents (infatuation), the love in friendships, the more mature love of a couple that has been together for thirty or so years, and a mother's love for a child. Companionate love was depicted as well as empty love. In addition, the love of best friends (same- and other-sex friendships), consummate love, fatuous love, and romantic love were depicted in the film. Love was characterized nonverbally throughout the movie as selfless, giving, and unconditional. According to Hooli (2010), "The movie *Valentine's Day* has a message that a person can find love at any age. It is meant for people of all ages. The movie cuts across generations from a childhood crush to teenage angst and old age in showing the sweet and messy sides of either approaching or avoiding love" (1). This movie captures what research by Diamond, Fagundes, and Butterworth (2010) reported: "Through adolescence, emerging adulthood, middle adulthood, and late life, the individual's developmental status shapes the quality and functioning of his or her intimate relationships" (379).

> Grow old along with me, the best is yet to be.
>
> Robert Browning

The movie *The Notebook* also addresses love over the life cycle, but in this case the movie features one couple together from adolescence through later adulthood, from the "in-love stage" to a deep love that took thirty plus years to achieve. All forms of interpersonal love identified above are portrayed in this film. A main message of the movie is that passionate, everlasting love conquers everything, including illness, and is immortal. This movie deals with love of a partner who has Alzheimer's disease, who often does not remember her husband, their children, or grandchildren. The husband stays by her side because she is his "sweetheart." The male protagonist states, "I am no one special; just a common man with common thoughts, and I've led a common life. There are no monuments dedicated to me and my name will soon be forgotten. But in one respect I have succeeded as gloriously as anyone who's ever lived: I've loved another with all my heart and soul; and to me, this has always been enough." Thus this movie describes consummate love.

> And think not you can
> Direct the course of love,
> For love,
> If it finds you worthy,
> Directs your course.
>
> Kahlil Gibran

This definition of love, a love that remains through death, was a theme of *The Bridges of Madison County* and *Love Story*. *Bridges* depicts a middle-aged couple who have to come to terms with infidelity in marriage and the choices they make and later regret in relationships as older adults. The film depicts interpersonal love in stages, as does *The Notebook:* from affection to emotional intimacy, passion, reciprocation, and commitment. *Bridges* asks viewers to consider commitment to a love without physical intimacy in the form of living together, that is, romantic love. For example, Francesca, the female protagonist, wants to be with Robert but decides to remain in her marriage to Richard (companionate love) in order to provide a good role model for her teenage children. "But love won't obey our expectations," she states. "Its mystery is pure and absolute. What Robert and I had, could not continue if we were together. What Richard and I shared would vanish if we were apart. But how I wanted to share this. How would our lives have changed if I had? Could anyone else have seen the beauty of it?"

The last scene depicts Francesca's family and friends heeding her request to spread her ashes over the area in which she and Robert (with whom she only spent four days) spent romantic encounters before they each returned to their separate lives. Her request: "I gave my life to my family. I want what is left to go to Robert."

We may be more likely to accept the death of lovers in movies such as *The Notebook* and *Bridges* because death is typically associated with older adulthood. However, this is not the case with *Love Story*, which chronicles the early stages of love and marriage in twenty-something individuals. The movie begins with the male protagonist summing up the theme of the movie: "What can you say about a twenty-five-year-old girl who died? That she was beautiful and brilliant? That she loved Mozart and Bach, the Beatles and me?" The film was unsettling for many viewers when it was initially released; it remains so today. Viewers see the movie's ending as unfair, most likely because all forms of interpersonal love or of Sternberg's triangular theory of love did not have an opportunity to be experienced and expressed because of the female protagonist's, Jennifer's, untimely death. Romantic love is expressed by the protagonists; they wanted to experience consummate love. Viewers were drawn to this film's ending so much that "Jennifer," the female protagonist's name, was the most popular name for girls in the United States from 1970 to 1984 (Gibbons 2009).

THEMES IN ROMANTIC MOVIES: HIDDEN MESSAGES

A man falls in love through his eyes, a woman through her ears.
Woodrow Wyatt

In addition to illustrating theories of love, the films I watched conveyed hidden messages about love. For example, the maintenance of traditional gender-role behavior was expected in all aspects of interpersonal love. Men pursued women, men proposed to women, and women didn't "give in" to the men at first so they wouldn't be considered nonvirginal. Women who were independent thinkers and activists were considered unattractive. *The Way We Were* captures the theme of how romantic love and fatuous love never grow into consummate love when women speak their own voice. In one scene in this movie, the protagonists, Katie and Hubbell, highlight this theme:

> *Katie:* I don't have the right style for you, do I?
> *Hubbell:* No, you don't have the right style.
> *Katie:* I'll change.
> *Hubbell:* No, don't change. You're your own girl, you have your own style.
> *Katie:* But then I won't have you. Why can't I have you?

Movies such as *The Proposal* and *The Devil Wears Prada* convey the message that career women sacrifice healthy romantic relationships in order to be successful at their career, a message not conveyed about men in Hollywood movies. For men, having a relationship and a career is not seen as incompatible; for women, it is. Furthermore, most of the women characters, even those who are independent in their careers, are forever in search of the perfect man to fulfill their all of their needs (for example, characters in *Valentine's Day* and *Sex and the City*). And when their needs are not fulfilled, they engage in destructive behavior such as overeating, including overeating chocolate candy, of which, as one character in *Valentine's Day* comments, there is an overabundance on Valentine's Day.

Themes related to the maintenance of gender-role stereotypical behavior are reminiscent of research findings from Kay Deaux and Randel Hanna (1984). They reviewed eight hundred personal advertisements from four newspapers circulated on the East and West Coasts: the *Village Voice*, *National Single Register*, the *Wishing Well*, and the *Advocate*. Lesbian, gay, and heterosexual advertisements were included in their research. The advertisements were coded for the presence or absence of words/terms in the following categories:

1. Attractiveness (good-looking, cute, muscular, handsome, beautiful)
2. Sexuality (passionate, lustful, erotic, potent, butch, stacked)
3. Physical characteristics (weight, height, hair color, bearded, eye color)
4. Financial security (affluent, financially secure, well established)
5. Sincerity (dependable, loyal, trustworthy, honest)
6. Personality traits (intelligent, sense of humor, spiritual, caring, sensible, mature)
7. Hobbies/interests (likes to cook, art lover, athletic)
8. Occupation (career woman, lawyer, executive)
9. Demographic variables (race/ethnicity, marital status, age)
10. Interest in marriage (marriage-minded)
11. Interest in permanent relationship (long-term relationship, lasting relationship)
12. Request for photograph
13. Request for telephone number

Deaux and Hanna reported that, in general, women were interested in the psychological aspects of a potential relationship and men were concerned with objective and physical characteristics. Heterosexual women were concerned with financial security, specific occupational information, and sincerity. Lesbian women placed less emphasis on physical characteristics and offered more information about their interests, hobbies, and their own sincerity. Women were less likely to focus on preferring an attractive partner.

Similar findings were reported by Goode (1996), who reviewed the responses to fictional advertisements that were placed in four personal columns. The advertisements were seeking "a beautiful waitress," "an average looking female lawyer," "a handsome cabdriver," and an "average looking male lawyer." For example, the advertisement for "beautiful waitress" received 668 responses; the ad describing the "average looking female lawyer" received 240. The advertisement describing the "average looking male lawyer" earned 64 responses; the "handsome cabdriver" ad received 15 answers. Results suggest that men were more influenced by a physical attraction than by success and women were more influenced by occupational success than by physical attraction.

MALE DOMINANCE AND FEMALE PASSIVITY IN FILM: VIOLENCE AS NORMATIVE

Love means not ever having to say you're sorry.

Love Story

Judy: Love means not ever having to say you're sorry.
Howard: That's the dumbest thing I've ever heard.

What's Up, Doc?

Many women and men have been socialized to believe that a woman's love for a man is equated with a woman's submission to the man. This aspect of a relationship contributes to role strain for women, who report being pressured to be active and passive simultaneously. Simone de Beauvoir (1961 [1949]) described this gender role pressure: "Shut up in the sphere of the relative, destined to the male from childhood, habituated to seeing in him a superb being whom she cannot possibly equal, the woman . . . will dream . . . of amalgamating herself with the sovereign. . . . She chooses to desire her enslavement so ardently that it will seem to her the expression of her liberty. . . . Love becomes for her a religion" (604).

These studies suggest that within heterosexual romantic relationships, gender-role stereotypes are being played out by both women and men in the establishment stage of the relationship and in the continuation of the relationship. Men are dominant; women are passive if the relationship is to survive. And Rubin (1976) referred to men and women in romantic relationships as "intimate strangers." This statement also refers to the unequal power in many romantic relationships.

Furthermore, this theme of dominance and passivity extends to violence played out in so-called romantic movies. The violence is portrayed as normative. In addition, the movies perpetuate myths regarding rape and intimate-partner violence. For example, *Gone with the Wind* is on every "most romantic movies" listing, and the relationship between Scarlett and Rhett in this 1939 movie is portrayed in reviews, for example, in *Women's World* (2011), as a "tumultuous romance" (47). However, the movie depicts a marital rape of Scarlett by Rhett. The movie combines romance and rape, making them indistinguishable from each other. According to Eaklor (2002), "Scarlett's high spirits in the morning-after scene, apparently denoting satisfaction, reinforce both this view of romance/rape and the corresponding myth that women, despite their protests, want and need to be conquered" (5). And xojuje's (2010) analysis of *Gone with the Wind* is similar:

> When Scarlett goes against the expected feminine identity, Rhett sees it as his duty to tame her. One of the ways Scarlett is pushed back into the expected feminine role is through force. The scene begins with Scarlett and Rhett standing at the bottom of the stairs. He begins to kiss her, and she struggles in protest. Refusing to be told no, Rhett picks her up and brings her upstairs, presumably to have sex with her. Since the last glimpse of Scarlett before they go upstairs is of her trying to get away from him, it can be implied that what goes on upstairs is sexual assault. (1)

Concluding this analysis, xojuje states, "If a man forcing a woman into sex is romantic, a woman's choice becomes irrelevant" (1). The fact is that most filmgoers view the scene as romantic, not as rape. Rape is not sex.

The belief that rape is romance is a myth. Gratification for rapists comes from gaining power and control and discharging anger, not sex. Rhett apologizes for his behavior, blaming it on his drinking. This act feeds into another rape myth: that women should relabel the violence as anything but what it is—rape. Similar myths exist with respect to intimate-partner violence. Rhett's apology is a common response of men who beat women; in fact, a cyclical pattern of beating is common. Walker (1979) identified three phases within this cycle. In the tension-building phase, there are battering incidents. The woman attempts to avoid escalation of the battering by trying to "calm" her mate and by staying out of his way. Tension builds too high to be controlled by these efforts, and the batterer responds with an acute battering incident in the second phase. In phase three, the tension from the first two phases is gone and the batterer becomes charming toward the woman. He delivers apologies and promises to never batter again. The phases are repeated, however, and the battering continues.

Disney's *Beauty and the Beast* has been identified as one of the most romantic movies, but the film teaches children that girls should tolerate intimate-partner violence and remain with their batterers. The male character screams at the female, imprisons her, throws her father out of the door, and keeps her away from her family. For example:

Beast: Where is she?

Mrs. Potts: She's not coming.

Beast: What? I thought I told you to come down to dinner.

Belle: I'm not hungry.

Beast: You'll come out or I'll . . . break down the door.

Mrs. Potts: Gently, gently.

Beast: Will you come down to dinner, please?

Belle: No thank you.

Beast: You can't stay in there forever.

Belle: Yes I can.

Beast: Fine. Then go ahead and starve! If she doesn't eat with me, she doesn't eat at all!

Media Education (2001) reported responses from interviews with girls who had seen this movie about what they would tell their friends who were in an abusive relationship. Girls' responses included the following:

"If Belle was my friend and I saw what happened to her, yelling and romantic, I'd be happy for her because she found someone who she liked, and I'd be happy for her that she liked the beast, and that she would stay with him. But I would also feel bad for her because she gets yelled at a lot." (Abigail, nine years old, p. 9)

"If Belle was my friend and I'd seen her go through this whole thing, I probably would say, keep being nice and sweet as you are, and that probably will change him and in the movie he does." (Melina, nine years old, p. 9)

Many girls and women formulate ideas about their roles in North American culture from media content and report feeling inadequate when they compare themselves with media portrayals of femininity (Paludi 2010). Media Education (2001) summarized girls' responses to *Beauty and the Beast:* "This is a movie that is saying to our children, 'overlook the abuse, overlook the violence, there is a tender prince lurking within, and it's your job to kiss that prince and bring it out, or to kiss that beast and bring the prince out. That's a dangerous message" (9).

MOST ROMANTIC MOVIES: ETHNOCENTRIC, HETEROSEXIST, AND ABLEIST

The only abnormality is the incapacity to love.

Anaïs Nin

There is a notable absence of movies on the "most romantic" list that include people of color, people with disabilities, and lesbian, gay, bi, and transgendered protagonists (e.g., Fowdur, Kadiyali, and Prince 2010; McIntosh et al. 2003; Paludi, in press). For example, Hollywood movies have been heterosexist; they assume that a heterosexual sexual orientation is normative, while gay, lesbian, bisexual, transsexual, transgendered, or questioning individuals are deviations from that norm. *Valentine's Day* does identify a relationship between two men; however, the viewer only sees the men together at the last few seconds of the film. Their romance was never discussed or shown. In fact, while other relationships were depicted in the movie's trailer, the gay couple was omitted (Smith 2009). *Variety* described one of the couple as "a quarterback struggling over the decision of whether to retire" (Smith 2009, 1). The romantic relationship was omitted. Kennedy (in Smith 2009) asked, "Is it really impossible to market an ensemble romantic comedy to the masses with a gay couple in it?" (1).

In addition, *Brokeback Mountain* was not included in lists of the most romantic movies of all time during the Valentine's Day celebration. However, the movie *is* a romantic drama that deals with romance and sex between two men. Unlike other movies considered romantic, *Brokeback Mountain* has been the brunt of jokes and parodies and has been used in bullying gay students (Bowles 2006). This movie is listed under categories of best gay movies. Yet other films discussed here are not listed under the category of best heterosexual movies. Why should there be a separate category for movies depicting gay romantic relationships?

More recently, the movie *A Single Man* also deals with a long-term relationship between two men, one of whom is trying to deal with his partner's untimely death from an auto accident. Promotions for the film focused on a heterosexual friendship rather than the love relationship between two men.

Individuals with disabilities represent the largest minority group in the United States (Mertens, Wilson, and Mounty 2007). However, lists of Hollywood romantic movies reveal a lack of representation of individuals with disabilities. This means that the lives of people with disabilities remain hidden from able-bodied individuals (Banks 2010; Schriempf 2001). Furthermore, when individuals with disabilities are portrayed in movies, they are done so in stereotypical ways and are frequently met with jokes based on their perceived lack of attractiveness and their inability to have a significant social and intimate relationship with someone because of that lack of attractiveness (Keller, Galgay, and Ryan 2010). In addition, most of the women portraying disabled individuals in the media are able-bodied who commonly exaggerate ways women with disabilities behave in relationships (Paludi, in press).

One movie considered one of the most romantic films of all time, *An Affair to Remember*, does include a female protagonist who is injured in a car accident. She is unable to walk. However, the romance portrayed in the movie happens prior to the accident. At the end of the movie, after the accident, viewers are left wondering if the relationship will survive. Another movie, *Children of a Lesser God*, features a hearing-impaired woman in a romantic relationship, but it has not been listed as one of the most romantic movies.

Campbell (2001) noted that individuals with disabilities endure "ableism," a type of discrimination defined as a "network of beliefs, processes and practices that produces a particular kind of self and body (the corporeal standard) that is projected as the perfect, species-typical and therefore essential and fully human. Disability is cast as a diminished state of being human (a corporeal standard) that is projected as the perfect" (44). This ableism is found in movies, where disabilities are ignored, trivialized, or omitted.

Furthermore, people of color are rarely protagonists in romantic movies. *Ghost*, a movie considered one of the most romantic films of all time, did include an African American woman in the plot, but she was not involved in a romantic relationship. In addition, interracial relationships have also been omitted in most romantic movies. According to Ivory Road (2010),

> Even films that do pair a white woman with a man of color tend to keep the relationship platonic or avoid showing any intimacy in their relationship. . . . Interracial weddings are rarely seen or celebrated on-screen, even though weddings are a particularly popular tool used in Hollywood films to end a movie. . . . Since weddings legitimize and solidify relationships, the avoidance of legitimizing interracial unions through marriage can be read as a symbolic ban. (1)

Some movies based on novels that addressed interracial sexual relationships— for example, *The Pelican Brief*—altered the story lines in order to eliminate interracial romantic relationships.

THE VOLUMES

In order to provide scholarly responses to the question "What is love?" I invited colleagues to contribute chapters about the definition, cultural meaning, and typologies of love as well as the many forms and rewards of love. Their work greatly assists us in understanding the psychology of love.

The book set consists of four volumes: *The Many Forms and Rewards*, *Emotion and Romance*, *Meaning and Culture*, and *Research and Literature*. Contributors focus on friendships, dating relationships, dissolution of relationships, communication in relationships, stages of love, and abuse in love relationships. In addition, we take a multicultural approach to the psychology of love, including modern love in China, same-sex relationships in New Zealand, and gender and romantic love in Australian love letters. We also offer readers resources on the psychology of love, including abuse in relationships.

I hope this book set provides answers to questions you are asking about love and relationships. The contributors to these four volumes share their own definitions, experiences, and research on love. And they share Leo Buscaglia's sentiment:

Perfect love is rare indeed—for to be a lover will require that you continually have the subtlety of the very wise, the flexibility of the child, the sensitivity of the artist, the understanding of the philosopher, the acceptance of the saint, the tolerance of the scholar and the fortitude of the certain.

REFERENCES

Amyfabulous. 2008. Definition of love—as told by children. http://amyfabulous.wordpress .com/2008/07/29/definition-of-love-as-told-by-children/. Accessed February 12, 2011.

Banks, M. 2010. 2009 Division 25 presidential address: Feminist psychology and women with disabilities: An emerging alliance. *Psychology of Women Quarterly* 34:431–442.

Beauvoir, S. de. 1961 [1949]. *The second sex.* New York: Bantam.

Bowles, S. 2006. Brokeback Mountain: Milestone or movie of the moment? http://www .usatoday.com/life/movies/news/2006-02-21-brokeback_x.htm/. Accessed February 11, 2011.

Buss, D. 2008. The evolution of love. In *The new psychology of love*, edited by R. Sternberg and K. Sternberg, 65–86. New Haven, CT: Yale University Press.

Campbell, F. 2001. Inciting legal fictions: Disability's date with ontology and the ableist body of the law. *Griffith Law Review* 10:42–62.

Deaux, K., and R. Hanna. 1984. Courtship in the personals column: The influence of gender and sexual orientation. *Sex Roles* 11:363–375.

Diamond, L., C. Fagundes, and M. Butterworth. 2010. *Intimate relationships across the life span: The handbook of life-span development.* New York: Wiley.

Eaklor, V. 2002. Scarlett, the feminine and the masculine. http://www.imagesjournal .com/2002/features/gwtw/text2.htm/. Accessed February 12, 2011.

Fehr, B. 1994. Prototype-based assessment of laypeople's views of love. *Personal Relationships* 1:309–331.

Fletcher, G., and M. Clark, eds. 2003. *Blackwell handbook of social psychology: Interpersonal processes.* Malden, MA: Blackwell.

Fowdur, L., V. Kadiyali, and J. Prince. 2010. Racial bias in expert quality assessment: A study of newspaper movie reviews. *Johnson School Research Paper Series No. 7—2010.* http://papers.ssrn.com/so13/papers.cfm?abstract_id=1483835&http://search.aol .com/aol/se/. Accessed February 12, 2011.

Gibbons, J. 2009. *Jennifer: The name, the noun, the myth.* http://www.redroom.com/blog/ jenniferkate/jennifer-the-name-the-noun-the-myth/. Accessed February 13, 2011.

Goode, E. 1996. Gender and courtship entitlement: Responses to personal ads. *Sex Roles* 34:141–169.

Graham, J., and K. Christiansen. 2009. The reliability of romantic love: A reliability generalization meta-analysis. *Personal Relationships* 16:49–66.

Hendrick, C., and S. Hendrick. 2008. Styles of romantic love. In *The new psychology of love*, edited by R. Sternberg and K. Sternberg, 149–170. New Haven, CT: Yale University Press.

Hooli, S. 2010. *Valentine's Day*—Review. http://entertainment.oneindia.in/hollywood/ reviews/2010/valentines-day-review/. Accessed February 10, 2011.

Ivory Road. 2010. Black men, white women and the Hollywood shuffle. http://ivoryroad
.wordpress.com/2010/01/27/black-men-white-women-and-the-hollywood-shuffle/.
Accessed February 11, 2011.

Keller, R., C. Galgay, and D. Ryan. 2010. Disability microaggressions: Increasing sensitivity to subtle forms of ableism. http://www.ahead.org/uploads/conference/2010/
Concurrent%20Session%202/2.5_Disability%20Microaggressions%20Powerpoint
.pdf/. Accessed December 27, 2010.

Kelly, H. 1986. *Chaucer and the cult of Saint Valentine*. Leiden: Brill.

Kenrick, D. 2008. The dynamical evolutionary view of love. In *The new psychology of love*,
edited by R. Sternberg and K. Sternberg, 15–34. New Haven, CT: Yale University
Press.

McIntosh, W., R. Murray, J. Murray, and D. Sabia. 2003. Are the liberal good in Hollywood?
Characteristics of political figures in popular films from 1945 to 1998. *Communication Reports* 16:57–67.

Media Education. 2001. *Mickey Mouse monopoly: Disney, childhood and corporate power*.
Northampton, MA: Media Education Foundation.

Mertens, D., A. Wilson, and J. Mounty. 2007. Gender equity for people with disabilities. In
Handbook for achieving gender equity through education, edited by S. Klein, 583–
604. Mahwah, NJ: Erlbaum.

Oruch, J. 1981. St. Valentine, Chaucer and spring in February. *Speculum* 56:534–565.

Paludi, M. 2010. "When I am an old woman I shall wear purple": The Red Hat Society:
Empowering older women? Paper presented at the New York Academy of Sciences
and Pace University's Conference on Women, Power and Aging. September, New
York, NY.

Paludi, M. In press. Women with disabilities: Mental health impact of disabilities and ableism. In *Women and mental disorders*, edited by P. Lundberg-Love, K. Nadal, and
M. Paludi. Westport, CT: Praeger.

Rubin, L. 1976. *Intimate strangers: Men and women together*. New York: Harper & Row.

Rubin, Z. 1970. Measurement of romantic love. *Journal of Personality and Social Psychology*
16:265–273.

Schmidt, L. 1993. The fashioning of a modern holiday: St. Valentine's Day, 1840–1870. *Win-
terthur Portfolio* 18:209–245.

Schmitt, D. 2008. Evolutionary and cross-cultural perspectives on love: The influence of
gender, personality and local ecology on emotional investment in romantic relationships. In *The new psychology of love*, edited by R. Sternberg and K. Sternberg,
249–273. New Haven, CT: Yale University Press.

Schriempf, A. 2001. (Re)fusing the amputated body: An interactionist bridge for feminism
and disability. *Hypatia* 16:53–79.

Smith, H. 2009. Did the *Valentine's Day* trailer go out of its way to hide a gay couple? http://
jezebel.com/. Accessed February 11, 2011.

Sprecher, S., A. Aron, A., E. Hatfield, A. Cortese, E. Potapova, and A. Levitskaya. 1994. Love:
American style, Russian style and Japanese style. *Personal Relationships* 1:349–369.

Stassinopoulos, A. 2004. *Gods and goddesses in love: Making the myth a reality for you*. New
York: Pocket.

Sternberg, R. J. 1988. *The triarchic mind: A new theory of human intelligence*. New York:
Viking.

Walker, L. 1979. *The battered woman*. New York: Harper & Row.

Woman's World. 2011. What does your favorite movie couple say about you? *Woman's World*, February 14, 47.

xojuje. 2010. Rape culture: *Gone with the Wind*. http://www.allvoices.com/contributed-new/5912560-rape-culture-gone-with-the-wind/. Accessed February 7, 2011.

Chapter 1

What Is Love?

Benita Zahn

"What is love?" is the question before me. And that question begets another question: How do you define something that, I think, is like catching breath with your hands? And love changes, like our breath, through the stages of our lives. So come, join me as I reflect on my perception of love.

When we're children we take love for granted, assuming that everyone loves us. In our immature minds that means people will care for us, treat us as if the world revolves around us, and that our wishes will be granted. When the concept of sharing is introduced to our lives, our understanding of love begins to change. We can no longer point to a set amount of something and say, "This is love." For example, when a child is routinely given two cookies by his mother, he may view those two cookies as love. But then, perhaps, a sibling enters the picture, or a friend, and he is given only one cookie. That becomes a childhood "aha" moment about love. With the help of a caring adult, we learn that it's the act of providing the cookie that underlies love, not the amount of what we receive. Thus we begin to develop a mature view of love, that it's the intent, not necessarily the final action, that defines love.

As we age, we enter the rebellious teen years. We want to test the bounds of our own emotional fabric and begin to give our own hearts, and we may believe parental love is childish, that we don't need it. It's too early in our lives to realize we can both accept the love that has endured and embark on sharing a new love. And what is that new love? Romantic love is that cauldron of emotions that bubbles up and over, fueled by hormones. It unleashes a storm of powerful feelings, often reducing our ability to reason. It can trigger dizzying highs and shattering lows.

Remember, hormones are powerful chemicals, but I think romantic love speaks to something beyond this. I think "beings" have a need to connect with someone. It may be we're seeking to re-create that love from childhood when nothing was required of us. It may be that we're looking for a connection that will allow us to share the emotional security we got as children. Even the most unloved child has, at some point, enjoyed the security of a person's arms, and that brief encounter is enough to trigger an understanding of connection, of love.

When the whirlwind of romantic love slows, we enter into another phase of love, what I call the "time of connectedness." It's a time when we are with someone who understands the nuances and idiosyncrasies of our life and accepts them. In some way those quirks feed us, we find them charming, and I suspect they keep a modicum of the heart-quickening, romantic love alive.

Can love die? Of course. That's because the underpinning of love is trust. To give of oneself when "in love" and to accept the love of another means you are exposing a need—the need to connect on a level that does not require words. If that trust is shattered, I think love is dealt a death blow.

I know. You're thinking that for some people, quantity remains a priority in love. True. And for some, no matter how many times their trust is abused, their love remains alive. But I think these folks have underlying emotional issues that I'm not equipped to address. As for addressing love, hey, it's like any other opinion: We're all welcome to have one. I can only hope you love me for mine.

Oh, and remember to breathe.

Chapter 2

Yes, We Do. Even at Our Age

Nieli Langer

Love, sexual intimacy, and sexuality are characteristics that help define individuals and often contribute to how well they will continue to live and age. Enhanced knowledge and healthy attitudes about the sexual needs and feelings of older adults living in the community or in long-term care settings may help to dispel negative myths, stereotypes, and self-fulfilling attitudes in older adults and in the general public. This awareness will support the perception that full sexual expression is part of the entire extent of adulthood.

At a time when almost every kind of physical intimacy is discussed with increasing candor, the sexual intimacy of older men and women in the community and in long-term care settings remains a taboo subject. But there is nothing unusual or deviant about romance among older people. The details of love and intimacy may change with age, but our basic physical and psychological needs do not. It is a disservice to older people, as well as to younger, to view any form of safe sexual expression that persists into later life as anything but healthy (Lachs 2010).

THE BEGINNING OF WISDOM IS THE DEFINITION OF TERMS (SOCRATES)

Love is a universal human emotion that may be experienced throughout the life cycle. Love is a word. It requires commitment, care, responsibility, and respect. It requires enjoyment, trust and we-ness, that is, a shared relationship and, often, a shared history. Love does not require youth. As the Beatles reminded us, "All you need is love, all you need is love / All you need is love, love, love is all you ever need" (Beatles 1967).

Sex is a primary human drive and can be considered alongside thirst, hunger, and avoidance of pain. We are sexual beings from birth to death. Older people *can* and *do* make love, although there may be decreased levels of arousal and a lessening of intensity along with a slowing down of response. *Sexual intimacy* between couples involves mutual affection; *sexual drive* is typically manifested by feelings, fantasies, and seeking out sexual activity. Desire in the emotionally mature person comes out of wholeness, a faith in oneself as powerfully loving and lovable. Sexual expression from this perspective leads to self-validated intimacy rather than other-validated intimacy, a more emotionally mature position. Self-validated individuals are confident of their worth even without confirmation by a partner. Schnarch (1997, 2002) suggests that reaching this point in one's sexual potential rarely happens before middle or late life. For humans, the most important part of sexual experience is the meanings they attach to it. It takes well-developed humans who take responsibility for their own experience of sexual intimacy to create passion, to spark eroticism.

Sadly, our culture has continually promoted the idea that love and sex are only for the young. The whole issue of intimacy among older people distracts discussion from a deeper truth, that simple, tender intimacy is very important as we age, the sort of concept our youth-oriented culture tends to minimize. Older people across past decades have also been well acquainted with the notion that sexual expression for them is not tolerated. The stereotype of the sexless older person continues to influence public policy as well as research agendas (Gott and Hinchliff 2003).

Society has perpetuated the notion that "we think our parents are too old to; we think our kids are too young to; our kids think we are too old to; so, who in the heck is supposed to have sex?" The best response? Everyone who wants to experience positive, ongoing sexuality throughout the life cycle (Langer 2006). Even though sex for older people may not be quantitatively identical to that experienced by younger people, older couples' need for sexual expression endures: "When the old folks make love, / each makes a space for the other to enter freely. / They write, 'I love you,' on each other's skin again and again like a poem" (Nymark 2002).

Belonging for an older couple signifies identification as a couple, sharing of values, comfortable interaction, and a sense of safety and security. Lummis Indians of the Pacific Northwest saw old age as the proper time to fall in love: "It was the proper time to suffer romances, and jealousy, and lose your head—old age, when you felt things more, and could spare the time to go dead nuts over a person, and understand how fine a thing it was" (Dillard 1992; 175).

Sexuality refers to an individual's self-perception of being attractive as a sexual partner. The ways we dress, speak to others, and daydream are all affected by sexuality and sexual identity. Sexuality reflects gender identity, body image, and desire. An essential part of psychological well-being for older adults is their interest in and ability to express their sexuality, regardless of physical or mental health. There is no age at which sexual activities, thoughts, or desires must end, although the way in which sexuality is expressed may change. The more positive the person's beliefs and values are about sexuality, the greater the person's desire to engage in sexual activities. For older people, sexuality often provides the opportunity to express not only passion but also affection and loyalty (Heath 1999). Throughout the life cycle, the ability to experience warmth, caring, physical intimacy, and connection to significant others contributes to an adult's self-esteem.

WHY HAVE LOVE AND INTIMACY FOR OLDER ADULTS NOT BEEN SERIOUSLY ADDRESSED?

We have listened to and perpetuated myths fed by misinformation about late-life love and sexual intimacy. Older people are

1. physically unattractive and, therefore, undesirable;
2. physically incapable of making love even if they wanted to;
3. lacking in sexual desires; and
4. weird or deviant if they are sexually active.

Myths are created to explain what we don't understand. These myths form the basis for many comments that trigger disdain or set off snickers on the topic of sexuality in older adults. Values, experiences, families, peers, the media, and religious beliefs all influence sexuality, gender roles, and sexual behaviors. With restrictive guidelines regarding appropriate sexual behavior and taboos against other forms of sexual activity, it is sometimes harder for older adults to engage in sexual expression. They have difficulty overcoming guilt and shame in light of societal pressures and ingrained childhood exhortations against sexual intimacy. Many researchers have found that older individuals are ashamed, if not reluctant, to discuss themselves as sexual beings (Gibson 1993).

The widely held view in our society that sexual interaction between older persons is socially unacceptable and even physically harmful may have negative consequences for older people. Many older people believe they have become ugly and undesirable and begin to dislike the way they look as a result of the aging process. They often worry that they can no longer meet social expectations of beauty and performance. Fearing laughter or criticism, many older people may unnecessarily withdraw from all forms of sexual expression long before they need to, thereby depriving themselves and often their partners of the energy and vitality inherent in sexuality (Kessel 2001). When older people give up on themselves and their sexuality, they give up on sensual pleasure, physical intimacy, and heightened self-worth. For many, open communication about sex and sexuality has been and continues to be inappropriate. As people age and society counts them out of the game of life, if they do not resist society's views, they can learn to hate themselves.

The sociocultural context in which older adults were raised and the prevailing cultural stereotypes, misconceptions, and humor about old age and sexuality can negatively influence older adults' attitudes toward sexual intimacy. Societal standards of physical appearance and beauty also influence sexuality. Since sexuality tends to be equated with youthful standards of attractiveness, definitions of older people as asexual are heightened for older women and men who are suffering from chronic illness, disability, and general loss of positive physical attributes.

A double standard still exists relative to men and women and the aging process. Men are victims of a lifelong excessive emphasis on the frequency and potency of their sexual performance. While older men are described as gray and distinguished, mature women are seen as sliding away from youth and beauty. The predominant message for older women has come from a widespread assumption that only the young are attractive. As a result, older men reject the possibility of romantic encounters out of fear that they will be unable to physically satisfy their partner while women feel that they are no longer sexually attractive (Gibson 1993). Friedan (1993) argued that older persons are then placed in an untenable situation; not only do they feel guilty about wanting to have sexual relationships, but they fear they will be unable to perform by cultural standards. This situation leaves no real option but to have their sexual needs and wants left unmet.

Adult children and grandchildren often convey the message that sexual expression between older couples is shameful and perverse; they do not accept sexuality in their parents' lives. They selfishly define their parents in purely parental roles. Adult children seeing parents on the current disabled list cannot imagine that they were once sought out as physically and/or sexually attractive men and women. Older adults' romantic relationships are constrained by a lack of privacy in a new romantic pairing or even in conjugal relationships between married partners if they share housing with adult children. Older adults' integration into a family structure, therefore, can inhibit the development or continuity of committed romantic relationships. Given the many benefits of a close family structure, this leaves older adults with multiple relational dilemmas. Negative societal attitudes, coupled with adult children's feelings about their parents' sexual intimacy, are often more potent reasons why older adults refrain from sexual intimacy than the biological changes they experience with aging.

Love in the Time of Cholera (García Márquez 1988) is a love story between two older people. Without guilt or shame and in spite of their shocked middle-aged children, who believed that "there was an age at which love began to be indecent," Fermina and Florentino "exchanged unhurried kisses; they enjoyed the rapture of caresses." This older couple embraced their love and did not back away: "They can all go to hell. . . . If there is any advantage it is that there is no one left to give us orders" (359–360).

Religion shapes sexual values with a "sacred" law that articulates a range of acceptable sexual behaviors and practices (whom an individual can marry, the types of sexual expression allowed, the use of contraception, etc.). In the Judeo-Christian tradition, the Old and New Testament prohibitions against sexuality in both its specific and general forms have proven to be immensely powerful forces. They have demanded and justified repression of sexual thought and conduct and have provided heavy burdens of guilt and shame (especially about nakedness, masturbation, and homosexuality).

The current cohorts of older adults grew up during a time when sexual behavior was not discussed, when encouragement of sexual feelings was suppressed, and when instruction in sex education was minimal; open communication about sex and sexuality was considered inappropriate. However, for future generations, the misinformation and shame associated with a discussion of sexually charged issues were forever unmasked with the publication of the first of Alfred Kinsey's volumes, *Sexual Behavior in the Human Male* (Kinsey 1998 [1948]) and with the release of *Sexual Behavior in the Human Female* (Kinsey 1998 [1953]). Kinsey's surveys of human sexuality produced a social explosion with the methodical dissection of Americans' sex life. Despite the flaws of the known sampling techniques of the time, the broad conclusions Kinsey drew from his data (approximately eighteen thousand interviews) changed the way Americans conversed and behaved around the topic of sex and sexuality (Langer 2006).

As a result of societal and familial pressure, many older people may have unnecessarily withdrawn from all forms of sexual expression long before they needed or wanted to. We now acknowledge that as people age, personal relationships take on increased importance and are a significant variable in healthy aging. Despite the personal nature of many of the questions in the University of Chicago's National Social Life, Health and Aging Project (NSHAP) (Lindau et al. 2007), study participants were very forthcoming about their responses. In a remark by one of the researchers, participants were more likely to refuse questions about income than they were about sex. Study results revealed that most people ages fifty-seven to eighty-five think of sexuality as an important part of life; men and women remain sexually active well into their seventies and eighties. For older people, emotional security, being able to depend upon and trust a significant other, mutual respect, and admiration are the keys to happy love relationships in later life.

WHY AND HOW BABY BOOMERS WILL DISPEL MYTHS ABOUT LATE-LIFE SEXUALITY

The Baby Boom generation can be defined by its place in history. All were born into post–World War II society with its revolution in social values and customs. They have defined their generation at every step of their lives—from the time their parents created suburbs to raise them, to their own working years, and now into retirement. These individuals "constitute the largest number of persons ever born in a single generation from 1905 until the end of the twentieth century in the United States" (Maples and Abney 2006). This generation has experienced an unprecedented rate of divorce and the growing acceptance of gay and lesbian relationships. They have seen the development, acceptance, and accessibility of oral contraceptives, thereby encouraging earlier and more frequent sexual activity for self-expression and pleasure rather than for reproductive function alone. Likewise, they have witnessed the discovery and spread of human immunodeficiency virus (HIV).

The world inhabited by this cohort can be characterized by greater sexual freedom, increased empowerment of women and minorities, and an attitude of anti-authoritarianism that extends to all groups and professional bodies that challenge them. The sixties generation got everything right but the drugs. They supported civil rights, gay and lesbian rights, and women's rights and helped to create an environment of entitlement and choice. This cohort will be far more confident about being old—a confidence derived from being part of the largest cohort in the history of humankind that has enjoyed huge strides in education and technology. These men and women are healthier, more affluent, and better educated than any generation before them. They are accustomed to being focused on as a driving force in society. A more open-minded attitude about sex compounded by the sheer number of people in this cohort (approximately seventy-eight million) suggests that they will be far less willing to accept the notion that their sexual expression is invalid. The subject of sexual intimacy will be prominent in their lives as well as for their families, eventual care providers, and society at large (Langer 2006).

MARRIAGE: GROWING OLDER TOGETHER

Older couples have grown old together. The couple relationship tends to be the focal point in married people's lives. Khalil Gibran's passage from *The Prophet* (1923) describes the kind of marriage that unites but does not consume the identity of each partner:

> Give your hearts, but not into each other's keeping.
> For only the hand of Life can contain your hearts.
> And stand together, yet not too near together,
> For the pillars of the temple stand apart,
> And the oak tree and the cypress
> Grow not in each other's shadow.

Many older couples report that they are sexually active and have experienced an increase in the spontaneity of sexual expression since their children have left the nest and they now have more unhurried quality time to express their love and sexual drive. Most couples report enjoying sex because it gives each partner feelings of desirability, completion, and of being loved and loving.

Most long-term couples plan their sexual experiences. For these couples, the mind leads the body more than the body leads the mind. McCarthy and McCarthy

(2003) have written that healthy, mutually pleasuring sex helps strengthen the bond between couples. An unsurprising result is that the more often a person has sex, the happier he or she is. This could be because people who have sex often are more likely to be healthy and enjoying a good relationship. Sexual intimacy for older couples is the most powerful way to demonstrate love of self and love for someone else. As a Chinese proverb states, "Married couples who love each other tell each other a thousand things without talking."

At the turn to the twentieth century, more than half of all marriages were interrupted by the death of one spouse, usually the husband, before the last child left home. Today, most married couples look forward to the post-parenting years as opportunities for increased closeness and companionship. The couple relationship is a source of great comfort and support as well as the focal point of everyday life, especially with the departure of adult children. Older couples are survivors who reflect the aging of our society whose unprecedented number are marching toward Golden Pond together. Since they have had few role models, they are explorers mapping out new territory on what it is like to grow old today as individuals and as a couple. They are grateful for the support and love of a lifelong partner—someone who remembers them as they once were and who continues to care for them as they are now. This bond is an irreplaceable attachment to the person who has shared his or her history with you. What always matters is the way two people feel about each other, and with that the hope that either or both partners will be willing to take the steps in order to weather the challenges of later life together.

Married and heterosexual are the most common types of couples among middle-aged and older men and women. Yet many older homosexual couples share a closed-couple relationship in which members tend to be sexually exclusive. Many of these couples, denied legal marriage in most of the United States, are only now openly acknowledging the true importance of their relationship. Older gay and lesbian couples often consider themselves married in every sense of the word. Life partners are an essential part of gay and lesbian elders' support systems and need to be recognized for the importance they play in each other's lives. Not having had role models of their own, older gay and lesbian couples often realize that they may be called upon to be role models for future generations.

WIDOWHOOD

Although many older people maintain a desire to continue or initiate sexual activity, an acceptable partner may not be available. Men may have multiple opportunities for sexual partners, whereas women, with the uneven ratio of older men to older women, may have very few. Older men are more likely to be married, and older women are more likely to be widowed, thus affecting the opportunities for sexual expression in an ongoing, intimate relationship.

A profound emotional and sexual situation facing older women revolves around the possibility of finding themselves alone—widowed, divorced, separated, or single as they grow older. Female longevity has consistently been the barrier to sexual activity for older women. Women live longer than men and generally marry men at least three years their senior. This means that women may expect to live at least a decade as a widow. It is not always possible for an older woman to have a sexual partner. Husbands die or move on to younger women, and many women face the prospect of being either self-sexual or nonsexual. The effect of the feminist movement coupled with the sheer number of well-educated confident women who are socialized to the workplace today will greatly influence their lives as they age: "The truth about 'older' women is that we love the stage of life we are in, and we are actively exploring new frontiers of experience; that includes sex" (Braun Levine 2005, 12). Women hopefully will feel far freer than today's older adults to enter nontraditional intimate relationships—an advantage for women, for whom the risk of isolation in late life is greater than it is for men (Langer 2006).

REMARRIAGE AND DATING 101

A substantial number of older couples are formed in later life with the desire for companionship as the motivating factor in their union. The desire to be in an intimate relationship with another person seems to persist throughout life: "Two ageing people, unwilling to face the evening of their lives in solitude. . . . Eva shuddered at the prospect. But friendship, love, intimacy, and above all, trust. . . . All was darkness, and she had been full of fear and apprehension, and then the sun had peeped through the clouds once more" (Fallada 1947, 373).

Individuals who share an attachment relationship appear to be better able to withstand the inevitable losses of later life. The recent greater diversity of relationship and marital experiences across adulthood may leave older people feeling more comfortable with dating. Whether a couple chooses to marry becomes secondary to the desire for closeness and companionship that they seek. Widowers and divorced older people often ask how long they should wait to get involved in a new relationship. It is different for each person, but if they are interested, they need to be visible and available.

Older people form all sorts of relationships—from partners to live-in companions to couples who marry. In addition, many late-life romantic relationships will likely increase because the Internet has made it easier for older singles to meet. In recent decades the number of couples of all ages cohabiting without marriage has dramatically increased, as has society's acceptance of these living arrangements.

Living apart together (LAT) is a new family form in which couples do not share a household but nonetheless view themselves as committed to the relationship (Levin 2004). They identify themselves as a couple, as do their family and friends. In interviews, they claim to have greater autonomy by not sharing a single household. As Baby Boomers age, we can expect to read more about LAT and other creative approaches to late-life love and intimacy.

In *remarriage*, many couples are interested not only in romantic love but also in building a relationship based on companionship, lasting affection, and respect. They are even willing to risk alienating adult children by remarrying so as not to spend their last years alone. Sexual attraction is as much a part of the relationship for an older couple as it is for two younger people. Is the nature of a new love in late life different from a love relationship shared over fifty years?

Although men often seek younger women, many younger men have no problem dating older women. Romance between older men and younger women has been so commonplace on screen that the age difference often passes without comment. Today, however, more women are seeking out relationships with younger men. They find men of their generation stuck in outdated, non-egalitarian modes, and they are eager for gender equality. An older woman often brings a wealth of experience, confidence, competence, and power to a relationship—of the sort a younger woman can not imagine. Whether a couple chooses to marry becomes secondary to the desire for closeness and the companionship they seek. Whether a couple is young or old, the euphoria and desire to be with the other person is much the same.

INTIMACY: IN THE COMMUNITY AND IN LONG-TERM CARE

Sexual health and physical health are often closely related. Obstetrician-gynecologists are both primary care providers and specialists. As primary care providers with a special focus and knowledge, they often provide continuity of care throughout the life cycle of the female patient for a wide variety of problems while addressing preventative care and health maintenance. Unfortunately, studies show low rates of sexual health assessment by primary care providers (Gott, Hinchliff, and Galena 2004). Many providers may underestimate patient risk, and/or lack the knowledge and comfort to discuss questions about sexual dysfunction or satisfaction with older patients (Spivak 2008). Medical practitioners often fall prey to the same ageist stereotypes and attitudes about love and intimacy among older adults that are prevalent in our society. The discomfort medical providers may experience when encountering sexuality in older persons creates barriers that can limit the free expression of sexuality and intimacy in their older patients (Langer Most and Langer 2010).

Care providers' discussion of sexuality with their older patients would improve patient education and counseling as well as the ability to clinically identify a highly prevalent spectrum of health-related and potentially treatable sexual problems. The willingness and ability of care providers to acknowledge and address sexuality in older patients' lives could contribute to patients' ability to continue to experience warmth, caring, physical intimacy, and connection to significant others (Langer Most and Langer 2010).

When physicians and other health-care providers assume their older patients are not engaging in any sexual behaviors, they miss the chance to educate them and to properly diagnose HIV and other sexually transmitted infections. Older individuals can and do engage in unsafe sex, whether knowingly or not, and need accurate information and encouragement to protect themselves. In the Web-based survey of over three thousand women, 40 percent said they did not seek help from a provider for sexual function problems they experienced; 54 percent said they wanted to see a provider. Those who did seek help did not rank highly the attitude or services provided (Lindau et al. 2007).

By addressing issues of sexuality, the care provider informs the patient that it is appropriate to discuss sexual problems. Medical care providers play an instrumental role in assessing and managing normal and pathological aging changes to improve the sexual health of older women and their partners by providing guidance, education, and acceptance (Nussbaum, Singh, and Pyles 2004). The expression of one's sexuality is a fundamental mental health need of all individuals, regardless of age and gender. Through further empirical study of the relationship between knowledge/attitudes, aging sexuality, and the factors that mediate it, effective intervention strategies can be developed in order to maximize delivery of medico-psycho-social health-care needs (Langer Most and Langer 2010).

One of the most humanitarian services professionals in the health, social work, and religious fields can provide is to help families and providers of long-term care realize the great opportunity and privilege there is in supporting an older person's right to be a sexual human being (Schlesinger 2000). Residents in long-term care facilities, in general, tend to be the most powerless, voiceless, and invisible groups in our society. Doris Hammond (1987), a researcher in sexuality and aging, has suggested such residents have a greater need than other older adults for sexual intimacy. Having experienced so many cumulative losses related to disability, widowhood, finances, social roles, and so on, emotional closeness can be of considerable benefit to a resident's self-esteem.

The lack of privacy often presents an obstacle to sexual expression for older residents, especially those who live in facilities ill equipped to provide seclusion for spouses or unmarried partners. The lack of privacy, in fact, is often an intentional institutional decision to not address this issue for religious/ethical reasons or for fear of incurring the wrath of adult children. Sometimes, too, since the continuing sexuality of older people is often an uncomfortable reality for staff members, some staff may demean older residents by teasing or ridiculing them when they show interest in expressing their sexuality.

Since more facilities are finding that there is more intimacy among residents regardless of living arrangements and mental or marital status, they have begun to have staff discussions and role playing in order to examine the meaning of the behavior of the "dirty old man" and the "shameless old woman." Even those residents suffering from dementias are capable of romantic attachments and sexual feelings. However, these attachments often raise personal and ethical questions that pit individual rights against professional and family values. One overall challenge is to help individuals develop and sustain the relationships they desire within the boundaries of their current lodgings and individual medical/psychological circumstances.

The Hebrew Home for the Aged in Riverdale, New York, has continually been in the forefront of addressing major issues related to long-term care. In 1995, the home introduced a set of policies and procedures concerning sexual expression among the residents. An explicit training video was created to educate staff on how to address sexual rights and the needs of residents. The video has been shown in connection with educational training programs at other, similar institutions.

CONCLUSION

Society has made assumptions about aging and sexuality that are now outdated. Perhaps, like old wives' tales, these assumptions were useful at one time, but today they no longer serve a purpose. One cannot choose to "not have sexuality as part of one's life any more than one can choose not to breathe or sleep" (Haffner 1994). Love and sexual intimacy are as normal and natural for older adults as they are for those in early adulthood. The only thing age has to do with sexual intimacy is that the longer you love, the more you learn. There is no age at which sexual activities, thoughts, or desires must end, although the way in which these are expressed may change. As we age, personal relationships take on increased importance. Sexual intimacy is a way to reaffirm the love of life.

Older adults are sexual people, even in the face of extraordinary changes in physical and mental functioning. Love and a sexual turn-on do not occur just because of youth or outer beauty. With an older couple, married or dating, loving each other is a turn-on in itself. Sexual intimacy at any age will be achieved by those with the ability to give and receive love, and to cherish and be cherished by a partner.

Someday, after we have mastered the winds, the waves, the tides and gravity, we shall harness the energies of love. Then, for the second time in the history of the world, man will have discovered fire. (Teilhard de Chardin 1978, 395)

REFERENCES

The Beatles. 1967. All you need is love. By John Lennon and Paul McCartney. Prod. George Martin. Parlophone, UK.

Braun Levine, S. 2005. *Inventing the rest of our lives*. New York: Penguin Books.

Dillard, A. 1992. *The living*. New York: Harper Collins.

Fallada, H. 1947. *Alone in Berlin*. Great Britain: Penguin.

Friedan, B. 1993. *The fountain of age*. New York: Simon and Schuster.

García Márquez, Gabriel. 1988. *Love in the time of cholera*. New York: Penguin.

Gibran, K. 1923. *The prophet*. New York: Alfred A. Knopf.

Gibson, H. B. 1993. Emotional and sexual adjustment in later life. In *Ageing, independence, and the life course*, edited by S. Arber and M. Evandrou, 104–118. London: Jessica Kingley.

Gott, M., and S. Hinchliff. 2003. How important is sex in later life? The views of older people. *Social Science & Medicine* 56:1617–1628.

Gott, M., S. Hinchliff, and E. Galena. 2004. General practitioner attitudes to discussing sexual health issues with older people. *Social Science & Medicine* 58:2093–2103.

Haffner, D. 1994. Love and sex after 60: How physical changes affect intimate expression. *Geriatrics* 49:20–28.

Hammond, D. 1987. *My parents never had sex.* Buffalo, NY: Prometheus Books.

Heath, H. 1999. Intimacy and sexuality. In *Healthy ageing: Nursing older people*, edited by M. Heath and B. Schofield, 341–366. London: Mosby.

Kessel, B. 2001. Sexuality in the older person. *Age and Ageing* 30:121–124.

Kinsey, A. 1998 [1948]. *Sexual behavior in the human male.* Bloomington: Indiana University Press.

Kinsey, A. 1998 [1953]. *Sexual behavior in the human female.* Bloomington: Indiana University Press.

Lachs, M. 2010. Desire in the twilight of life. *Wall Street Journal*, November.

Langer, N. 2006. *Love and sex: Are we ever too old?!?* Victoria, BC: Trafford.

Langer Most, O., and N. Langer. 2010. Aging and sexuality: How much do gynecologists know and care? *Journal of Women and Aging* 22:283–289.

Levin, I. 2004. Living apart together: A new family form. *Current Sociology* 52:223–240.

Lindau, S. T. T., L. P. Schumm, E. O. Laumann, W. L. Levinson, C. A. O'Muircheartaigh, and L. J. Waite. 2007. A study of sexuality and health among older adults in the United States. *New England Journal of Medicine* 357:762–774.

Maples, M. F., and P. C. Abney. 2006. Baby boomers mature and gerontological counseling comes of age. *Journal of Counseling and Development* 84:3–9.

McCarthy, B., and E. McCarthy. 2003. *Rekindling desire: A step-by-step program to help low-sex and no-sex marriages.* New York: Brunner/Routledge.

Nusbaum, M. R., A. R. Singh, and A. A. Pyles. 2004. Sexual healthcare needs of women aged 65 and older. *Journal of the American Geriatric Society* 52:117–22.

Nymark, N. 2002. When the old folks make love. *Aging Today,* 1 May 2003.

Schlesinger, B. 2000. The sexless years or sex rediscovered. In *Intersections of aging: Readings in social gerontology*, edited by E. W. Markson and L. A. Hollis-Sawyer, 52–59. Los Angeles: Roxbury.

Schnarch, D. 1997. *Passionate marriage: Love, sex, and intimacy in emotionally committed relationships.* New York: Norton.

Schnarch, D. 2002. *Resurrecting sex: Resolving sexual problems and rejuvenating your relationship.* New York: Norton.

Spivak, B. 2008. Discussing sexuality with older patients. *Clinical Gerontology* 16:8–9.

Teilhard de Chardin, P. 1978. *The heart of matter.* New York: William Collins Sons & Harcourt.

Chapter 3

Psychological Definitions of Love

Jennifer F. Hsia and William E. Schweinle

Superficially, love seems like an easy concept to define. However, once we started exploring the scientific and creative literature and examining our own thoughts and feelings, we found that developing a comprehensive and exhaustive definition of love was quite a challenge. Part of the difficulty is that psychological researchers, like us, attempt to apply objective and quantifiable terms to what is a fundamentally subjective experience. Nevertheless, psychologists have developed several thoughtful and empirically supported theories of love. Among these are Lee's styles theory (1977), Sternberg's triangular theory (1986), and Hazan and Shaver's attachment styles theory (1987). These three theories dominate the psychological literature (Ahmetoglu, Swami, and Chamorro-Premuzic 2010; Hendrick and Hendrick 1989; Madey and Rodgers 2009; Myers and Shurts 2002).

Lee (1977) proposed that people adopt six basic romantic love styles, with eros, ludus, and storge delineated as the primary styles and mania, agape, and pragma as secondary styles. With the eros style, the individual seeks a lover whose physical appearance matches the image in the individual's mind. Individuals with a ludus style tend to have numerous short-term relationships. Those who have the storge style tend to develop affection and companionship gradually and expect long-term commitment. The mania style is characterized by obsession, jealousy, and strong emotional intensity. The agape style is altruistic; individuals love the other person without expecting anything in return. Pragma-style individuals consciously and deliberately evaluate the demographic characteristics of their loved one (Lee 1977).

Drawing on attachment theory (Bowlby 1969), Hazan and Shaver (1987) identified secure, avoidant, and anxious/ambivalent attachment styles. Those who are securely attached tend to associate positive feelings such as happiness and trust with important love experiences and report accepting and supporting the people they love in spite of personal faults. Avoidant individuals fear intimacy. They experience large fluctuations in emotional intensity and jealousy in their relationships. They also tend to be skeptical of romanticized notions of love, such as the possibility of falling head over heels for someone, the enduring nature of love, and the ability to find someone to love. Anxious/ambivalent individuals tend to experience love as obsessive and emotionally intense. They also tend to want unification and reciprocity with high levels of sexual attraction. These individuals report that they fall in love with relative ease, though they rarely find what they consider to be true love (Hazan and Shaver 1987).

In contrast to the two previously discussed theories, which focus only on romantic love, Sternberg (1986) proposes that all types of love are based on a triangular combination of three components: intimacy, passion, and commitment. Intimacy leads to warmth in the relationship. It is characterized by "feelings of closeness, connectedness, and bondedness in loving relationships" (Sternberg 1986, 119). Passion includes sexual chemistry, physical attraction, and romance. The commitment component involves the decision to love another in the short term and to sustain that love in the long term. Thus each of the three components addresses a different aspect of love: intimacy develops from the emotional bond, passion comes from desire, and commitment represents a conscious decision-making process (Sternberg 1986).

According to the triangular theory, different combinations of intimacy, passion, and commitment produce eight types of love. Nonlove results when all three components are absent. Liking is the type of love that exists in most friendships and results when intimacy is present while passion and commitment are absent (Sternberg 1986). Infatuated love, or "love at first sight" (Sternberg 1986, 124), results when passion is present in the absence of intimacy and commitment. Empty love occurs when only commitment is present without passion or intimacy and can occur in stagnant romantic relationships. Romantic love results when passion and intimacy are present without commitment. Companionate love is characterized by intimacy and commitment without passion and tends to develop in long-term marriages. Fatuous love results when passion combines with commitment in the absence of intimacy, and this type of love characterizes whirlwind romances whereby two individuals marry shortly after meeting. Consummate love involves the presence of all three components and is considered the type of love that most people strive to achieve (Sternberg 1986). Together, these eight types can describe all interpersonal relationships.

While many attempts have been made to develop a comprehensive definition, love remains an elusive psychological construct. Overall, Ahmetoglu, Swami, and Chamorro-Premuzic (2010) argue that Sternberg's model of love has demonstrated higher empirical reliability than Lee's model, and recent literature appears to focus most on testing Sternberg's theory. However, this model may still miss some of the complexities and nuances present in many relationships. Thus even though a theory or definition may capture general characteristics, generating a definition of love to include all the subtleties may not be possible or even desirable because love is ultimately a subjective experience. As such, fully describing this experience may eliminate the mystery that underlies its appeal.

REFERENCES

Ahmetoglu, G., V. Swami, and T. Chamorro-Premuzic. 2010. The relationship between dimensions of love, personality, and relationship length. *Archives of Sexual Behavior* 39:1181–1190. DOI: 10.1007/s10508-009-9515-5.

Bowlby, J. 1969. *Attachment and loss.* Vol. 1, *Attachment.* New York: Basic Books.

Hazan, C., and P. Shaver. 1987. Romantic love conceptualized as an attachment process. *Journal of Personality and Social Psychology* 52:511–524. DOI: 10.1037/0022-3514 .52.3.511.

Hendrick, C., and S. S. Hendrick. 1989. Research on love: Does it measure up? *Journal of Personality and Social Psychology* 56:784–794. DOI: 10.1037/0022-3514.56.5.784.

Lee, J. A. 1977. A typology of styles of loving. *Personality and Social Psychology Bulletin* 3:173–182.

Madey, S. F., and L. Rodgers. 2009. The effect of attachment and Sternberg's triangular theory of love on relationship satisfaction. *Individual Differences Research* 7:76–84.

Myers, J. E., and W. M. Shurts. 2002. Measuring positive emotionality: A review of instruments assessing love. *Measurement and Evaluation in Counseling and Development* 34:238–254.

Sternberg, R. J. 1986. A triangular theory of love. *Psychological Review* 93:119–135. DOI: 10.1037/0033-295x.93.2.119.

Chapter 4

Platonic Couple Love: How Couples View Their Close Couple Friends

Geoffrey L. Greif and Kathleen Holtz Deal

Little is known about the nature of couples' platonic friendships with other couples. In order to learn more, seventy-six couples were asked to select a couple with whom they were close and answer a series of questions about that relationship. Generally, couples felt least comfortable talking about sex with their close friends, and more than half admired their friends' demonstrations of loving, caring, and sharing. The race of the couple, the number of years married, and the length of the friendship were related to what was shared. Implications for therapy and marriage enrichment include educating couples about the impact of time on friendships as well as trusting other couples, being able to discuss many but not all intimate topics, and emulating other couples' relationships.

PLATONIC COUPLE LOVE: HOW COUPLES VIEW CLOSE COUPLE FRIENDS

Research has consistently demonstrated that social support, often operationalized as friendships with individuals (Allgood, Crane, and Agee 1997), is beneficial to one's health (e.g., Biesanz, West, and Millevoi 2007; Hayslip, Han, and Anderson 2008). Research also has shown that people who are married live longer, healthier lives (e.g., Waite and Gallagher 2000). Yet little is known about the specific qualities and potential benefits of friendships between two couples who are considered close, platonic friends. Some research has looked at couples' friendships with individuals and family members (e.g., Liebler and Sandefur 2002; Kalmijn and Bernasco 2001), but not friendship between two couples. This topic bears attention, as platonic affection between two couples can theoretically assist a couple in the way that an individual friendship might not. An individual friendship might pull one member of a couple away, while a friendship that allows the couple to both be with each other and sustain a relationship with another couple could reenforce the couple's relationship with each other. In this chapter, we look specifically at how couples, who identify another couple as close friends *as a couple*, manage that friendship.

LITERATURE REVIEW

Social networks refer to "structural properties of the social milieu that reflect regular patterns in the organization of the social system (i.e., patterned interconnections of members)" (Bost et al. 2002, 518). Individual friends have been defined operationally as people one trusts, one depends on, and by whom one feels supported and understood (Greif 2009). Friends, along with family, are a part of an individual's or couple's social network or support system. Couples may have individual friends, share friends in common, or engage as a dyad with another couple.

While no studies look specifically at couple friendships with other couples, some examine the role that social support networks, including friends, play in a couple's marriage. For example, marital success in long-term marriages has been found to be related to husbands and wives receiving support for their marriage from friends and family (Brandt and Conger 1999). Over time, a couple's social networks tend to become more overlapping, that is, they share more friends in common (Kalmijn 2003), a phenomenon related to marital satisfaction (Allgood, Crane, and Agee 1997; Hansen, Fallon, and Novotny 1991; Kearns and Leonard 2004). Couples tend to form these overlapping friendship networks primarily prior to and during their first year of marriage, after which the interdependence of husbands' and wives' networks remains fairly stable (Kearns and Leonard 2004).

The phenomenon of couples sharing overlapping social networks is complex, however. On the one hand, intensity of interactions can be a problem—if the networks are too small and the interactions too intense, the couple may experience depression and anxiety (Hansen, Fallon, and Novotny 1991). On the other hand, having shared lifestyles where friends are held in common can help keep couples together because the cost of breaking up is greater (Kalmijn and Bernasco 2001).

Gender differences have been found in the ways men and women seek out support from friends (Allgood, Crane, and Agee 1997). Men are likely to talk to their male friends until a great deal of self-disclosure is needed, at which point they stop talking to those friends. Men's help-seeking is likely to be more cognitive in nature and more likely to involve action rather than sharing feelings (Barusch and Peak

1997). Women are more emotionally expressive with friends than are men and have a larger friendship network involving more women (Shye et al. 1995). Husbands are more apt to rely on their wives for emotional support and less apt to rely on male friends (Allgood, Crane, and Agee 1997; Liebler and Sandefur 2002). Some other differences have been found between men's friendships with men and their friendships with women. With female friends, men have been found to be more empathic, understanding, appreciative, connected, and supportive than they are with male friends (Parker and de Vries 1993; Rose 1985; Vonk and von Nobelen 1993).

When men are with their partners, they may feel more comfortable with emotional expressiveness. Slatcher (2010), in a laboratory situation, experimented with couples by randomly assigning them to two groups—one that participated in self-disclosure tasks and one that made small talk. Those who participated in self-disclosure were more likely to want to see the other couple after the experiment than those who shared small talk.

These findings raise questions about how mixed-gender dyads (heterosexual couples) relate to one another, that is, to what extent couple friendships reflect the emotional expressiveness women tend to bring to relationships or the action-orientation men appear to prefer. One possibility these findings regarding differences between men's same- and cross-sex friendships suggest is that, in a couple-to-couple friendship, men may experience greater freedom to express support and emotional connectedness because they are in the company of women to whom they feel close—their wives and close female friends.

Babchuk's (1965) study (which we cite with reservations as significant changes in roles have occurred since it was undertaken) explored middle-class couples' primary friends and whether those friends became friends of both members of the couple. In interviews with 117 heterosexual couples, almost half did not have an individual or primary friendship other than their spouse. Husbands took the lead more often than wives in establishing friendships for the couple. Wives became less willing to make friends through their husbands as the length of the marriage increased. At three years of marriage, mutual friends were often married and the couple became friends with the newly formed couple. Three years into the marriage, the couple was also meeting more couples and forming friendships together (486). Of further note, the "interviews showed that respondents were not always equally close to both individuals. Inclusion of both spouses as primary friends stemmed from the patterns of visiting which most often took place on a couple basis" (487). Also, one husband stated during the interview that if you were close with one member of a couple, it was hard not to be close with the other. In a handful of interviews, however, both partners identified one member of the couple but not the other as a primary friend. Of final note, during the interviews couples were apt to initially say they were equally close to both members of the couple but, later in the interview, would single out the same-sex member of the other couple as the person with whom they were closer. Equality of closeness between all four members was not "morally appropriate," a position supported by the majority of those interviewed.

Differences in friendship maintenance for couples appear based on age. Agnew, Loving, and Drigotas (2001) found that young, dating couples who have a higher proportion of joint versus individual friends were more committed to and satisfied with their relationship, findings similar to those relating to the network overlap referenced above. Sherman, de Vries, and Lansford (2000) found that younger couples communicate more in face-to-face interactions than older couples, who tend to rely more on the telephone and mail. Matthews (1988) describes the friendship-making process newlyweds go through, noting that, before the wedding, the partners are concerned with whether they will be accepted by their partner's friends. After the wedding, they consider how much they like their partner's friends. They begin to consider who will stay friends with one of them and who will become friends with both of them. By extension, the friends of the partner's partner also are considered within the realm of friendship.

Differences also were found in married versus partnered couples. Partnered couples in the Netherlands who were not yet married were found to spend less time together than married couples, due, it is believed, to the uncertainty of the future of their relationship (Kalimijn and Bernasco 2001).

Parenthood is often linked to being a member in a couple. Adjustment to parenthood for the couple can be a developmental milestone that affects social networks. In a study of 137 couples, those who described greater network support prior to the birth of their first child were more likely to report having larger and more supportive networks two years postpartum (Bost et al. 2002). The authors found that contact with family members, referenced above in relation to overly intense social networks, varied based on the needs of the couple, such that couples who were having emotional difficulties were more likely to have contact with their family and, by extension, their social network than those who were adjusting well. Need may drive the contact so that less frequent network contact may not necessarily be related to poor adjustment in the couple. Gender differences also appeared. The number and quality of friendships declined during this two-year period for fathers but not for mothers, and both mothers and fathers who expressed satisfaction with their friendships were less apt to experience depression.

Liebler and Sandefur (2002), studying social support at midlife from data in the Wisconsin Longitudinal Study, found, consistent with other research, that women are more likely than men to give and receive emotional support. Men in middle age are more apt to value their friendships more highly and speak about them in greater depth than younger men (Fox, Gibbs, and Auerbach 1985). Tolerance of friends increases with age for both men and women, and people will make greater attempts to resolve differences as they age (Antonucci and Akiyama 1995, as cited in Berk 1998; Fox, Gibbs, and Auerbach 1985).

In addition, race-based differences regarding friendship-related behavior have been explored. According to Ellison (1990), African American men and women disclose more personal information to their friends than whites. This may be linked to whites' greater focus on individualism as compared with blacks' collectivism (Coleman, Ganong, and Rothrauff 2006). Collectivism would include the notion that people take care of one another within the family and within the community (Boyd-Franklin 2005). It could be anticipated that African Americans would place a greater emphasis on networking with others than would whites, though a study by Griffin et al. (2006) found that black women had fewer friends and levels of support than white women. Differences between black women and black men are similar to those between white women and white men, that is, black women have larger social support systems than black men (Barker, Morrow, and Mitteness 1998).

Despite the research on couples and their social networks, no one has looked specifically at how couples interact with other couples. By exploring how couples maintain their friendship with one particular couple, we will gain a picture of "best friends" and how that applies to our understanding of friendships in general.

METHODS

The data for this study are drawn from a mixed-methods convenience study of seventy-six couples who were interviewed about their couple friendships with other couples for part of a larger study (Greif and Deal, under contract). The sample was gathered by seventeen master of social work students who varied in age, race, and gender. Following Institutional Review Board approval for the study, the students passed university-required Web-based training on the ethics of research and HIPAA (Health Insurance Privacy and Portability Act) compliance. Students were trained as research interviewers in qualitative methods and were asked to interview five couples about their friendships with other couples using a fifteen-question qualitative interview guide. Many interviewed couples they knew or were friends of people they knew. They were instructed to not interview couples they knew to be in marital distress because harm could potentially befall such couples if the interview raised issues that were unsettled between them. A thirty-one-item written questionnaire was also completed separately by each member of the couple while the couples were together; interviews were conducted jointly, with both members of the couple present. Seventy-six useable couple interviews and 152 individual questionnaires, derived from contacts with heterosexual couples, were the sample frame.

Asking open-ended questions in a qualitative interview is a frequently used form of naturalistic inquiry that is similar to the therapeutic interview in that emotionally laden material may emerge (Padgett 2008). The open-ended questions are broad enough to allow subjects to respond in a variety of ways. With virtually no information available on these couple relationships, we chose a mixed-methods approach to gain an exploratory understanding of their unique nature.

The students audiotaped and transcribed their interviews. They then discussed their findings and impressions of the meaning of the data with other students during class meetings. This process helped each student to better understand possible ways of interpreting the questions to the interviewees and of interpreting the respondents' answers. This iterative process is common when research teams approach a topic.

Data from the written questionnaires were entered into Microsoft Excel; the qualitative interviews were coded independently and also entered into Excel. The principal investigators (PIs) and a research assistant independently coded for themes from the couples based, in part, on understandings gained from the students' work and from the corollary literature. The two PIs had a high level of agreement (95%) on the codes and resolved differences, where they appeared, through discussion. This verification process and triangulation are common in qualitative research.

During the qualitative interview, after couples were asked about couple friendships in general, the couple was asked to identify one couple with whom they have a good friendship and to answer a series of questions. Couples tended to agree on a couple who were their best friends as a couple. These were rarely family members. For this chapter, the responses to ten open- and closed-ended questions (one question had nine parts to it) were selected. These items were chosen because we believe they provide a broad description of the way these close couple friendships function. The following questions were used for this analysis:

1. Describe how the friendship started. (This item was intended to learn whether couple friendships are started mutually or by one member of the couple.)
2. Do you talk about your friendship as a couple with them? (This item was intended to learn how open the couples were with each other about their friendship.)
3. Who tends to initiate getting together? (This question was intended to learn how these friendships are maintained, whether their time together is mutually initiated or whether one couple believes they are the initiators.)
4. Do you trust both members of the couple?
5. Are both members equally likeable? (This was used as a cross-check to ensure that the couple chosen was usually a couple that was close friends though some variation in response was expected given the nature of the question.)
6. Would you feel comfortable discussing any of the following with them—child's problems; health problems; sexual issues in your marriage/relationship; money issues in your marriage/relationship; family issues in your extended family; work issues; issues with other friends; political issues; religious issues?
7. Do you have a favorable view of the marriage/relationship of the couple you identified?
8. What aspects, if any, of their marriage/relationship do you admire?
9. Do you wish your marriage was more like theirs?
10. Are they affectionate with each other?

We then explored whether the following were correlated with the responses to dependent variables selected from the questionnaire and the coded responses to the qualitative interviews: the age of the individual (as well as the total age of the couple), the race and socioeconomic class of the couple, whether the couple was married versus partnered, and the number of years married or partnered.

As this is one of the first studies conducted on this topic, we consider these findings to be preliminary and in need of verification through future research. The fact that this is a convenience sample is both a strength and a limitation of the study. While the sample is not random (getting a random sample for this topic may be highly difficult), the significant number of interviewers resulted in a fairly diverse nonclinical sample. The generalizability of the study's findings is limited by its use of people who agreed to be interviewed on this topic and who were known by the interviewee. However, this study is unique in that it represents an effort to begin exploration of an important and underresearched area using a mixed-methods design.

THE SAMPLE

The seventy-six couples (152 respondents) ranged in age from twenty-one to ninety-five. The mean age of the individual respondents was forty-one, and the median combined ages for the couple (we added up both her and his age) was sixty-seven, indicating a typical couple was in their early to mid-thirties. The sample was largely white (71.1%) and African American (23.7%), with a small percentage of others (5.3%). Six of the seventy-six couples are interracial. Almost half (45.6%) are Protestant, 26.2 percent are Catholic/Eastern Orthodox, 8.7 pecent are Jewish, 14 percent did not identify a religion, and the remaining handful were split between agnostic and atheist. The number of years married/partnered ranged from 1 year (the minimum to participate in the study) to 55 years. The mean number of years together is 14 and the median is 7.25 years. Over half the couples (58%) have children in the home or have had them in the home. When asked to identify their socioeconomic class, 18.6 percent gave their class as lower or lower middle class, 52.4 percent as middle class, and 28.9 percent as upper middle class or upper class. Almost one-fourth (23.3%) completed high school only, 12 percent had some college, 40 percent completed college, and 24.7 percent had some graduate school education. One in five (20.8%) are blue-collar workers, 47 percent are white-collar employees, 15.4 percent are professionals, 10.1 percent are retired, 4 percent are students, and 2.7 percent are unemployed. Respondents had lived in the area where they were interviewed for between three months and 62 years, with 17.1 as the mean number of years. Nearly 66 percent (65.8%) reported this was their first marriage or partnering, and 67.8 percent were married while 32.2 percent were partnered.

Forty-two percent indicated on the questionnaire that couple friendships are very important, 36 percent said they are somewhat important, and 22 percent said they are slightly/not important. One in seven respondents (14.7%) answered that they do not have enough couple friends and wished they had more. The other respondents either had enough friends but wanted more (48.7%) or had enough friends and did not want more (36.7%). The median number of couple friends the couple identified during the qualitative interview was five. Time together with friends is usually spent around food, either eating at a couple's house or out at a restaurant, going to movies, or getting together at someone's house. In identifying a particular couple to talk about in the interview, the range of years of having known at least one member of the couple was between 1 and 55 years. The mean number of years was 12.4, and the median number was 8.

THE FINDINGS

Describe how the friendship started. For 89 percent of the couples, this particular couple friendship was based originally on an individual friendship started by one person. Typical friendships in this group were ones in which close high school or college friends each found a partner and then the two couples became friends. For the other 11 percent, the couple friendship was begun as a mutual relationship between the four people. These friendships were often formed around their children or within a religious context.

Do you talk about your friendship as a couple with them? Over three-fifths of the sample (61%) answered that they have talked about the nature of their friendship with the other couple, and the other two-fifths (39%) replied the nature of the friendship had not been discussed.

Who tends to initiate getting together? Seventy-seven percent replied socializing was initiated mutually, 12 percent believed the other couple initiated socializing, and 11 percent felt they were responsible for approaching the other couple about socializing.

Do you trust both members of the couple? A high degree of trust exists between the two couples, with 90 percent saying they trusted both members, 6 percent replying that it depends on the topic, and 4 percent replying they do not trust one member of the couple..

Are both members equally likeable? The vast majority, 87 percent, thought both members were equally likeable, with the other 13 percent saying they were not equally likeable or, in one case, the couple did not agree on whether they were equally likeable.

Would you feel comfortable discussing any of the following with them? Figures represent the couples' yes responses: child's problems, 89 percent; health problems, 88 percent; sexual issues in your marriage/relationship, 23 percent; money issues in your marriage/relationship, 48 percent; family issues in your extended family, 84 percent; work issues, 98 percent; issues with other friends, 79 percent; political issues, 90 percent; and religious issues, 90 percent.

Do you have a favorable view of the marriage/relationship of the couple you identified? While 80 percent said they had a favorable view, the rest were mixed in their view (16%) or held an unfavorable view (4%).

What aspects, if any, of their marriage/relationship do you admire? Respondents could give more than one answer: Fifty-four percent admired their friends' demonstrations of loving, caring, and sharing, 20 percent admired the freedom that the partners allowed each other to pursue their own interests, 19 percent admired the couple's perseverance or sticking together through tough times, 18 percent admired the other couple's always having fun together and doing interesting things as a couple, 17 percent admired how they interacted with their children and/or their relationship with their children, and 12 percent gave other answers.

Do you wish your marriage was more like theirs? Despite the fondness for the other couple, 76 percent said they "never" wish their marriage was like the other couple's. Of the remaining couples, most said they "rarely" wish their marriage was like the other couple's, with a few saying they "sometimes" wish their marriage was like the other couple's.

Are they affectionate with each other? Forty-three percent said their couple friends were usually affectionate with each other, 25 percent said sometimes, and 32 percent said they were rarely or never affectionate.

We explored whether selected demographic variables—race, age, years married, friendship length, class, partnered versus married, and whether one or both partners have children—were related to the responses the couples gave. We will present statistically significant results for race, age (along with years married and friendship length, which are often related to age), class, and whether the couple is married or partnered.

In relation to race, because of the small cell sizes for Asian and Latino respondents, we only compared couples in which both partners were white and couples in which both were African American. This left a sample size of sixty-four couples. In general, white couples seem more willing to talk about specific issues with their close couple friends than African American couples. When couples were asked if they would feel comfortable discussing a series of issues with their close couple friends, whites would feel more comfortable discussing health problems ($x^2 = 13.55$; df = 1; p < .001), family issues ($x^2 = 6.02$; df = 1; p < .014), their relationships with other friends ($x^2 = 5.20$; df = 1; p < .03), and religion ($x^2 = 7.08$; df = 1; p < .008) than would African American couples. In relation to sex, money, children, work, and politics, there were no significant differences in the responses.

For the number of years married, respondents were grouped by those married one to three years (29%), four to nine years (32%), and ten-plus years (39%). The longer a couple was married or partnered, the less comfortable they would feel talking about sex: 25 percent of those married/partnered one to three years would feel comfortable talking about sex with their couple friends, but only 8 percent of those together ten years or more would feel comfortable talking about sex ($x^2 = 6.36$; df = 2; p < .05). By a similar measure, we looked at the length of the friendship and grouped people by those who were friends with at least one member in the couple for ten years or less (63%) or more than ten years (37%). The longer the friendship, the more comfortable the couple would feel talking about the following:

their child's problems (x^2 = 5.62; df = 1; p < .02), health problems (x^2 = 6.17; df = 1; p < .013), and family issues (x^2 = 4.82; df = 1; p < .03). The longer the marriage, the more likely they are to say they wish their marriage was more like that of their friends (x^2 = 4.14; df = 1; p < .05). A similar finding appeared for the number of years married (older people would tend to be married longer) with those married longer more likely to say they wished their marriage was more like their friends' (x^2 = 8.44; df = 2; p < .02).

The only significant difference in the responses of those married from those partnered is that partnered couples felt more comfortable talking about sex (x^2 = 4.50; df = 1; p < .04) with their close couple friends. The presence of children was not related to any of the questions explored. Race, age, years married, married versus partnered, and class were not related to whether members were equally likeable in the other couple or in the amount of affection observed in the other couple. In terms of what they admire in another couple, when we analyzed the data by the first response given in relation to what they admired, we found no significant differences. When analyzed by whether a response was given at all about what they admired (respondents could give more than one response), we also found no significant differences.

DISCUSSION AND CLINICAL IMPLICATIONS

The responses and analyses draw a picture of the way a couple, as part of a non-clinical sample, maintains and considers a friendship with another couple with whom both members of that couple feel close. While research on how couples manage friendships with an individual friend is available (e.g., Kearns and Leonard 2004), our finding that 89 percent of couple friendships with a close couple are initiated by one partner and not mutually offers a rare window into how these particular relationships start. It does not mean that all couple friendships start this way, just those that are mutually agreed upon as being a close couple. Similarly, the couples viewed themselves and their close couple friends as equally taking the initiative to socialize (76%), rather than one couple usually taking the lead. It may be that this mutuality of responsibility for getting together is one reason the other couple is chosen as couple friends. The level of discussion about the friendship (62% comment on it), along with the general likeability of both members (86%) and the high level of trust felt (90%), are other indications as to how a close couple friendship operates.

Another way to look at how these friendships operate is to consider what topics are discussed. Of the range of topics that couples would feel comfortable discussing with the other couple, relationships with family members and friends are included (along with health, children, religion, work, and politics). These findings, when considered along with the tendency of couples in this study to openly discuss their friendship with each other, suggest that men, when they are socializing with their spouse or partner, may engage more frequently in the kind of "relationship talk" common to women's friendships (Basow and Rubenfeld 2003; Wright and Scanlon 1991). These are not relationships driven solely by traditional male topics of discussion (e.g., sports). Most topics are on the table. Further investigation of the relationship patterns within couple-to-couple friendships could benefit from examining whether these friendships have characteristics typically seen in male or female friendships or some unique variation.

Despite the high level of trust and the mutuality in the relationship both in terms of initiating contact and how likeable both members are, some topics remain off limits for some of the couples. Sexual issues in particular are off limits to three-quarters of the couples. Money issues are off limits for half of the couples. When probing further in the qualitative interviews, couples often said that sex would be discussed between the women in the couple and not between the men. Money was occasionally mentioned as a topic of discussion between the men, while women rarely or never mentioned money as a topic they would save for their same-sex friendships.

Couples' close couple friends' marriage or partnership was generally viewed favorably (only one couple said they did not admire anything), though five (all with friends of twelve years' duration or more) said they wished their marriage was like that of their friends. Over half of the couples said they admired the other couple's demonstrations of loving, sharing, and caring for each other, consistent with viewing their friends' relationship as usually or sometimes affectionate. Approximately the same percentages of respondents admired the couple's willing-ness to allow each other freedom to pursue their own interests and to do fun things together as a couple, although no couple reported admiring both these aspects of their friends' relationship.

All couples need to internally balance closeness with each other and individua-tion, and it appears that couples, when they were asked what they admire in the other couple, viewed both qualities as strengths. Some research suggests that couples with too much freedom or separateness may not be considered as having a joint lifestyle (Kalmijn and Bernasco 2001) and may have a less satisfying marriage (Kingston and Nock 1987). However, another study, which found that husbands and wives who maintained separate same-sex friendships reported high levels of marital satisfac-tion, hypothesized that using these friendships as supplemental sources of support and assistance enhances the marital relationship (Stein et al. 1992). Couples may also look to their couple friends to see how they manage tensions within their marriage as almost one-fifth (19%) of the couples interviewed admired their couple friends' perseverance in sticking together through difficult times.

The findings in relation to race were unexpected. Given the collective nature of African Americans compared with whites (Coleman, Ganong, and Rothrauff 2006), we had expected them to feel more comfortable than whites in raising personal issues. We do not know if the declining marriage rates among African Americans compared with whites (Boyd-Franklin 2005) or the added pressures on African American couples (Black 2000) suggest that when couples are together with their friends they wish to focus on positive topics or keep the discussions on a lighter note.

The results of the impact of time on the couple friendship are mixed as three different independent variables were used—number of years married, length of friendship, and age. First, the longer married, the less apt a couple is to talk about sex. It could be that sex talk in general is more prevalent among recently wed and partnered people (if they are younger) as their sex lives are generally more active than the sex lives of older couples. It could be that people who have been married/partnered longer are more circumspect in what they wish to talk about as they were raised in an age where sex was not treated as openly as it is now. Second, the longer married/partnered, the more likely a couple is to have children with the potential for problems and to encounter health issues for themselves and their family that emerge and become topics of discussion. Third, older couples who have more established relationships may feel more comfortable discussing the pros and cons of their friends' marriage as well as admiring the marriage without the discussion threatening their own relationship. Allgood, Crane, and Agee (1997) found a correlation between those who openly talk about their marital problems and stability in marriage; openness between older established couples in admiring the marriage of close friends may represent another indication of marital stability.

Partnered people were more open to talking about sex and politics with the couple they identified and tended to wish their relationship was more like that couple's. One possibility is that the openness of partnered couples compared with married couples is due to partnered couples having a less permanent and more permeable boundary—that is, fewer issues are considered to belong to the couple only. Their level of self-differentiation as a couple, where roles and responsibilities are developed, may not be as developed (Zwirn and Jessee 1987). From our data, we are unable to tell if wishing their relationship was more like the other couple was related to their own status as being partnered and not married. We did not ask the marital status of the identified couple friends.

CONCLUSION

We have attempted to describe an important relationship that has been ignored in the literature yet may be very important to health and happiness: a couple's platonic relationship with another couple. Through interviews and questionnaires from a nonclinical sample of seventy-six couples, we have a beginning understanding of the importance of these friendships, how they are started and maintained, what topics may be discussed, whether both partners in a couple are considered likeable and trustworthy, and one couple's perception of another couple's marriage.

As Degges-White and Borzumato-Gainey (2011) write, "Having a variety of others in our social network, kin or non-kin, is important, but the quality of the relationship we have with our partner, out of any other social relationship (including both family and friends), is the one most highly associated with our well-being" (227–228). Couples who have couple friends get to spend time with each other and nurture their primary relationship while also socializing and having new experiences with others. The more we understand how these relationships typically function, the more we can help couples understand and enhance their own relationships.

REFERENCES

Agnew, C. R., T. J. Loving, and S. M. Drigotas. 2001. Substituting the forest for the trees: Social networks and the prediction of romantic relationship state and fate. *Journal of Personality and Social Psychology* 81:1042–1057.

Allgood, S., M. D. R. Crane, and L. Agee. 1997. Social support: Distinguishing clinical and volunteer couples. *American Journal of Family Therapy* 25:111–119.

Babchuk, N. 1965. Primary friends and kin: A study of the associations of middle-class couples. *Social Forces* 43:483–493.

Barker, J. C., J. Morrow, and L. S. Mitteness. 1998. Gender, informal social support networks, and elderly urban African Americans. *Journal of Aging Studies* 12:199–223.

Barusch, A. S., and T. Peak. 1997. Support groups for older men: Building on strengths and facilitating relationships. In *Elderly men: Special problems and personal challenges,* edited by J. L. Kosberg and L. W. Kaye, 262–278. New York: Springer.

Basow, S.A., and K. Rubenfeld. 2003. "Troubles talk": Effects of gender and gender typing. *Sex Roles* 48:183–187.

Berk, L. E. 1998. *Development through the lifespan.* Boston: Allyn and Bacon.

Biesanz, J. C., S. G. West, and A. Millevoi. 2007. What do you learn about someone over time? The relationship between length of acquaintance and consensus and self-other agreement in judgments of personality. *Journal of Personality and Social Psychology* 92:119–135.

Black, L. W. 2000. Therapy with African American couples. In *Couples on the fault line: New directions for therapists,* edited by P. Papp, 205–221. New York: Guilford.

Bost, K. K., M. J. Cox, M. R. Burchinal, and C. Payne. 2002. Structural and supportive changes in couples' family and friendship networks across the transition to parenthood. *Journal of Marriage and Family* 64:517–531.

Boyd-Franklin, N. 2005. *Black families in therapy: Understanding the African American experience.* 2nd ed. New York: Guilford.

Brandt, C. M., and R. D. Conger. 1999. Marital success and domains of social support in long-term relationships: Does the influence of network members ever end? *Journal of Marriage and the Family* 61:437–450.

Brehm, S. S. 1985. *Intimate relationships.* New York: Random House.

Coleman, M., L. H. Ganong, and T. C. Rothrauff. 2006. Racial and ethnic similarities and differences in beliefs about intergenerational assistance to older adults after divorce and remarriage. *Family Relations* 55:576–587.

Degges-White, S., and C. Borzumato-Gainey. 2011. *Friends forever: How girls and women forge relationships.* New York: Rowman & Littlefield.

Ellison, C. G. 1990. Family ties, friendships, and subjective well-being among black Americans. *Journal of Marriage and Family* 52:298–310.

Fox, M., M. Gibbs, and D. Auerbach. 1985. Age and gender dimensions of friendship. *Psychology of Women Quarterly* 9:489–502.

Fraenkel, P., and S. Wilson. 2000. Clocks, calendars, and couples: Time and the rhythms of relationships. In *Couples on the fault line: New directions for therapists*, edited by P. Papp, 63–103. New York: Guilford.

Greif, G. L. 2009. *Buddy system: Understanding male friendships.* New York: Oxford University Press.

Greif, G. L., and K. H. Deal. Under contract. *Couples and their couple friendships: The seekers, keepers, and nesters.* New York: Routledge.

Griffin, M. L., M. Amodeo, C. Clay, L. Fassler, and M. Ellis. 2006. Racial differences in social support: Kin versus friends. *American Journal of Orthopsychiatry* 76:374–380.

Hansen, F. J., A. E. Fallon, and S. L. Novotny. 1991. The relationship between social network structure and marital satisfaction in distressed and nondistressed couples: A pilot study. *Family Therapy* 18:102–114.

Hayslip, B., G. Han, and C. Anderson. 2008. Predictors of Alzheimer's disease caregiver depression and burden: What noncaregiving adults can learn from active caregivers. *Educational Gerontology* 34:945–969.

Kalmijn, M. 2003. Shared friendship networks and the life course: An analysis of survey data on married and cohabiting couples. *Social Networks* 25:231–249.

Kalmijn, M., and W. Bernasco. 2001. Joint and separated lifestyles in couple relationships. *Journal of Marriage and Family* 63:639–654.

Kearns, J. N., and K. E. Leonard. 2004. Social networks: Structural interdependence, and marital quality over the transition to marriage: A prospective study. *Journal of Family Psychology* 18:383–395.

Kingston, P., and S. Nock. 1987. Time together among dual earner couples. *American Sociological Review* 52:391–400.

Liebler, C. A., and G. D. Sandefur. 2002. Gender differences in the exchange of social support with friends, neighbors, and co-workers at midlife. *Social Science Research* 31:364–391.

Matthews, A. M. 1988. *Why did I marry you, anyway? Good sense and good humor in the first year . . . and after.* Boston: Houghton Mifflin.

Padgett, D. K. 2008. *Qualitative methods in social work research.* 2nd ed. Los Angeles: Sage.

Parker, S., and B. de Vries. 1993. Patterns of friendship for women and men in same and cross-sex relationships. *Journal of Social and Personal Relationships* 10:617–626.

Rose, S. 1985. Same- and cross-sex friendships and the psychology of homosociality. *Sex Roles* 12:63–74.

Sherman, A. M., B. deVries, and J. E. Lansford. 2000. Friendship in childhood and adulthood: Lessons across the life span. *International Journal of Aging and Human Development* 51:31–51.

Shye, D., J. P. Mullooly, D. K. Freeborn, and C. R. Pope. 1995. Gender differences in the relationship between social network support and mortality: A longitudinal study of an elderly cohort. *Social Science & Medicine* 41:935–947.

Slatcher, R. B. 2010. When Harry and Sally met Dick and Jane: Creating closeness between couples. *Personal Relationships* 17:279–297.

Stein, C. H., E. G. Bush, R. R. Ross, and M. Ward. 1992. Mine, yours and ours: A configural analysis of the networks of married couples in relation to marital satisfaction and individual well-being. *Journal of Social and Personal Relationships* 9:365–383.

Vonk, R., and D. von Nobelen. 1993. Masculinity and femininity in the self with an intimate partner: Men are not always men in the company of women. *Journal of Social and Personal Relationships* 10:627–630.

Waite, L. J., and M. Gallagher. 2000. *The case for marriage: Why married people are happier, healthier, and better off financially.* New York: Doubleday.

Wright, P. H., and M. B. Scanlon. 1991. Gender role orientations and friendships: Some attenuation, but gender differences abound. *Sex Roles* 24:551–566.

Zwirn, B., and E. Jessee. 1987. A resistant couple. In *Casebook: Structured enrichment programs for couples and families*, edited by L. L'Abate and L. Young, 327–338. New York: Bruner Mazel.

Chapter 5

Sexual and Romantic Interests in Opposite-Sex Friendships

April Bleske-Rechek

Anyone with an opposite-sex friend has probably received the following question from curious outsiders: "Are you two dating, or are you just *friends?*" The frequency with which people pose this question to opposite-sex pairs demonstrates that "friendship" is a relationship that is typically not defined as a reproductive or romantic partnership. In fact, opposite-sex friendship has been described as a voluntary, cooperative, *nonromantic* alliance between members of the opposite sex (Werking 1997). Arguably, however, the most consistent finding in the short history (approximately two decades) of research on opposite-sex friendship is the existence of either one-sided attraction or mutual attraction between friends. This chapter reviews briefly the history of research on romantic and sexual attraction in opposite-sex friendship, theoretical explanations for its existence, and the potential benefits and costs of attraction between opposite-sex friends.

PREVALENCE AND INTENSITY OF ATTRACTION IN OPPOSITE-SEX FRIENDSHIP

In one of the first theoretical papers on opposite-sex friendship, O'Meara (1989) proposed that opposite-sex friends confront four major challenges: determining

the type of emotional bond shared, facing sexuality in the relationship, presenting the relationship as an authentic friendship to outsiders, and addressing equality in the context of gender inequality. Numerous studies have demonstrated that
opposite-sex friends confront the first three of these challenges (Afifi and Faulkner
2000; Baxter and Wilmot 1984; Bleske-Rechek and Buss 2001; Cupach and Metts
1991; Guerrero and Chavez 2005; Kaplan and Keys 1997; Messman, Canary, and
Hause 2000; Reeder 2000; Sapadin 1988; Swain 1992), all of which reflect the core
issue of sexuality between friends (O'Meara 1989).

The frequency and intensity with which mating interests manifest in opposite-
sex friendships vary from study to study; for example, Reeder (2000) reported
that just 20–30 percent of young men and women experience physical or sexual
attraction to their opposite-sex friends, whereas Kaplan and Keys (1997) reported
that the majority of young adults reported at least slight sexual attraction to an
opposite-sex friend and Afifi and Faulkner (2000) reported that about half of
young men and women have had sexual intercourse with an opposite-sex friend.
Some of the variability in response from study to study may be a product of how
opposite-sex friends are defined for participants. For example, in some studies
participants are simply asked to think of an opposite-sex friend, in others they are
asked to think of a friend of the opposite sex with whom they are not romantically involved, and in some they are asked about a *member* of the opposite sex
with whom they are not romantically involved. Some of the variability in response
may also be a product of the type of attraction in question: Some researchers ask
participants to report their level of sexual attraction, others ask about romantic
attraction or physical attraction, and still others (e.g., Sapadin 1988) ask about
sexual tension in the friendship.

Some of the variability in response may also be related to the age of participants. Specifically, a number of studies with higher estimates involve college students; levels of romantic attraction seem to be lower among middle-aged adults
(Bleske-Rechek et al., under review), for a number of potential reasons that need
to be explored. For example, attraction to opposite-sex friends may be lower
among middle-aged adults because these men and women are more likely to be
have serious commitments (e.g., marriage) and thus may be more "blind" to alternatives (Simpson, Gangestad, and Lerma 1990), or because they spend less time
with their friends than younger men and women do, or because they have friends
who are about their age and thus might inspire lower levels of sexual attraction.
Or perhaps men's and women's opposite-sex friends in middle adulthood are less
likely to be selected by direct choice but instead are tied to spouse, their workplace,
or the friend and activity choices of their children. Given the myriad variables that
are likely to be systematically tied to the prevalence and intensity of attraction
between friends, it is notable that the issue surfaces in investigations of friendship regardless of how it is presented, and even when it is not presented at all.
In one study that asked men and women to list ways in which their opposite-sex

friendships enhance their lives and complicate their lives, comments about attraction and sexual tension came up spontaneously in both types of lists, among both emerging adults and middle-aged adults (Bleske-Rechek et al., under review).

THEORETICAL EXPLANATIONS FOR ATTRACTION IN OPPOSITE-SEX FRIENDSHIP

In explaining attraction in opposite-sex friendship, a common starting point is that opposite-sex friendships as we know them are a relatively modern phenomenon (Monsour 1997). In many parts of the modern world, genetically unrelated men and women of reproductive age interact together in unprecedented ways: They work together, entertain their children together, play sports together, and pursue vocational training and hobbies together. If these interactions are unique to modern society, what are people relying on to navigate them? A constructionist explanation emphasizes culture and society forces. According to Monsour (2002), for example, the media instills in men and women the suggestion that they should be attracted to their opposite-sex friends. The media portrays "normal" relationships between men and women as sexual, and hence nonsexual relationships between men and women as strange. This attitude is demonstrated in some of the most popular American television series and movies of the 1980s, 1990s, and 2000s—*Moonlighting, Cheers, When Harry Met Sally, Friends, The Office, Scrubs, He's Just Not That into You*—all of which thrive on the romantic tension and excitement portrayed between opposite-sex "friends" who end up either in a romantic partnership or a temporary attempt at one.

Evolutionary theorists have focused more on biological underpinnings of attraction in friendship (Bleske and Buss 2000; Koenig, Kirkpatrick, and Ketelaar 2007). For example, one possibility is that humans have psychological adaptations specific to opposite-sex friendship, and these adaptations guide men's and women's behaviors in the formation, maintenance, and termination of opposite-sex friendships (Bleske 2001). This adaptationist perspective requires that our human ancestors engaged recurrently in friendships with members of the opposite sex. It also requires that engaging in those friendships served as an effective strategy for solving one or more problems of survival or reproduction, such as gaining physical protection or sexual access, such that individuals who engaged in opposite-sex friendships outreproduced, on average, individuals who did not.

An alternative evolutionary hypothesis is that men's and women's perceptions of their opposite-sex friends are a manifestation of their evolved human mating adaptations operating in a modern environment. That is, attraction in opposite-sex friendship is a byproduct of humans' evolved mating strategies being activated in a novel social context (Bleske-Rechek et al., under review). According to this byproduct hypothesis, humans' evolved mating strategies facilitate involvement in opposite-sex friendships and also lead to attraction to friends—even when not intended. This explanation has two requirements: first, that what people generally define as opposite-sex friendship is unique to recent human history; and second, that humans have evolved mating strategies.

There is no doubt that modern cultural influences and the dynamics of personal relationships over human ancestral history will both be relevant for a full understanding of why and when men and women experience attraction to their opposite-sex friends. These different influences may also interact. To the extent that evolved aspects of the human psyche influence men's and women's perceptions of their relationships, they may also influence men's and women's creation of, and susceptibility to, different cultural and environmental influences.

A number of findings on opposite-sex friends do coincide, however, with the suggestion that evolved mating strategies are a key piece of the puzzle. Gender and context effects on attraction in opposite-sex friendship replicate those seen in the mating literature. First, across a number of samples, men report more sexual interest in their friends than women do (Bleske and Buss 2000; Kaplan and Keys 1997), even when the samples include pairs of friends (Bleske 2001; Bleske-Rechek et al., under review; Koenig et al. 2007). Second, as predicted from research on evolved biases in cross-sex mind reading (Haselton and Buss 2000), men overestimate their female friends' attraction to them; women underestimate (Bleske-Rechek et al., under review; Koenig et al. 2007). Third, as predicted from research on sex differences in interest in short-term mating (Schmitt 2005), single and involved young men alike experience moderate sexual and dating interest in their opposite-sex friends, whereas involved women report less interest in their friends than single women do (Bleske-Rechek et al., under review).

POTENTIAL IMPLICATIONS OF ATTRACTION IN OPPOSITE-SEX FRIENDSHIP

Many scholars have noted and documented that individuals vary widely in their response to sexual attraction in their opposite-sex friendships (Bell 1981; Rawlins 1992; Sapadin 1988). Opposite-sex friends provide a host of positive elements, like advice and support, that occur in both friendships and romantic relationships, so adding attraction to the mix may lead to uncertainty about the status of the relationship as platonic or romantic (Guerrero and Mongeau 2008). Presumably, how people feel about attraction varies depending on whether it is mutual or one-sided; it may also vary widely across friendships, such that the same individual might perceive attraction as adding zest to one opposite-sex friendship but tension to another; and perceptions might also vary over time in the context of the same friendship, such that attraction might be stronger or more favorably received when the members are single than when they are involved. These speculations have not yet been probed systematically.

There is some research to suggest that, overall, men and women frequently experience sexual attraction as a challenge, but that addressing it is associated with friendship maintenance as opposed to dissolution (Halatsis and Christakis 2009), perhaps because addressing it can reduce relational uncertainty. Among both young and middle-aged adults—women, in particular—attraction in friendship is nominated as a cost or complication of friendship far more often than it is nominated as a benefit (Bleske-Rechek et al., under review). That said, some adults do nominate it as a benefit, with men doing so more often than women. Perhaps the prevalence of nominations of attraction as a cost or complication is tied to how attraction can impact or is perceived by people's other relationship partners. For example, in the aforementioned study, 25 percent of middle-aged men and 38 percent of middle-aged women spontaneously mentioned jealousy from their current romantic partner as a cost of having opposite-sex friendships; moreover, that jealousy may not be misplaced: men and women who reported more attraction to a current opposite-sex friend in their life reported lower levels of satisfaction in their current romantic relationship (Bleske-Rechek et al., under review). The data are correlational and do not clarify whether attraction to a friend can negatively impact romantic relationship dynamics or whether dissatisfaction in one's romantic relationship can lead to increased involvement with and attraction to an opposite-sex friend.

Perhaps future research that systematically follows just-initiated friendships over time will help to distinguish between those possibilities. Longitudinal studies will also help resolve many questions about the contexts under which male and female friends experience attraction to each other, the circumstances under which they choose to discuss it or act on it, and whether their friendship is strengthened as a result.

REFERENCES

Afifi, W. A., and S. L. Faulkner. 2000. On being "just friends": The frequency and impact of sexual activity in cross-sex friendships. *Journal of Social and Personal Relationships* 17:205–222. DOI: 10.1177/0265407500172003.

Baxter, L. A., and W. W. Wilmot. 1984. "Secrets tests": Social strategies for acquiring information about the state of the relationship. *Human Communication Research* 11:171–201. DOI: 10.1111/j.1468-2958.1984.tb00044.x.

Bell, R. R. 1981. Friendships of women and men. *Psychology of Women Quarterly* 5:402–417.

Bleske, A. L. 2001. The benefits and costs of friendship. Unpublished PhD diss., Department of Psychology, University of Texas at Austin.

Bleske, A. L., and D. B. Buss. 2000. Can men and women be just friends? *Personal Relationships* 21:131–151.

Bleske-Rechek, A. L., and D. M. Buss. 2001. Opposite-sex friendships: Sex differences and similarities in initiation, selection, and dissolution. *Personality and Social Psychology Bulletin* 27:1310–1323. DOI: 10.1177/01461672012710007.

Bleske-Rechek, A., E. Somers, C. Micke, L. Erickson, L. Matteson, B. Schumacher, C. Stocco, and L. Ritchie. Under review. Benefit or burden? Attraction in cross-sex friendship. *Journal of Social and Personal Relationships*.

Cupach, W. R., and S. Metts. 1991. Sexuality and communication in close relationships. In *Sexuality in close relationships,* edited by K. McKinney and S. Sprecher, 93–110. Hillsdale, NJ: Erlbaum.

Guerrero, L. K., and A. M. Chavez. 2005. Relational maintenance in cross-sex friendships characterized by different types of romantic intent: An exploratory study. *Western Journal of Communication* 69:339–358. DOI: 10.1080/10570310500305471.

Guerrero, L. K., and P. A. Mongeau. 2008. On becoming "more than friends": The transition from friendship to romantic relationship. In *Handbook of relationship initiation,* edited by S. Sprecher, A. Wenzel, and J. Harvey, 175–195. New York: Taylor and Francis.

Halatsis, P., and N. Christakis. 2009. The challenge of sexual attraction within heterosexuals' cross-sex friendship. *Journal of Social and Personal Relationships* 26:919–937.

Haselton, M. G., and D. M. Buss. 2000. Error management theory: A new perspective on biases in cross-sex mind reading. *Journal of Personality and Social Psychology* 78:81–91. DOI: 10.1037/0022-3514.78.1.81.

Kaplan, D. L., and C. B. Keys. 1997. Sex and relationship variables as predictors of sexual attraction in cross-sex platonic friendships between young heterosexual adults. *Journal of Social and Personal Relationships* 14:191–206. DOI: 10.1177/0265407597142003.

Koenig, B. L., L. A. Kirkpatrick, and T. Ketelaar. 2007. Misperception of sexual and romantic interests in opposite-sex friendships: Four hypotheses. *Personal Relationships* 14:411–429. DOI: 10.1111/j.1475-6811.2007.00163.x.

Messman, S. J., D. J. Canary, and K. S. Hause. 2000. Motives to remain platonic, equity, and the use of maintenance strategies in opposite-sex friendships. *Journal of Social and Personal Relationships* 17:67–94. DOI: 10.1177/0265407500171004.

Monsour, M. 1992. Meanings of intimacy in cross- and same-sex friendships. *Journal of Social and Personal Relationships* 9:277–295. DOI: 10.1177/0265407592092007.

Monsour, M. 1997. Communication and cross-sex friendships across the life cycle: A review of the literature. In *Communication yearbook 20,* edited by B. R. Burleson and A. W. Kunkel, 375–414. Thousand Oaks, CA: Sage.

Monsour, M. 2002. *Women and men as friends: Relationships across the life span in the 21st century.* Mahwah, NJ: Erlbaum.

O'Meara, J. D. 1989. Cross-sex friendships: Four basic challenges of an ignored relationship. *Sex Roles* 21:525–543. DOI: 10.1007/BF00289102.

Rawlins, W. 1992. *Friendship matter: Communication, dialects, and the life course.* New York: Aldine de Gruyter.

Reeder, H. M. 2000. "I like you … as a friend": The role of attraction in cross-sex friendships. *Journal of Social and Personal Relationships* 17:329–348. DOI: 10.1177/0265407500173002.

Sapadin, L. 1988. Friendship and gender: Perspectives of professional men and women. *Journal of Social and Personal Relationships* 5:387–403. DOI: 10.1177/0265407588054001.

Schmitt, D. P. 2005. Sociosexuality from Argentina to Zimbabwe: A 48-nation study of sex, culture, and strategies of human mating. *Behavioral and Brain Sciences* 28:247–311.

Simpson, J. A., S. W. Gangestad, and M. Lerma. 1990. Perception of physical attractiveness: Mechanisms involved in maintenance of romantic relationships. *Journal of Personality and Social Psychology* 59:1192–1201.

Swain, S. 1992. Men's friendships with women: Intimacy, sexual boundaries, and the informant role. In *Men's friendships*, edited by P. Nardi, 153–171. Thousand Oaks, CA: Sage.

Werking, K. 1997. *We're just good friends: Men and women in nonromantic relationships.* New York: Guilford Press.

Chapter 6

Disinterested Love in Cross-Class Romance Films, 1915–1939

Stephen Sharot

Cross-class romance films continue to be made, but the number of such films in recent years cannot compare with the considerable number that was released from 1915 to the late 1930s. The 1920s and 1930s differed greatly economically and in what may be called the "mood" of the nation, but both the partial prosperity of the 1920s and the Depression of the 1930s appear to have been conducive to what is often perceived as the "escapism" of the cross-class romance. Steven Ross (1998) writes that between 1921 and 1929 the total of "cross-class fantasy" films numbered over four hundred, or about 7 percent of all features. Lary May (2000) provides even higher estimates in a graph that shows that, of a sample of the films reviewed in the trade journal *Motion Picture Herald* between 1915 and 1940, films featuring marriage or romance across class lines varied from 10 percent to almost one-quarter. May's graph shows that after 1938, the number of cross-class romance films dropped rapidly. There is only one cross-class romance film in May's sample for 1946, and although the graph shows some increase in the early 1950s, this is followed by another drop with no cross-class romance film in 1958, when his survey ends. These estimates may be high, but there can little doubt that the period from World War I to the mid-1930s was a peak period for cross-class romance films.

Two characteristics of cross-class romance films stand out from an examination of a sample that I have built up of 203 cross-class romance films released between 1915 and 1939. First, in most films (84 percent), the rich protagonist is male and the poor protagonist is female. Second, most cross-class romance films (80 percent) end successfully with marriage or the promise of marriage. The proportion of films with unsuccessful outcomes was somewhat higher in the 1929–39 period (24 percent) compared with the 1915–1928 period (17 percent), and these were more evident in the male rich–female poor romances than in the female rich–male poor romances. In a number of films of the 1930s with rich females, their relationship is not with a working-class man but with a middle-class man, often a reporter, and in these, mainly screwball comedies of the 1930s, the romance is almost inevitably successful. If we exclude from the sample the films of rich heiresses and middle-class men (including the well-known films *It Happened One Night*, *Libeled Lady*, *Holiday*, and *Bringing Up Baby*), the overall proportion of unsuccessful cross-class romances of the 1930s rises to about a third of the total, twice the proportion of the earlier period.

An understanding of the popularity of the cross-class romance films and their characteristics requires a review of the contexts of cultural and social changes, especially those that relate to social class and gender. One important context was the spread throughout the class structure of the "disinterested" ideal of romance. Another was the gendered inequality of the work force as the number of women in particular sectors of the work force increased. A third relevant development was the advance of consumerism and its linkage with romance.

DISINTERESTED LOVE

The cross-class romance culminating in marriage or the expectation of marriage has been a common plot line throughout the history of not only film but also the novel. In literature, it appears in Samuel Richardson's *Pamela or Virtue Rewarded* (1740), regarded by many as the first true novel in the English language. The inclusion of "Virtue Rewarded" in Richardson's title points to a trope that is present in a great many subsequent cross-class romances: the poor character, most often a female, demonstrates virtues that are finally rewarded by marriage to the wealthy character, most often a male. The virtues of Richardson's heroine, a maid, are demonstrated by her struggle against the sexual advances of Mr. B, a member of the landed gentry. Pamela does not succumb to Mr. B's threats, violence, and promises, including his offer to make her economically independent, and he only acquires her through her consent and his acceptance of the norms of modern love. The theme of an upper-class male redeemed by the love of a woman lower than him in class became common in the English novel and popular romances (Armstrong 1990).

The major virtue of the twentieth-century heroine of the cross-class romance is not her sexual purity, although this remained a factor in the early decades of the century, but her disinterested love for the wealthy man. The integrity of the heroine was less focused on her body than it was on her indifference to material and other considerations of class and status, which are entirely subordinated to the overwhelming value and emotion of love. On his part, for the sake of love the wealthy man is willing to forego his class and status, as would occur, for example, if the opposition of his family takes the form of disinheritance. The love of the wealthy male for the poor female is generally accepted as sufficient reason to explain his choice, despite the frequent opposition of status-conscious parents, but in a rare admission in *Working Girls* (Paramount, 1931), the wealthy male explains to his buddy the benefits of a union with a poor girl to the male's ego. He tells his friend that "little working girls have something that society girls have not got." He would give up his wealthy fiancée for the poor girl because the wealthy girl has had everything she has wanted and would not get excited at whatever a man did for her, whereas the poor girl (the "little kid") looks up to him.

Although a link between romantic love and marriage can be traced back to earlier centuries, it was in the nineteenth century that romantic expectations began to be commonly attached to marriage, and it was only at the end of the nineteenth century that the disinterested ideal of love can be said to have spread throughout the class system. Around the turn of the century it became less common to openly acknowledge that marriage was principally an economic transaction, an agreement between families to a favorable alliance that would reflect or strengthen their economic interests and status in society. This principle had been especially important among the upper middle and upper classes, who in order to retain or increase their family property or capital had regulated their children's choice of potential marriage partners through the institution of "calling." This institution came to be replaced by "dating," an institution that was expected to be conducted in accord with the disinterested ideal of love and was understood to transcend class boundaries (Illouz 1997; Bailey 1988).

The adoption of the romantic ideal has made little difference to the practice of homogamy or class endogamy. The vast majority continue to marry or cohabitate with people from their own class, and in those cases where there is class-crossing the couples tend to come from adjacent classes. This does not mean that people lie to others and perhaps to themselves concerning their romantic motivations. It is rather that people do fall in love disinterestedly but they do so with people of their own class because these are the people they meet more frequently in their workplaces, neighborhoods, and social gatherings and with whom they find common interests (Illouz 1997). Moreover, instrumental considerations are still present in the choice of partners. A number of recent studies have found that whereas males are more likely to emphasize physical attractiveness in the choice of spouses, women are more likely to consider class, status, and ambition. More women than men admit that they are willing to marry regardless of love (Peplau and Gordon 1985; Malakh-Pines 1999; Cox 2009). It is possible that these gender differences were even greater in the interwar period, when there were greater inequality of the sexes and fewer educational and occupational opportunities for women.

With the diffusion of the norm of disinterested love utilitarian considerations in the choice of spouses were less likely to be admitted openly, and people who were seen to be so motivated were often subject to moral condemnation. In the cross-class romances of popular culture, the person from the lower class whose love for the upper-class person is genuinely disinterested is most often rewarded by both love and wealth, but the calculating person, such as the "gold digger" who seeks to gain wealth by a romantic tie or marriage, most often fails or is punished in some way.

GENDERED INEQUALITY AND MOBILITY

Although the cross-class romance films provided escapist solutions, they were grounded in a reality of class and gender inequality. The phenomenon of the social mobility of women through marriage was particularly common at a time when women were entering certain sectors of the work force but the opportunities for their occupational mobility were severely limited. The overall proportion of women who worked outside the home increased from 23 percent in 1920 to 24 percent in 1930 and to 28 percent in 1940. As a percentage of the total labor force, women represented 20 percent in 1920, 22 percent in 1930, and 25 percent in 1940. The percentage of married women who worked remained low, 12 percent in 1930 and 15 percent in 1940, and although the Depression induced more married women into the work force, even at the lowest income levels only a quarter of married women worked in the 1930s. There were considerable changes in the occupational distribution of women: a decline in the proportion employed as domestics and an increase in the proportion employed in clerical and sales occupations. By the end of the period, women outnumbered men in the lower ranks of clerical work but they had made little headway in the professions in which they had experienced a setback during the Depression years. The Depression was a blow to many women who believed they might rise in class through their own endeavors. Many dropped their academic or vocational pursuits, lowered their career goals, and sought security in marriage (Ware 1982; Kleinberg 1999; Chafe 1991; Scharf 1980).

It was taken for granted by most men and women during this period that a man should earn enough to support a wife and that a wife was not required to work. The economic and normative constraints meant that the major means of upward mobility for women was through marriage. Even for the small proportion of women who received a higher education, it appeared entirely rational for women with aspirations of class rise to set their sights on a good marriage rather than on the pursuit of a career in business or the professions. Mobility for women through marriage rather than work was legitimized by what a social critic, Ruth McKenney, called in 1940 the "immense body of propaganda for the dream world of romantic love" (Hapke 1995, 126). Most films, like most popular literature, promoted this "dream world." Working women appeared in films of the 1930s more frequently than in later decades, but the message conveyed by the films was that even if a woman was successful in her profession or in business, she would only be happy and find meaning in her life if she gave up work outside the home for love, marriage, or her husband's esteem (Dalton 1977; Galerstein 1989).

CONSUMERISM AND ROMANCE

The consumer society did not begin in the 1920s, but this was the decade of a clear shift from a producer to a consumer economy. New social norms of consumption became pervasive, and the consolidation of mass merchandising marked the decisive advent of "modern consumer society" (Horowitz 1985; Leach 1993; Rhodes 1998). Although the Depression impoverished large sectors of the population, it did not stem the development of consumerism and there were considerable advances during the 1930s in the standardized marketing of goods and mass-mediated culture. Although many still based their sense of self on a work ethic and having very little was nothing new for a large part of the population, the belief in entitlement to the good (consumer) things of life was taking greater hold. The experience of scarcity did not immunize Americans against dreams of abundance, which were encouraged by the advertising of consumer goods (Susman 1984; Barnard 1995; Cohen 1993; Cross 2000).

Consumption had long been associated with women, and changes in the 1920s, especially an increase in the number of young, unmarried women with money to spend, reinforced this association. The assumption of a gender division between men as producers and women as consumers was not shaken by the increase in the number of women in the work force. Women's work was understood by many as a period in women's lives prior to their marriage and motherhood.

Romantic love was initiated within the appropriate patterns of consumption while dating, and it was sustained, and even strengthened, through the use of appropriate commodities in marriage. The "commodification of romance" occurred largely within the framework of commercialized leisure, which had developed extensively across the class structure around the turn of the century. Although dating provided greater opportunities for class mingling, the commodities and forms of entertainment consumed in dating were largely determined by access to wealth and leisure time. Women required resources to make themselves attractive through clothes and beauty products, but the customary practice of "treating" a woman meant that the costs of dating fell most heavily on the man. The costs of theater and movie tickets, flowers, chocolates and taxi rides, items that had become central to the seduction process, meant that many lower income men were disadvantaged in the new economy of love.

In addition to having the money to purchase commodities and leisure activities, it was advantageous to be conversant with the rituals of consumption, and help in such matters was provided by etiquette books, which provided advice on appropriate behavior in such settings as expensive restaurants and hotels (Illouz 1997). Thus representations of love became associated with new forms of social distinction based on the acquisition and appropriate consumption of commodities and leisure activities. These changes were reflected in the changing contexts provided for cross-class romances in films. Whereas many of the poor heroines of the pre-1917 cross-class romance films worked in factories, the heroines of the cross-class romance films of the 1920s were more likely to be white collar, working in offices and department stores. Of nine cross-class romance movies I have identified in 1915, five occurred in a factory context and two in department stores; in 1916, out of nineteen cross-class romances, eight occurred in a factory context and three in department stores. After 1920, none of the cross-class romances in my sample occurred in a factory, but department stores, offices, and luxury hotels continued to be common contexts throughout the 1920s and 1930s (Sharot 2010).

MOTIFS IN CROSS-CLASS ROMANCE FILMS

The plots of cross-class romances revolved around, and provided solutions to, the dilemmas and tensions between disinterestedness in love and the costs and rewards of class and status arising from the cross-class tie. In many of the unsuccessful cross-class romances, the character from a poor background decides to leave, sometimes after marriage, her rich partner, whom she discovers she does not really love, for "true" love with a nonwealthy, generally more worthy, partner. In *Home* (Louis Weber Productions, 1919), the daughter of a plumber visits her wealthy classmate's country residence, where she hopes to find a rich husband, but she returns to her old sweetheart after her disillusionment with the mores of high society. She discovers that the wealthy guest to whom she almost succumbed was conducting an affair with her friend's stepmother. Another example of this type is *The Triflers* (Universal, 1920), in which the department store clerk heroine returns to her poor but honest boyfriend after she discovers the shallowness of socialites during a splurge vacation in a fashionable hotel.

The abandonment of a rich man for true love with a poor man appears to have been particularly common in films of the Depression years. Examples include *Bought* (Warner Bros., 1931), *Bed of Roses* (RKO, 1933), and *The Gilded Lady* (Paramount, 1935). In *Sinners in the Sun* (Paramount, 1932) and *Hands Across the Table* (Paramount, 1935), the poor female and the poor male succeed in capturing rich partners, but they decide that love is more important than money and they end up with each other. A reversal of the pattern of a heroine giving up a rich man for a poor man is found in *Ten Cents a Dance* (Columbia, 1931) and *Honor Among Lovers* (Paramount, 1931). In both of these films, the girl refuses the attentions of a rich businessman, who at first offers her arrangements that do not include marriage, for a poor man who turns out to be a womanizer, weak, and dishonest. The girl leaves the poor man for the rich man, who turns out to be decent and ready to marry her.

Another demonstration of disinterested love was provided by the narrative of the poor protagonist who accepts the wealthy protagonist only after he or she is divested of their money. In *Her Great Chance* (Select Pictures, 1918), the department store salesgirl accepts a proposal of marriage from a millionaire's son only after he is disinherited. Forsaking wealth was also the theme of *The Girl Who Wouldn't Work* (Shulberg, 1925), in which a rich philanderer spends his entire fortune in obtaining the acquittal of the girl's father from the charge of murder. Some wealthy protagonists or those who married rich people in cross-class romance films of the 1930s sought to prove their worthiness to their loved one by demonstrating that they could live without their money or the money of their spouses. The steelworker who marries the daughter of the factory boss objects to becoming one of the *Kept Husbands* (RKO, 1931), and he eventually convinces her to live on his salary without the help of her wealthy father. The wealthy heiress who marries a working-class man in *Saleslady* (Monogram, 1938) accepts his refusal of her father's offer to help them out. The riveter in *The Hot Heiress* (First National, 1931) tells the wealthy girl that they will live on his wages and insists that she will not work. In order to prove his love, the wealthy man in *The Idle Rich* (MGM, 1929) and its remake *Rich Man, Poor Girl* (MGM, 1938) moves in with his secretary and her family, where he learns of the struggles of the lower middle class.

It was rare for a cross-class couple to end up poor, but before she was rewarded by wealth, many a poor heroine proved her disinterested love by her willingness to sacrifice her love when she is convinced, often by one of the hero's parents, that her marriage would impede the son's career or social status. In *A Coney Island Princess* (Famous Players, 1916), the exotic dancer lies, saying she never loved the wealthy sportsman, so that he can marry someone from his own class. In most cases in which the heroine is willing to sacrifice her love, the rich hero persists and overcomes her concerns, as in *Sally in Our Alley* (Peerless, 1916) and *Her Social Value* (Katerine MacDonald, 1921). The poor heroine's sacrifice may include attempting to deceive her loved one by putting on an act that she is unworthy of him. After the wealthy father tells the poor girl in *My Best Girl* (Mary Pickford Company, 1927) that her marriage to his son could ruin his career, the girl pretends to her loved one that she was only after his money. Maggie, the girl played by Mary Pickford, smears lipstick on her mouth, tries to puff a cigarette, and dances to the song "Red Hot Mama." The son and his father look on, recognizing that it is only an act, and Maggie finally breaks down, stating her love for the son.

The theme of attempted sacrifice of love that is rewarded by union with the wealthy protagonist remained popular in the 1930s. In *Love among the Millionaires* (Paramount, 1930), the railroad magnate father says he wants nothing else to do with his son if he intends to go through with his intended marriage to a waitress. When Pepper (Clara Bow), the waitress, realizes how much the son's work in the development of the railway network means to him, she decides to break up their relationships by acting in an obnoxious manner at a party given by the father. She pretends to be drunk and makes fun of the upper-class guests, complete with a phony English accent. It is this performance that convinces the father that Pepper really loves his son and she would be the perfect wife for him.

In *Ladies of Leisure* (1930, Columbia), the wealthy mother tells Kay Arnold (Barbara Stanwyck), a former "party girl," that she believes Kay loves her son Jerry, and that it is because Kay loves him that she should give him up. The mother explains that Kay would be a handicap to her son and that although she, the mother, would understand, others, her son's "people, his world," would not. In an attempt to alienate Jerry's affections Kay sets off for Havana with his dissolute friend, but in despair she tries to commit suicide by jumping off the ship. She is saved and Jerry comes to her bedside to tell her that everything will be all right.

The sacrifice made by the "dime a dance" girl, Madeleine McGonegal (Nancy Carroll) in *Child of Manhattan* (Columbia, 1933), occurs after her marriage to Paul Vanderkill (John Boles), a middle-aged widower and one of the richest men in New York. Madeleine had agreed to become Paul's mistress because of Paul's concerns about the impression that a marriage to a dance hall girl would have on his daughter. We are given to understand that it is the mistress's task to prevent pregnancy because when Madeleine becomes pregnant she apologizes profusely to Paul and is surprised when Paul proposes marriage. They marry secretly, and when the baby dies shortly after birth, Madeleine's sacrifice is to leave for Mexico in order to obtain a quick divorce. Madeleine believes that Paul only married her out of a feeling of obligation, but after some misunderstanding Paul arrives in Mexico and, after overhearing Madeleine's true love for him, the couple is reunited.

Even without the pressures of rich parents or other family considerations, heroines from poor backgrounds were willing to sacrifice their love for the sake of the man's career or social status. The character played by Joan Crawford in *Possessed* (MGM, 1931) persuades the lawyer whom she loves that she plans to wed another in order not to handicap his chances of being nominated for governor. In *Gambling Lady* (Warner Bros., 1934), the heroine Lady Lee (Barbara Stanwyck) pretends that she is leaving the wealthy Gary for alimony when, in fact, this is the only way for her rival to agree to give Gary an alibi when he is falsely accused of murder. Gary's father accuses her of being a fortune hunter, but after he discovers the truth he is instrumental in reconciling the couple.

Proof of the disinterested love of the poor character is provided when the poor character falls in love with the rich character before she discovers that he is rich. It was common for a poor heroine to be rewarded for her goodness, virtue, constancy, and disinterest in wealth by discovering that her supposedly poor sweetheart is really a millionaire. *A Little Sister of Everybody* (Anderson-Brunton 1918), living in an East Side tenement in New York with her socialist grandfather, discovers that her factory worker sweetheart is really the owner of the factory who was posing as a laborer in order to understand why his workers were threatening to strike. The owner agrees to improve conditions in the factory, wins the respect of the grandfather, and finds happiness with the girl. *Subway Susie* (Al Rockett Productions, 1926), a salesgirl, postpones her wedding with a subway guard when her firm promotes her to the position of buyer and asks her to sail to Paris. After Susie misses her boat because of a stalled train, the subway guard reveals that his father is president of the subway, and Susie agrees to journey to Paris for a honeymoon rather than as a buyer.

Miss Nobody (First National, 1926), a former heiress, now penniless, falls in love with a hobo who is revealed to be a famous, wealthy author who has donned rags in search of inspiration. In *Home James* (Universal, 1928), the department store clerk mistakes the son of the store owner for a chauffeur, in *Orchids and Ermine* (First National, 1927), the hotel telephone receptionist mistakes the wealthy young oilman for his valet, and in *My Best Girl* (Mary Pickford Company, 1927), the department storeroom girl discovers that her sweetheart, co-worker in the storeroom, is the son of the store's owner. A double class disguise variation was played out in *The Duchess of Doubt* (Metro Pictures, 1917), in which a maid poses as a duchess and then falls for a ribbon clerk who turns out to be the son of the department store owner.

The frequent class disguise or class passing in cross-class romance films represents the class hierarchy as a fluid system in which it takes little more than a change in clothing for a person from one class to be accepted in another. The ambitious young career woman in *A Man of Sentiment* (Chesterfield, 1933) jilts a wealthy man for a poor man only to find that he is the errant son of a wealthy family who eventually accept him back with his bride. The heiress in *The Luckiest Girl in the World* (Universal, 1936) falls in love with a resident of the cheap boardinghouse in which she lives because of a bet with her father that she can make it alone in New York without his assistance. The unemployed girl in *If You Could Only Cook* (Columbia, 1936) assumes that the man sitting on a park bench with her is as desperate as she is. He is, in fact, wealthy, but he does not disclose his identity when the girl talks him into passing as her husband in order to secure work as a cook and butler. In *Hard to Get* (Warner Brothers, 1938), the rich girl changes places with the maid as part of her elaborate plan to seek revenge against an attendant at a gas station who had made her clean the rooms of the station's adjoining motel when she had no cash on her to pay for the petrol he put in her car. Of course, she falls in love with him, and he is the one that has to be persuaded to marry her.

There is the double disguise theme in *The Gay Deception* (Fox, 1935), in which the prince obtains work as a bellhop in order to learn about American hotels and the small-town stenographer, after winning five thousand dollars in a lottery, stays at the exclusive Waldorf-Plaza in New York and is mistaken for a rich girl. The double disguise was resolved by an intraclass union when both protagonists take on the identity of, or are mistaken as persons from, another class, only to find that they are, in fact, from the same class. The department store workers in *Young Romance* (Lasky, 1915) pose as wealthy persons in a seaside resort, part when each feels they are unequal to the other in class, and find happiness when they discover each other's true identity. In *The Maid's Night Out* (RKO, 1938), a milk magnate's son works as a milkman as a bet with his father, and he mistakes a socialite for a housemaid. They keep their identities secret from each other for fear that class differences will disturb their relationship, but they are both happy when they discover the truth.

The wealthy son in *The Maid's Night Out* does not appear to notice that the girl he believes to be a maid is wearing well-tailored, obviously expensive clothes. In cross-class romance films it is more often the poor characters that are slow to identify indications of class differences. The dance hall girl in *Child of Manhattan* believes at first that Paul, who is remarkably well dressed, is unemployed and hard up. The difference in their clothes is soon overcome when Paul buys Madeleine an entire wardrobe and the major class difference between them is represented as accent and speech: a lot is made of Madeleine's low-class Brooklyn accent and that she does not understand Paul's sophisticated way of talking. These differences are understood as part of the appeal the characters have for each other, but in some other films the absence of cultural capital proves a hindrance to the acceptance of the poor characters. The dress shop model in *Hard to Get* (First National, 1929) finds that she has to put on phony airs for the wealthy man and she realizes that she will be happier with the garage mechanic. The brashness of the Jean Harlow character in *Red Headed Woman* (MGM, 1932) does not endear her to her rich husband's friends. The loud clothes and vulgar behavior of *Stella Dallas* (Samuel Goldwyn, 1925 and its remake 1937) make her an inappropriate wife and mother in the cultured upper middle class into which she married.

THE REDEMPTION OF GOLD DIGGERS

In most cross-class romance films, the heroine is not a gold digger at any stage of the narrative. She is, rather, a morally guided young woman whose love for the wealthy man is, from the beginning, genuinely disinterested. Gold diggers were a prominent minority in cross-class romance films, but in most cases they underwent redemption through disinterested love.

The literary roots of the woman who uses sexual allure in order to advance her economic situation or class may be traced at least as far back as Daniel Defoe's 1722 novel *Moll Flanders*, but the term "gold digger" only came into use about 1915. It was used by a journalist to refer to Peggy Hopkins Joyce, a showgirl who married wealthy men. In her investigative book *My Battle with Vice* Virginia Books (1915) notes that the term was used among the working class to refer to girls who came to a dance hall with the purpose of obtaining material benefits from the young men. In popular entertainment, an association between gold diggers and chorus girls was established in 1919 in Avery Hopwood's play *The Gold Diggers*, which ran for two years on Broadway and then went on tour. Warner Brothers produced a film version in 1923 and a musical version, *Gold Diggers of Broadway*, in 1929, followed by *Gold Diggers of 1933, 1935*, and *1936*. A common plot line in which chorus girls succeeded in marrying wealthy men was made credible by the knowledge that real-life chorines from the Ziegfeld reviews, Peggy Hopkins Joyce and Marion Davis, had married fabulously wealthy men (Markantonatou 2006).

The chorus girls were represented as independent women who used their sexual allure to earn a living and to triumph over men in their off-stage relationships. It was also evident that they were dependent on men, both as the providers of their work and as husbands.

The number of gold-digger characters in films increased as the decade of the 1920s advanced; according to the American Film Institute (AFI) list, of the twenty-eight films with gold diggers from 1923 to 1928, eleven appeared in the films released in 1928. They were rarely the central characters (the 1928 film *Gentlemen Prefer Blondes*, based on Anita Loos's 1920 best-seller, was an exception in that respect), and they were often portrayed unsympathetically as women who led men astray from their wives or faithful sweethearts to whom the men invariably returned. Gold diggers appear more frequently, often as central characters, in the early 1930s; 1933 was a peak year according to the AFI catalogue, which lists fourteen films with gold-digging characters in that year. Musicals continued the association of gold diggers with chorus girls, but gold diggers appeared in a range of occupations and milieus. The addition of sound provided more opportunities for the gold-digging characters to demonstrate, often through wisecracks, their cynical view of the relationships between the sexes, and the gold diggers of the 1930s tended to use their sexual charms on men in a more aggressive, unashamed, and calculating manner than those of the 1920s. It is the films with sexually experienced, exploitative women, such as *Red Headed Woman* (MGM, 1932) and *Baby Face* (Warner Bros., 1933), which have remained the best-known and most discussed films of the period. One reason for this is that these films encountered protests from sectors of morality who objected to the association of class rise and female sexuality, and there were problems of censorship, which, as in the case of *Baby Face*, resulted in cuts and a tacked-on moral ending.

The prominence of the morally ambivalent gold digger in film history, popular and academic, has given the impression that most of the films portraying cross-class sexual relationships in the 1930s were of this type. As I have shown, this was not the case; many of the cross-class romance films were little different from those of the 1920s. Moreover, it was not unusual for a gold digger to undergo a change and forego her predatory ambitions for disinterested love. Lea Jacobs (1997) states that, in most of the gold-digger films in which the gold digger is triumphant, the ending is at odds with the more typical romantic or sentimental classical happy end, but her own analysis of the films shows that happy endings with gold diggers who have retained their cynicism were the exception rather than the rule. "Sentimental" endings were tacked on in response to censorship pressures in the cases of *The Easiest Way* (MGM 1931) and *Baby Face*. The one film in which the gold digger remains unreformed through disinterested love is *Red Headed Woman*; although she does not achieve her goal of acceptance into upper society, she is last seen with a bearded old sugar daddy in a car driven by her lover-chauffeur. The industry censors had let the film pass, hoping that the film's comedy would make palatable the theme of an unredeemed gold digger who did not pay for her sins.

In films with more than one gold digger, the redemption through disinterested love of one was offset, to some extent, by the continuing gold-digging spirit of another, usually a secondary character. *Bed of Roses* (RKO, 1933) begins with Lorry and Minnie released after a stretch in a reformatory with no signs of their having been reformed. Minnie immediately suggests the promise of sex to a driver for a lift into town. Lorry tricks a wealthy publisher who, although he comes to understand her manipulations, takes her as a mistress and sets her up in a luxury apartment. Lorry's redemption through love occurs when she falls for a barge owner and leaves the publisher, but because she feels unworthy of her true love, instead of going to him, she moves into a small one-roomer and finds work in a department store. Minnie brings them together again, but the last shot shows Minnie observing the couple and then admiring the bracelet on her wrist, which Lorry had refused to take from the rich publisher. Minnie has the last line in the film: "I like to see true love triumphant." This can be taken both as an expression of the material benefits that Minnie has gained from taking Lorry's place after she had rejected the rich man and the film makers' admission to the audience that they have followed the conventional formula.

Another, somewhat less cynical film with two gold diggers, in which one is reformed by love, is *Girls About Town* (Paramount, 1931). Wanda and Marie are paid well by Jerry as "escorts" to entertain and soften up his business associates. The difference between the two girls is established early on in the film when Wanda tells Marie how she is fed up with having to hire herself out for the evening and asks Marie if it doesn't make her sick "to be pawed by a bunch of middle-class Babbitts." Marie replies that she is always revived by the checks they receive, and Wanda acknowledges that someone's got to pay for her dress. Wanda falls in love with Jim, one of Jerry's wealthy clients, and when Marie tells her how she intends to get an emerald and money from Benjamin, Jim's friend, Wanda's response is that there are other things in the world apart from money. Marie asks Wanda if she is going straight on her. Wanda says that she is and loving it. She demonstrates her disinterested love for Jim by tearing up the check she receives for entertaining him. Jim comes to believe that Wanda cooperated with her ex-husband, who tricks Jim into giving him ten thousand dollars. In order to return the money, Wanda enlists Marie's help in auctioning their jewelry and furs to their gold-digging friends. After Jim asks Wanda to forgive him for his suspicions and they decide to marry, the last shot has Marie phoning Jerry to tell him that she will be working for him alone.

The true love found by one of the three gold diggers in *The Greeks Had a Word for Them* (Goldwyn/United Artists, 1932, rereleased as *Three Broadway Girls*) constituted a change from the original stage production in which all three girls were shown continuing their gold-digging activities at the end. The film emphasizes the differences among the girls: the one for whom it makes no difference if the man she loves will not inherit the wealth of his father, the manipulative one who double-crosses her friends in order to obtain wealthy men, and the one who, although she is quite willing to be supported by a sugar daddy, is good-hearted and supports her friend to obtain her true love.

The musical *Gold Diggers of 1933* (Warner Bros., 1933) contains a range of cross-class romances and gold-digging chorus girls. The purest disinterested love relationship is that of Polly for Brad, who she thinks is a penniless songwriter but is, in fact, a Boston blueblood. Two of her friends are genuine gold diggers, but whereas one of them, Trixie, is clearly only after the material benefits that can be provided by an elderly lawyer, Peabody, the other, Carol, finds romance as well as money with Brad's older brother, whom she at first was only interested in fleecing. Another chorus girl, Fay Fortune, is excluded from the rewards of matrimony because she offers sex too overtly as a bargaining commodity. The film divides the gold diggers into the good-hearted, whose circumstances account for their behavior and who are rewarded, and the cold-hearted, who resort to unacceptable methods. It is, however, a fine line dividing the predatory tactics of the more sympathetically portrayed Trixie and the unsympathetically portrayed Fay in their pursuit of Peabody.

As Jacobs (1997) has shown, the rapid rise in class and relatively easy class crossing, as represented by material accouterments such as clothes and jewels, of the heroines of the early 1930s films became less common after 1934. A number of changes, including the political climate and stricter censorship, brought an end to the representations of successful gold diggers. Jacobs's major example of the change is the remake of *Stella Dallas* (Goldwyn/United Artists, 1937), which, unlike the first silent version, transforms the class rise motif into one of maternal sacrifice. This was a theme that did not encounter problems of censorship, and in general, the dwindling number of cross-class romance films of the late 1930s provided few problems for the censors. The successful gold digger passed from the scene. The last film in my sample, *Fifth Avenue Girl* (RKO, 1939), has the heroine, unemployed but happy, only posing as a gold digger at the request of a wealthy older man who is neglected by his family. The girl has an impact on the members of the family, including the son who starts taking an interest in the family business as well as in the girl.

CONCLUSION

The cross-class romance has been a staple narrative of American cinema from the earliest period of the feature film to the present day, but its peak period was from World War I until the late 1930s. A number of social and cultural changes were conducive to its popularity. From World War I the class system became more fluid and class distinctions less obvious as consumerism developed and spread among wider sectors of the American population. Consumerism raised desires for the good things of life and contributed to the belief that class rise was possible.

However, the barriers to class rise through higher education and occupational mobility remained formidable for the lower middle and working classes, and they were especially formidable for women. The positive impact of World War I on the employment of women was short-lived, and until World War II there was no significant improvement in the occupational opportunities and status of women workers. There was a move in the female work force from domestic and manual to nonmanual occupations, with an increasing proportion of young unmarried women finding employment as saleswomen, secretaries, typists, and file clerks. These low-ranking positions held little chance of advancement, and that small proportion of women who acquired higher education or professional training were mostly limited to occupations and positions specifically set aside for women. Like other women, female college graduates were brought up to think of themselves, first and foremost, as future wives and mothers. The traits perceived as most conducive to winning a husband were understood as least conducive to securing success in a career, and most women who earned doctorates or entered the higher professions remained unmarried. Thus it was entirely rational for women with aspirations of class rise to set their sights on a good marriage rather than on the pursuit of a career in business or the professions.

Cross-class romance films were grounded in a social and gender inequality that resulted in a common pattern of women's mobility through marriage, but sociological studies have found that in the vast majority of cases the mobility of women through marriage has been short range; for example, if the woman's father had a manual occupation, her husband had a lower white-collar occupation (Kerbo 1983). The films diverged from the common pattern insofar as they represented mobility through marriage as long range, from the poor stratum or working class to the wealthy upper middle or upper class. Thus the films were both tied to contemporary reality and escapist.

The possibility of class rise through marriage was encouraged by the diffusion of the value of disinterested love, itself a consequence of the weakening of class boundaries. The tension between the desire for class rise through marriage and the principle of disinterested love was solved in the most economical way by cross-class romance films: Class rise through marriage was the reward that the character from the poor background received for his, or more frequently, her disinterested love. In one common narrative strategy, proof of disinterested love was provided by the poor character's belief that her or his love object was also poor when, in fact, he or she was rich. Many plots revolved around the suspicion, usually false, which arose from a misunderstanding or the manipulation of the rich protagonist's family, that the poor protagonist's admission of love was not disinterested. At the beginning of some narratives, the poor character had mercenary motives, but in most cases the character underwent a transformation and was given an opportunity to demonstrate her or his disinterested love. Where the narrative set up class rise and disinterested love as alternatives, it was the latter that generally won out, and when characters chose class rise over love, they were likely to regret their choice. Love alone was sufficient for happiness, but it was the combination of love and class rise that provided the happy end in most cases.

Sexual aggressiveness on the part of the female was contained, in most cases, within the confines of disinterested love, and with the stricter censorship from 1934, this containment was heightened. Despite some cynical narratives of class rise through sexual allurement in the early 1930s, the principle of disinterested love remained intact, and in the cross-class romance films, it continued to be rewarded by class rise.

REFERENCES

Armstrong, N. 1990. *Desire and domestic fiction: A political history of the novel.* New York: Oxford University Press.

Bailey, B. L. 1988. *From front porch to back seat: Courtship in twentieth-century America.* Baltimore: Johns Hopkins University Press.

Barnard, R. 1995. *The Great Depression and the culture of abundance: Kenneth Fearing, Nathanael West, and mass culture in the 1930s.* Cambridge: Cambridge University Press.

Books, V. 1915. *My battle with vice.* New York: Macauley.

Chafe, W. H. 1991. *The paradox of change: American women in the 20th century.* New York: Oxford University Press.

Cohen, L. 1993. The class experience of mass consumption: Workers as consumers in interwar America. In *The power of culture: Critical essays in American history,* edited by R. W. Fox and T. J. Jackson, 135–60. Chicago: University of Chicago Press.

Cox, F. D. 2009. *Human intimacy: Marriage, the family and its meaning.* Belmont, CA: Wadsworth.

Cross, G. 2000. *An all-consuming society: Why commercialism won in modern America.* New York: Columbia University Press.

Dalton, E. 1977. Women at work: Warners in the 1930s. In *Women and the cinema: A critical anthology,* edited by K. Kay and G. Peary, 267–81. New York: E. P. Dutton.

Galerstein, G. L. 1989. *Working women on the Hollywood screen.* New York: Garland.

Hapke, L. 1995. *Daughters of the great depression: Women, work, and fiction in the American 1930s.* Athens: University of Georgia Press.

Horowitz, D. 1985. *The morality of spending: Attitudes toward consumer society in America, 1875–1940.* Baltimore: Johns Hopkins University Press.

Illouz, E. 1997. *Consuming the romantic utopia: Love and the cultural contradictions of capitalism.* Berkeley and Los Angeles: University of California Press.

Jacobs, L. 1997. *The wages of sin: Censorship and the fallen woman film, 1928–1942.* Berkeley and Los Angeles: University of California Press.

Kerbo, H. R. 1983. *Social stratification and inequality: Class conflict in the United States.* New York: McGraw-Hill.

Kleinberg, S. J. 1999. *Women in the United States, 1930–1945.* London: Macmillan.

Leach, W. 1993. *Land of desire: Merchants, power, and the rise of new American culture.* New York: Vintage Books.

Malakh-Pines, A. 1999. *Falling in love: Why we choose the lovers we choose.* New York: Routledge.

Markantonatou, M. 2006. Gold-diggers. In *Encyclopedia of prostitution and sex work,* edited by M. Hope. Westport, Conn.: Greenwood Publishing.

May, Lary. 2000. *The big tomorrow: Hollywood and the politics of the American way*. Chicago: University of Chicago Press, 2000.

Peplau, L. A., and S. L. Gordon. 1985. Women and men in love: Gender differences in close heterosexual relationships. In *Women, gender, and social psychology*, edited by R. K. Unger and B. Strudler Wallston, 257–292. Hillsdale, NJ: Erlbaum.

Rhodes, C. 1998. *Structures of the jazz age: Mass culture, progressive educations, and racial disclosures in American modernism*. London: Verson.

Ross, S. 1998. *Workingclass Hollywood: Silent film and the shaping of class in America*. Princeton, N.J.: Princeton University Press.

Scharf, L. 1980. *To work and to wed: Female employment, feminism, and the Great Depression*. Westport, Conn.: Greenwood Press.

Sharot, S. 2010. Class rise as a reward for disinterested love: Cross-class romance films, 1915–28. *Journal of Popular Culture* 43:583–599.

Susman, W. 1984. *Culture as history: The transformation of American society in the twentieth century*. New York: Pantheon Books.

Ware, S. 1982. *Holding their own: American women in the 1930s*. Boston: Twayne.

Chapter 7

Sexual Script or Sexual Improv? Nontraditional Sexual Paths

Wind Goodfriend

Sex lies at the root of life, and we can never learn to reverence life until we know how to understand sex.

Havelock Ellis, 1859–1939

Havelock Ellis was one of the world's most influential sexual thinkers. An English physician, Ellis gained great insight into the wide variety of sexual behaviors common to men and women during his practice. This insight resulted in a six-volume publication called *Studies in the Psychology of Sex*, in which he suggested several ideas that were extremely controversial at the time (Yarber, Sayad, and Strong 2010). For example, many of Ellis's contemporaries believed that the act of masturbation could lead to a variety of physical and mental problems, even eventually resulting in insanity. Ellis, on the other hand, believed that sexual behaviors completed by adults, with everyone consenting and with no harm, were certainly not dangerous and could even have several positive results, such as relieved stress and tension (Yarber, Sayad, and Strong 2010). During the Victorian era, when most people were concerned with public appearances, strict standards of behavior, and making sure one was covered up from head to toe, Ellis was a pioneer in accepting nontraditional sexual paths in life. He noted that growing up with a certain culture's sexual norms and values didn't mean those were the only legitimate belief systems; in fact, he argued that sexual acts from other cultures or subcultures should be considered just as valid. In essence, Ellis believed in sexual diversity.

In this chapter I will discuss and define the traditional or stereotypical sexual path assigned to humans in modern society—the socially accepted "sexual script." Then I will present some brief data regarding modern attitudes about other options. Finally, I'll cover three nontraditional sexual paths some individuals may embark upon, all of which require stepping out of tradition to form a new sexual script—in essence, requiring sexual improvisation.

THE TRADITIONAL SEXUAL SCRIPT: SOCIETY'S EXPECTATION

In 1973, Gagnon and Simon offered the term "sexual script" to refer to the behaviors of most individuals in terms of their sexual lives. The metaphor of a script refers to the idea that most people live their lives like actors, playing out what they believe they are expected to perform according to the roles they have been assigned by society (Gagnon and Simon 1973). We rehearse our parts, in essence "practicing" for our opening night (i.e., loss of virginity). We learn what to expect from older, more experienced actors (parents, friends) and from what we see presented in the media through books, television, movies, and advertisements. The idea of social scripts—sometimes called schemas—in general is a well-known one in social psychology (e.g., Wyer and Srull 1994); we are familiar with the expected order of events and procedures for a variety of social encounters, such as introducing people for a business meeting, navigating the order of events when eating at a restaurant, and so on. But perhaps no script is as personal as the one for sexual encounters. In his 1977 textbook *Human Sexualities* (as cited in Kimmel 2007, xii), Gagnon writes, "In any given society . . . people become sexual in the same way as they become everything else. Without much reflection, they pick up directions from their social environment. . . . Their critical choices are often made by going along and drifting. People learn when they are quite young a few of the things that they are expected to be."

What is the traditional sexual script? In other words, what are we "expected to be"? We all have been taught the stereotype, starting from the earliest messages regarding parental roles. The order of events goes something like the following. In junior high or high school, we start dating casually. This might begin in group settings to take the pressure off individuals (or because not everyone has a car). Kissing, heavy petting, and other sexual exploration begin. It is assumed by everyone that everyone else is heterosexual, and that men should be the initiators/aggressors while women passively wait to be asked out. In late high school or college, true sexual exploration begins, with many people moving on to genital sex. We are expected to start being more selective in dating partners, potentially being exclusive and looking for a future spouse.

In our early twenties we get serious, finding a "true love." We might live together (this is becoming more accepted over time), but certainly it's expected that people who have been dating for over a year are eventually going to be legally married. Again, the man is the initiator; he asks the woman for marriage. After getting married in the early to mid-twenties, every couple will desire to have two or three children. Sexual encounters will be in a bed, in the missionary position, with no external devices, props, and so on. Couples will remain faithful, remain heterosexual, and will fall into a steady routine of having sex with only each other on weekends or on vacation. Sexual behaviors will slowly decline as we age, and eventually older couples are assumed to be basically asexual, now more like platonic friends. Then we die.

Undoubtedly, this script has worked well for thousands of people for thousands of years. But is there room to go off script? What if this path is unappealing? What if we discover that we were born as something other than heterosexual? This important personal crossroads is an essential moment in one's personal sexual journey. In an early feminist book on sexual scripts, Laws and Schwartz (1977, 24) note this moment of discovery in an eloquent way:

> We might predict that to the extent that the individual's sexual development and history correspond to the social scripts, sexual identity will be unproblematic. Conversely, exposure to experiences which are not in the script or which are out of sequence or out of synchrony with age mates will make sexual identity problematic. . . . In seeking to make sense of her experience, the exceptional individual may discover alternative constructions of reality. For some women, an alternative construction of sexuality may fit the subjective experience better than the standard script does. For these individuals, a transformation of identity occurs.

A TRANSFORMATION OF IDENTITY

It's been a long time since Ellis wrote about alternate sexual paths being socially acceptable. Behaviors such as premarital sex or cohabitation, oral or anal sex, or sexual fetishes have received popular attention. Are these nontraditional scripts perceived as real possibilities for young people today?

A sample of eighty-nine students (thirty-eight men, fifty-one women) completed a survey a few weeks before this chapter was written regarding their personal views of a variety of sexual behaviors. Some of these behaviors fit into the traditional script, and some offered alternatives. These students come from a small, rural, liberal arts college in Iowa and thus at least somewhat represent what "middle America" thinks about sexual options. The survey listed several possible sexual paths and asked each student to think about two questions relevant to each path: (1) Would *you personally* consider this path? and (2) Do you think *society in general* accepts this path? For both questions, responses were given on a 1–7 scale (see table 1).

Table 1
Response scale for questions related to sexual paths.

1	2	3	4	5	6	7
Definitely not acceptable or worth consideration			Neutral			Definitely acceptable or worth consideration

Definitions of each path were offered to the students in case they were unsure of some terms (these are available from the author if desired). The paths and all responses are listed in table 2. The first four paths fit reasonably well with the traditional script in varying degrees (casual dating, premarital sex, cohabitation, and marriage), while the rest of the table offers less traditional paths. There are several interesting results.

First, we can examine the most popular and least popular paths considered for the students' personal lives. For both men and women, the most popular path out of the sixteen options was legal marriage with one person for life. This is the ultimate traditional choice—the "happily ever after" image we are instructed to desire. Over half of both men and women wrote a "7" next to this option, as well as indicating that this path is also the one most accepted by general society. The other paths accepted by both men and women for their personal lives were casually dating several people before "settling down," premarital sex, cohabitation before marriage, and masturbation. While these paths may be frowned upon by certain pockets of more traditional or orthodox society, they are part of the expected script in modern times (in other words, at least some of these paths fall under the "Everyone does it, nobody talks about it" mentality). Both men and women had much lower numbers for any of the nontraditional paths, indicating both that they were less likely to consider these scripts and that they believed society may condemn them. Least likely to be considered were paths including prostitution, having an affair, open marriage, orgies, group marriage, and sexual communal living.

Another interesting thing to consider from the table is differences between men and women. In general there is agreement on the paths, but there are some paths in which one sex was more interested than the other. Men indicated that they were more likely to consider being single and sexually active for life (a perpetual "player"), masturbation, being in a threesome, being in an orgy, and group marriage or polygamy. These differences make sense in light of the well-known sexual double standard (Byers 1996; Laws and Schwartz 1977): Men are allowed to explore their sexuality and have more sexual behaviors and partners than are women; in contrast, women's virginity is prized. However, two paths chosen by women as more possible were homosexuality and bisexuality. Again, this

Table 2
Men's and women's views on possible sexual paths.

	Men's responses		Women's responses	
	Mean	SD	Mean	SD
Casually dating several people				
I would personally consider	4.87	1.42	5.51	1.91
Does society accept?	4.42	1.91	5.29	1.65
Premarital sex				
I would personally consider	5.58	1.59	5.35	1.88
Does society accept?	4.95	1.56	5.12	1.56
Cohabitation				
I would personally consider	5.84	1.39	5.49	1.74
Does society accept?	5.05	1.35	5.18	1.57
Legal marriage with one person for life				
I would personally consider	6.47	1.20	6.65	0.91
Does society accept?	6.18	1.27	6.29	1.14
Single and sexually active for life				
I would personally consider	3.79	1.93	3.00	1.80
Does society accept?	3.71	1.61	3.33	1.60
Single and celibate for life				
I would personally consider	2.08	1.88	2.67	2.10
Does society accept?	3.68	2.00	3.86	1.91
Masturbation				
I would personally consider	5.58	1.45	4.43	2.29
Does society accept?	4.53	1.75	4.45	1.60
Homosexuality				
I would personally consider	2.00	1.74	2.80	2.33
Does society accept?	3.11	1.20	3.53	1.60
Bisexuality				
I would personally consider	2.42	1.94	3.37	2.37
Does society accept?	3.29	1.16	3.47	1.45

(continued)

Table 2 *(continued)*

	Men's responses		Women's responses	
	Mean	**SD**	**Mean**	**SD**
Prostitution				
I would personally consider	1.92	1.53	1.29	0.94
Does society accept?	1.95	1.09	2.06	1.29
Having "an affair" or "cheating"				
I would personally consider	1.87	1.58	1.12	0.38
Does society accept?	1.92	1.22	2.39	1.44
"Open marriage" or "swinging"				
I would personally consider	1.89	1.57	1.75	1.52
Does society accept?	2.29	1.09	2.31	1.37
Being in a threesome				
I would personally consider	4.58	2.02	2.73	2.04
Does society accept?	3.32	1.42	3.59	1.87
Being in a group orgy				
I would personally consider	2.71	2.05	1.71	1.57
Does society accept?	2.42	1.29	2.39	1.36
Group marriage or polygamy				
I would personally consider	2.31	1.95	1.27	0.90
Does society accept?	2.08	1.30	1.84	1.03
Living in a sexual commune				
I would personally consider	1.87	1.55	1.39	1.20
Does society accept?	1.58	0.98	1.67	1.11

difference is reasonable due to society's greater acceptance of lesbians compared to gay men (e.g., Kite 1984; Whitley 1988).

Finally, it is important to see that individuals' consideration of each possible sexual script or path is highly correlated with whether they believe society in general accepts that script. For over half of the paths, the correlation between individual consideration and perceived social acceptance was statistically significant (at a level of $p < 0.05$). It is likely that as culture changes to accept different sexual paths more than in previous eras, more individuals will consider nontraditional scripts as possibilities for themselves.

THE ROADS LESS TRAVELED: OTHER OPTIONS

We all fall victim to stereotypes—both as the target and as the perpetrator of these social expectations. When it comes to sexual stereotypes, what happens to an individual who does not feel alignment with the traditional path laid out by culture, family, friends, and the media? There are many possible alternate paths. However, the second half of this chapter will focus on three specific paths that are not chosen but are instead determined for individuals from birth and thus call for a need for some creative sexual improvisation.

Alternative I: Ethnic Variations

There's an underlying, unstated assumption in the stereotypical sexual path described earlier: that you're white. In the United States and other, similar countries, the default ethnicity is white unless otherwise stated (Dalton 2008; Dyer 2008). This is part of the often unsaid, but universally understood, white privilege of our history. If one is of a different ethnicity, the cultural expectations are not necessarily as straightforward because the vast majority of media images are, again, white.

There is little research on sexual scripts specific to ethnic minorities, and it is certainly possible that some individuals of color may feel perfectly comfortable fitting in with the majority expectations. However, one article (Phillips and Stephens 2003) articulates the difficulty some African American women feel when they do not perceive a good fit. Phillips and Stephens note that while media representations of African American women have increased steadily over the years, these images still fall along stereotypes (Gillespie 1993, as cited in Phillips and Stephens 2003), and these racially based stereotypes have implications for expected sexual behavior. They note, "Differentiating African American adolescent women's sexuality from white women's reinforces their positions as individuals standing on the margins of society, clarifying its boundaries" (Phillips and Stephens 2003, 4–5). For some women of color, the choices displayed in the media may be just as confining as the traditional script and certainly perpetuate stereotypes. Stephens and Phillips (2003) list several alternative stereotypical paths for African American women, with a huge variance in specific sexual behaviors and perceived acceptance from general society. A few of the modern stereotypical scripts they describe are summarized below.

The Diva. An upper-class woman willing to spend money on her appearance, she is light-skinned, slender, and wears provocative clothing. Her hair and nails are always done perfectly. Her personality and general lifestyle are "high maintenance," and her sexuality is sultry and tempting but never overtly obvious.

The Gold Digger. A younger woman who is willing to barter sexual acts, or even marry, in exchange for material possessions or general wealth, the gold digger typically is not considered to bring anything else of value to the trade and thus is perceived as lacking in culture, education, and employment.

The Gangster Bitch. She's an aggressive, independent, strong woman. Despite her independence, she does not fight against patriarchy, however, and indeed often perpetuates it by supporting a man's dominance over her. Considered to have come from a relatively dangerous background herself, this woman may have turned to this sexual path as a survival mechanism, aligning with the strongest (and therefore most protective) man available.

The Sister Savior. A physically larger woman with a spiritual side, she nurtures and welcomes her family and community. Often involved in church activities, she is not asexual but follows sexual norms dictated by her religion (which is stereotypically Southern Baptist). She is similar to the "Earth Mother" archetype.

The Baby Mama. Possibly on welfare, this woman has been pregnant at least once (and possibly more) by men to whom she is not married, possibly on purpose. She desires a relationship with the father of the child, sometimes for emotional and personal reasons, sometimes as simply a role model for the child, and sometimes for financial reasons.

Phillips and Stephens note that not all African American women will fit these paths; as mentioned earlier, some will simply follow the traditional script and others will carve a new path for themselves as individuals. This final path (the individual road) requires the most sexual improvisation because there are no media models or cultural expectations—there are no stereotypes. The article notes, "She may also choose or need to not use the scripts; if she feels comfortable with herself, her sexuality, and her context, young women may not need the predictability of the sexual script behaviors to interact with males or make sense of herself" (Phillips and Stephens 2003, 35). They essentially praise any woman who can break out of the stereotypes laid down upon her and who can perform sexual improvisation outside of these preassigned roles.

Alternative 2: Orientation Variations

Ever since the famous Kinsey publications *Sexual Behavior in the Human Male* (Kinsey, Pomeroy, and Martin 1948) and *Sexual Behavior in the Human Female* (Kinsey et al. 1953), the American public has been obliged to admit that there are multiple sexual orientations and that nonheterosexuals are more common than many would like to believe. Kinsey famously suggested that sexual orientation is not categorical (homosexual, bisexual, or heterosexual) and instead falls along a continuum, where people can be partially homosexual and partially heterosexual (e.g., a 60/40 split) and can move along that continuum as life progresses, changing orientations from one year—or even one moment—to the next.

Again, unfortunately there is a dearth of research on the sexual scripts of nonheterosexuals. In the 1970s research began, but little followed. At that time, several scholars noted that journals and diaries from gay people included their internal struggle with their identities and sexual feelings, which were not in alignment with the traditional script and were, in addition, clearly not accepted by most social circles (Johnston 1973; Miller 1971; Millett 1974). Laws and Schwartz (1977) note that often individuals realize their nonheterosexual preferences in a first crush or by normal experimentation with a close friend. Later, emerging homosexual people might try going to a gay bar, but in gay bars the focus is on finding partners for single sexual encounters (just as in heterosexual singles bars), and thus the "education" one receives about sexual scripts is extremely limited to sexual behaviors and not necessarily to larger script themes such as relationships or what the future holds for the couple.

Laws and Schwartz (1977) do note that in one study of interviews with lesbians (Blumstein and Schwartz 1974), lesbians who had been practicing a lesbian script for several years were able to identify several benefits of the lesbian script over the traditional, heterosexual one, including

1. more egalitarian relationships (due to the avoidance of opposite-sex power struggles between men and women);
2. relationships that were less role-bound (e.g., with an equal division of labor at home);
3. more knowledge about each other's sexual needs; and
4. more orientation to a long-term relationship (as is more commonly found in general with women, as compared to men; e.g., Buss 1994).

However, in spite of these advantages, lesbians also noted several disadvantages to having to create their own sexual scripts, including

1. social stigma (living in fear of being outed or not being accepted by others);
2. fear of partner's sexual orientation (i.e., fear that one's partner is bisexual or may identify as heterosexual later in life and thus leave the relationship);
3. stress due to lack of established social roles (while this can be an advantage, as noted above, it can also lead to misunderstandings and arguments); and
4. lack of children.

A much more recent study (Power, McNair, and Carr 2009) focused on one more, very important potential disadvantage to the improvisational nature of the nonhetero script: increased risk for STIs. In junior high and high school sexual education courses, the assumed heterosexuality of every student is pervasive; this can lead some homosexual or bisexual people to feel that their sexual activities are therefore not risky. With the rise of HIV fear in the 1980s, some sexual health programs were focused on gay men avoiding STIs in general (and HIV specifically), but lesbians were left out once again. Power and her colleagues note, "Lesbians are unlikely to engage with sexual health promotion targeted toward gay men or heterosexual women, yet lesbian-specific sexual health promotion does not adequately construct an alternate discourse on safer sex that lesbians can relate to their own sexual practice" (Power, McNair, and Carr 2009, 67).

Note that while the studies above were all conducted with women, it is certainly reasonable that all of the same concerns would be found in gay men, who are even more socially punished than lesbians (Kite 1984; Whitley 1988) and thus may be even more reluctant to vary from the traditional heterosexual script, even when their biological destiny asks them to do so.

Alternative 3: Gender Variations

Psychology as a field has generally accepted the difference between the term "sex," as referring to biological determination of male versus female, and "gender," referring to psychological differences between masculinity and femininity (Bem 1974; Spence, Helmreich, and Stapp 1974). A biological man could have a female gender (i.e., be a feminine man), or vice versa, but the traditional sexual script calls for men to be the instigators, aggressors, and agents, while women are called upon as the passive recipients at each stage. Women wait to be asked out, women do not choose the date activity, women wait to be asked for marriage, and women are on the bottom of sexual positions such as the traditional missionary position.

Again, individuals who do not feel comfortable with these assigned roles are forced outside of tradition and must improvise a new script with which they feel at home. In 2000, a study focused on these gender outlaws and how their atypical genders caused sexual anxiety (Katz and Farrow 2000). While observers sometimes assume feminine men and masculine women are nonheterosexual, when these individuals *are* heterosexual, their lack of desire to fulfill traditional roles can lead to a variety of problems. In the Katz and Farrow study (2000), women who self-identified as agentic (or masculine) reported feeling increased sexual anxiety and less sexual desire compared to other women. In addition, men who self-identified as highly expressive (or feminine) also reported feeling less sexual desire. The authors argued these findings resulted from sexual partners treating individuals in the traditional way, expecting them to fulfill their sexist roles, and when the participants did not respond accordingly, stress was the result.

Even more recently, a separate study was completed using a group of heterosexual college men from New York City who were interviewed regarding their acceptance (or rejection) of traditional sexual roles (Dworkin and O'Sullivan 2005). While the traditional sexual script shows men being interested in aggression and conquest, this stereotype is the antithesis of general social fairy tales and fantasies involving love, romance, and emotional intimacy (e.g., Brod 1995; Seal and Ehrhardt 2003). The men interviewed by Dworkin and O'Sullivan (2005) noted that their most common sexual encounters were male-dominated and male-initiated. However, 60 percent of these same men stated their desire for more egalitarian encounters, and another 25 percent desired female-dominated encounters (thus only 15% preferred the traditional male-dominating script).

Dworkin and O'Sullivan (2005) list some quotes from their interviews, showing this male desire for a female sexual aggressor: "I've felt lonely—I know she's not gonna start it. I would like for her to come to me. It's hard to, um, just always initiate it myself. There were couple of times when she came to me and it was a rush, exciting" (153). And other man concurred, saying, "I would like her to be in control more. More dominant I guess. I think it's attractive. I remember one time . . . she actually grabbed my butt and threw me on the bed. It was a rush. It felt like . . . I guess the word is erotic or something" (153).

CONCLUSIONS

Just as Kinsey, years ago, noted that sexual orientation is on a continuum, almost any socially created variable is also on a continuum. Race and ethnicity were discussed above, but increasingly people are of mixed racial backgrounds. If a person is one-quarter African American, one-quarter Caucasian, one-quarter Chinese, and one-quarter Latino, where does that person fit in culturally accepted stereotypes and sexual expectations? Along similar lines, Sandra Bem (1974) suggested that masculinity and femininity are also not simple categories but are continua that result in multiple possible definitions of the self (one could be masculine, feminine, undifferentiated, androgynous, or anywhere in between). Although less discussed, more psychologists and biologists are suggesting that, indeed, biological sex is also not simply "male" or "female." There are a wide variety of sexual anomalies, such as people with Turner's syndrome, congenital adrenal hyperplasia, androgen insensitivity syndrome, Klinefelter's syndrome, and 5-alpha reductase syndrome. Some people are transsexual. The list of human variances and diversity goes on.

Stereotypes of any kind result in limited opportunities because they do not allow for this great diversity. When stereotypes are applied to sexual behavior in the form of traditional sexual scripts, they provide only one narrow path for individuals to explore. Clearly, the world of actual sexual behaviors is much wider than this path, and the traditional sexual script may need to be rewritten. It is even possible that the idea of a single, traditional sexual script may—in the future—be rejected as an unjust simplification of sexual possibilities. One hundred years ago, sexual thinkers and theoretical revolutionaries such as Havelock Ellis were suggesting that culture and social norms were arbitrary and potentially harmful in terms of dictating sexual behaviors and that the world needed to be open-minded to exploration. While current culture seems to be still largely bound by the traditional sexual script dictated by previous generations, it is possible that the future will welcome sexual improvisation and diversity in a manner never seen before.

REFERENCES

Bem, S. L. 1974. The measurement of psychological androgyny. *Journal of Consulting and Clinical Psychology* 43:155–162.

Blumstein, P., and P. Schwartz. 1974. Lesbianism and bisexuality. In *Sexual deviance and sexual deviants*, edited by E. Goode and R. Troiden, 278–295. New York: Diana Press.

Brod, H. 1995. Pornography and the alienation of male sexuality. In *Men's lives*, edited by M. Kimmel and M. A. Messner, 393–404. Boston: Allyn and Bacon.

Buss, D. M. 1994. *The evolution of desire: Strategies of human mating.* New York: HarperCollins.

Byers, E. S. 1996. How well does the traditional sexual script explain sexual coercion? Review of a program of research. *Journal of Psychology and Human Sexuality* 8:7–25.

Dalton, H. 2008. Failing to see. In *White privilege*, 3rd ed., edited by P. Rothenberg, 15–18. New York: Worth.

Dworkin, S. L., and L. O'Sullivan. 2005. Actual versus desired initiation patterns among a sample of college men: Tapping disjunctures within traditional male sexual scripts. *Journal of Sex Research* 42:150–158.

Dyer, R. 2008. The matter of whiteness. In *White privilege*, 3rd ed., edited by P. Rothenberg, 9–14. New York: Worth.

Gagnon, J., and W. Simon. 1973. *Sexual conduct: The social sources of human sexuality.* Chicago: Aldine.

Johnston, J. 1973. *Lesbian nation: The feminist solution.* New York: Touchstone.

Katz, J., and S. Farrow. 2000. Heterosexual adjustment among women and men with non-traditional gender identities: Testing predictions from self-verification theory. *Social Behavior and Personality* 28:613–620.

Kimmel, M. 2007. John Gagnon and the sexual self. In *The sexual self: The construction of sexual scripts*, edited by M. Kimmel, vii–xv. Nashville: Vanderbilt University Press.

Kinsey, A., W. Pomeroy, and C. Martin. 1948. *Sexual behavior in the human male.* Philadelphia: Saunders.

Kinsey, A., W. Pomeroy, C. Martin, and P. Gebhard. 1953. *Sexual behavior in the human female.* Philadelphia: Saunders.

Kite, M. E. 1984. Sex differences in attitudes toward homosexuals: A meta-analytic review. *Journal of Homosexuality* 10:69–81.

Laws, J. L., and P. Schwartz. 1977. *Sexual scripts: The social construction of female sexuality.* Hinsdale, IL: Dryden Press.

Miller, M. 1971. *On being different: What it means to be a homosexual.* New York: Random House.

Millett, K. 1974. *Flying.* New York: Ballantine Books.

Phillips, L. D., and D. P. Stephens. 2003. Freaks, gold diggers, divas, and dykes: The sociohistorical development of adolescent African American women's sexual scripts. *Sexuality & Culture* 7:3–49.

Power, J., R. McNair, and S. Carr. 2009. Absent sexual scripts: Lesbian and bisexual women's knowledge, attitudes and action regarding safer sex and sexual health information. *Culture, Health & Sexuality* 11:67–81.

Seal, D. W., and A. A. Ehrhardt. 2003. Masculinity and urban men: Perceived scripts for courtship, romantic, and sexual interactions with women. *Culture, Health & Sexuality* 5:295–319.

Spence, J. T., R. L. Helmreich, and J. Stapp. 1974. The Personal Attitudes Questionnaire: A measure of sex role stereotypes and masculinity-femininity. *JSAS: Catalog of Selected Documents in Psychology* 4:43–44.

Whitley, B. E. 1988. Sex differences in heterosexuals' attitudes toward homosexuals: It depends on what you ask. *Journal of Sex Research* 24:287–291.

Wyer, R. S., Jr., and T. K. Srull, eds. 1994. *Handbook of social cognition*. 2nd ed. Hillsdale, NJ: Erlbaum.

Yarber, W. L., B. Sayad, and B. Strong. 2010. *Human sexuality: Diversity in contemporary America*. 7th ed. New York: McGraw-Hill.

Chapter 8

Support and Interference from Social Network Members: A Conceptual Framework

Jacki Fitzpatrick

In this chapter I provide an overview of a conceptual framework for support and interference from social network members. The framework delineates a range of ways in which network members can provide support and/or interference in romantic relationships and acknowledges the potential role of network members' apathy toward romance. In addition, I note implications of the framework for future research.

SOCIAL CONTEXT OF ROMANTIC RELATIONSHIPS

Romantic relationships are commonly a primary relationship in young adulthood. In contrast to adolescent relationships, romances in young adulthood tend to be more stable, enjoyable, and mature (Shulman and Kipnis 2001). Such romances are meaningful social environments in which partners can develop deep bonds, interpersonal competence skills (Fitzpatrick, Feng, and Crawford 2003), and relationships that last a lifetime (e.g., Raley, Crissey, and Muller 2007).

However, it is important to remember that romantic relationships do not exist in isolation (Walker and Hirayama 2010). Rather, the romances exist in the context of partners' social networks. It is possible for romantic partners to spend a great deal of their time with individuals with whom they don't have a strong psychological connection (e.g., classmates, neighbors, store staff). Although interactions with such individuals are often necessary to complete daily tasks, these individuals might have little or no impact on their romances. Thus relationships with such individuals would be peripheral ties (Fingerman 2009).

However, some social network members are meaningful. Relationships with family and friends exist typically prior to the romances, and most individuals who are romantically involved want to maintain both romantic and network relationships (e.g., Agnew, Loving, and Drigotas 2001). Thus it is often not a choice of either family/friends or romantic partners but, rather, family/friends and romantic partners (Bryan et al. 2001). If family and friends are a central part of their lives that do not disappear when romances occur, then romantic partners might care about the ways in which these network members respond to the romances. These responses are conceptualized typically as social support or social interference.

SOCIAL SUPPORT AND SOCIAL INTERFERENCE

There has been extensive attention to social support in the close-relationship literature (Pierce et al. 1996). Social support refers to the assistive and cooperative resources given to others (Dressler et al. 1997; Overall, Fletcher and Simpson 2010) as well as the sense of inclusion within a community of close relationships (Kim et al. 2006). Types of support have been typically classified as emotional, informational/appraisal, and tangible (goods, services) resources (e.g., Coffman 2008; Dunkel-Schetter and Skokan 1990).

However, it should be noted that not every network response to romantic relationships is supportive or positive (Bryan et al. 2001). It is common that family/friends don't like or even loathe individuals' romantic partners or the relationships (e.g., ways in which they act as couples). Network members might also be displeased by the changes that occur when romantic relationships develop (Milardo, Johnson, and Huston 1983). For example, network members might perceive that they are less important or have less time with individuals. Alternatively, members simply perceive that individuals have "changed" in dissatisfying ways since entering the romances. In such situations, it is not logical to expect that network members are going to provide social support. Rather, it is possible that family/friends are going to provide social interference. Social interference is reflected in intrusion, impediments, or critical judgment that is offered to others (e.g., Richardson, Barbour, and Bubenzer 1991). It represents more than simply an absence or refusal to provide support. Rather, interference is the expressions (of affect, thought) and actions designed to interrupt or obstruct interpersonal relationships (e.g., Aquino and Thau 2009; Vinokur and van Ryn 1993).

Research has shown that the support or interference from network members can affect romantic relationships. For example, Blair and Holmberg (2008) reported that family approval was associated with greater romantic quality (e.g., satisfaction, trust). Similarly, Sprecher and Felmlee (1992) reported that support from female's network members was positively related to relationship stability. In contrast, friend disapproval has been associated with increased termination of relationships (Hughes, Morrison, and Asada 2005; Lehmiller and Agnew 2007). However, the network-romance linkages have not always been so direct or consistent across studies (e.g., Neyer and Voigt 2004). For example, Driscoll, Davis, and Lipetz (1972) reported a "Romeo and Juliet effect" (1) in which parental interference was associated with more love among romantic partners. A similar pattern has been reported in some studies (e.g., Jankowiak and Fischer 1992) but has been absent in other studies (e.g., Sprecher and Felmlee 1992). Similar inconsistencies have been found in examinations of social support.

One possible source of the inconsistencies is the variations in conceptualization of support and interference (Clark and Grote 1998; Sarason et al. 1987). There has been some diffusion in the ways in these network responses have been described and measured. If concepts such as "support" and "interference" do not have the same meanings across studies, then the inconsistent research results are not a complete surprise. Sarason and Sarason (2009) noted that the lack of conceptual clarity is problematic for the field and greater effort should be made to provide more precise constructs.

Traditionally, authors/researchers have focused on sources (family vs. friends, weak vs. strong ties—Fingerman 2009; Sinclair 2008), types (e.g., emotional, informational—Cutrona et al. 2007), and reactions (e.g., distress, satisfaction—Vinokur and van Ryn 1993) to support/interference. Another way to consider these constructs is the degree of intensity (e.g., serious to mild). It is possible that more intense forms of support or interference have stronger effects on romantic relationships (quality, stability). It is also possible that intensity might have implications for the ways in which these factors are defined and/or measured (Fitzpatrick 2009).

In an effort to contribute to the ongoing development of conceptualization, this chapter provides a delineation of support and interference constructs. The delineation is based on the degree of intensity. Three dimensions of support and three dimensions of interference are described. In addition, apathy from social network members is acknowledged. This delineation is followed by considerations for future advancements in conceptualization and research.

DIMENSIONS OF SOCIAL SUPPORT

Promotion

Promotion is an intense dimension of social support. Promotion by social network members represents their efforts to move relationships toward growth. This movement might be toward the initiation, transition (to "the next level"), or maintenance of romantic relationships. Promotion can be proactive, in that network members instigate relational events without the awareness or consent of individuals. In this way, family/friends might outpace (be ahead of) the romantic partners in their plans for relationship development. As family/friends know individuals well (e.g., traits, habits, preferences) and care about their quality of life, it is possible that family/friends feel free to act on behalf of the individuals. Given that family and friends play a primary role in the lives of young adults (e.g., Barry et al. 2009), it is possible that network and romantic relationships will be embedded in significant ways. Thus the network members might think that they know what is best for the individuals (and network group) and act accordingly.

One network action that is consistent with promotion is arranged marriages. In its traditional form, parents choose spouses (Zaidi and Shuraydi 2002) for their sons and daughters. These choices can be in the early years, before children have awareness of romances. As the children grow into young adulthood, they fulfill the marital commitments. Thus their marriages are a couple and community (network) process. In some communities, a modified form of arranged marriages has developed. The modification allows individuals to have some input in the process, but the role of network members remains strong. For example, groups in Trinidad and Tobago who practice arranged marriages will allow potential brides and grooms to meet, but male relatives make the decisions about who will marry (Seegobin and Tarquin 2003).

In contrast to arranged marriages, network members can provide promotions in less formal ways. For example, they can create conditions for individuals to meet potential partners (Sprecher et al. 2002) or directly make introductions. Family might arrange blind dates, or friends might take individuals to speed dating or group dating events (e.g., Guerrero and Mongeau 2008). Indeed, Scott (2002) noted that friends were identified as a source of pressure for some individuals to join a Mormon online dating site. Beyond initiation, network members might work to facilitate relationship progression. For example, family members might ask about plans ("When are you going to get serious about him/her?" "When are you going to get married?") with the intent to incentivize or pressure individuals into deeper commitments. Such questions can have important implications for relational and individual well-being. It should also be noted that network members might intervene to repair relationships. If there are romantic problems or conflicts, then family/friends might choose to intervene. Of their own initiative, they might serve as mediators, offer advice, or simply attempt to fix problems. Thus network members might see their roles in romances as quite substantial.

Facilitation

In contrast to promotion, facilitation is a less intense dimension of support. Facilitation by network members represents their efforts to help but not to change the status of romantic relationships (movement toward more growth). Rather than being proactive in attempting to influence romances, facilitation is reactive. Thus family/friends would respect the romantic partners' preferences for their relationships. Facilitation would reflect that network members are following the couples' lead rather than attempting to take charge of the romances on behalf of the couples. If members think they know what is best for couples, then family/friends might withhold this information until it is requested. If individuals never request the information, then they might not provide it.

If romantic partners request assistance, then network members might be quite generous with the support that they provide. Members might provide multiple types of support (e.g., emotional, informational, tangible) over a prolonged period of time (Pierce et al. 1996). It is possible that members might even provide support at some inconvenience to themselves (Kim et al. 2006). Thus facilitation does not represent a lack of care or concern for romantic partners but is a more passive approach to support than promotion.

It is important to note that sometimes network members have to wait for certain events to occur before support can be reasonably provided. For example, Copeland and Norell (2002) examined the transitional experiences of wives who move internationally (in response to their husbands' career demands). The specific nature, location, or time of the moves might not be known far in advance. Thus network members might be more effective in providing support after the move has been decided. Indeed, support might be unnecessary or impractical before the decision. Copeland and Norell reported that wives who received support after the moves had better adjustments to their new communities.

Similarly, family/friends might offer their advice when asked about romantic relationship events or problems (Klein and Milardo 2000). They might not intervene in relationships at the moment that they see problems but will respond when invited into the situation. Indeed, Agnew, Loving, and Drigotas (2001) noted that network members might have more accurate perceptions of relational issues than do romantic partners. Their research indicated that some members more accurately predicted the future of relationship stability (continuation vs. dissolution) than the partners. Thus relational insights might be an important type of informational support. Facilitation might be less intense than promotion, but it still has the power to influence romantic outcomes.

Approval

In contrast to promotion and facilitation, approval is the least intense dimension of support. Approval represents network members' efforts to sanction the relationships. This would be judgments in favor of the relationships, which might indicate inclusion in the larger family group or community. Approval would be reactive in nature (e.g., Sinclair 2008), similar to facilitation. Indeed, some network members (e.g., parents, grandparents) might not learn of romances until couples have already achieved a certain degree of closeness and commitment. Approval might not be sought for casual relationships (e.g., first dates), but only for serious relationships or significant transitions (e.g., engagement, marriage). Thus romantic relationships might have progressed significantly before approval is sought.

If network members provide approval, this could qualify as emotional support. If members provide an assessment of the relationship partners and relationship advice with approval, this would qualify as informational and emotional support. However, approval does not obligate members to provide other types of support (e.g., behavioral, material, financial). In addition, approval can be a singular event. Approval does not necessarily need to be repeated or prolonged (e.g., "I think that you are a good couple" need not be stated once per month). Thus approval requires less effort than facilitation or promotion from network members.

The approval process is consistent with the transitivity properties of social networks (e.g., Felmlee 2006). For example, family members would likely know their young adult children much better than the romantic partners. Based on a lifetime of experience with these individuals, they might value some of their qualities (e.g., honesty, kindness, loyalty). They might assume that these qualities allow the individuals to either find similar qualities in partners (e.g., partners are equally kind) or evaluate partners well (e.g., individuals' impulsiveness and partners' reserve provide good balance in the relationships). In either case, family members might trust the individuals' choices in romantic partners and provide approval. Thus the positive view of the individuals is extended to include their romantic partners (e.g., A trusts B, B loves C, A approves of B and C's relationship). This approval process is consistent with research on trust transferability in social networks (Ferrin, Dirks, and Shah 2006).

Despite its relatively low effort demands, the salience of approval should not be underestimated. The request of parental approval prior to a wedding proposal has been a longstanding tradition in several societies (Simmonds 2005). If elders are held in high esteem in their families or cultures, then their approval might be particularly important. Elders can be viewed as a source of wisdom from a lifetime of experiences (Falicov 1999), including romantic experiences. If individuals are from collectivistic cultures, then approval might indicate inclusion into the family or community groups. Even within the United States (a relatively individualistic culture), network approval has been associated with greater romantic stability (e.g., Sprecher and Felmlee 1992). If approval is the sole dimension of support for some romances, this dimension might be quite meaningful to them.

DIMENSIONS OF SOCIAL INTERFERENCE

Disruption

Disruption is an intense dimension of social interference. Similar to promotion, disruption is a proactive response from network members. That is, the family/

friends are engaging in efforts to affect or alter the pathways of romantic relationships. They might engage in such actions without discussing the actions with individuals. In contrast to promotion, however, members don't engage in disruptive actions to foster relationship growth (e.g., greater closeness, higher commitment). Rather, they are working to move relationships toward dissolution. In this process, they might work to damage the romances (e.g., undermine trust, cause conflict). Taken to an extreme, this would be consistent with the literature on social aggression or interpersonal harm in social networks (Duffy, Ganster, and Pagon 2002; Venkataramani and Dalal 2007).

An example from classic literature is Iago's disruption in *Othello* (Shakespeare 1993). Iago actively manipulates Othello to breed jealousy and fury. Based on how well he knows Othello, Iago works to exploit Othello's weaknesses (e.g., Taylor 2004). In this manner, Iago is able to negatively affect the trajectory of Othello's romantic relationship with Desdemona. There is some disagreement as to whether Othello and Desdemona's relationship would have survived without Iago's interference, or whether it was doomed to inevitable dissolution (e.g., Hunt 2003), but there is no doubt that Iago's deeds actively harmed the romance.

Some research has examined a phenomenon identified as "social undermining" (Westman and Vinokur 1998, 137). Some items used to measure undermining seem to be consistent with the disruption concept. These studies have identified that undermining is a separate phenomenon from social support rather than simply a low level of support (Vinokur and van Ryn 1993). Undermining has been associated with more distress and depression (e.g., Cranford 2004; Westman, Etzion, and Danon 2001). Research has identified a crossover process in which the negative actions of individuals affect the psychological states of others (e.g., depression). However, this research has focused primarily on the interactions between spouses rather on the disruptiveness by network members. In a review of employment issues, Bercovici (2006) noted that co-workers can engage in actions that sabotage the relationships and/or careers of individuals who engage in workplace romances. Sabotage also seems consistent with the principle of social disruption. Thus some aspects of disruption might already exist in the literature.

Hindrance

In contrast to disruption, hindrance is a less intense dimension of interference. Hindrance by family/friends represents their efforts to create discomfort for romantic partners or relationships. However, this discomfort is relatively passive (or passive aggressive). Their efforts do not overtly focus on romantic dissolutions. Rather, their efforts focus on either excluding the romantic couples/partners or making it more uncomfortable for romantic partners to maintain (or grow) their relationships. Thus network members do not have to be particularly proactive, intrusive, or direct in their actions. They can simply provide encumbrances or create exclusions. This hindrance principle is consistent with prior research on marginalized groups (e.g., Longwell-Grice 2003).

Hindrances can occur during critical periods in relationship development and can thus slow relationship growth or place couples at greater risk for future problems. For example, Brown, Orbuch, and Maharaj (2010) argued that too much contact with extended family during the early years of marriage interferes with marital development. The extended family members might not be actually trying to disrupt the marriages, but their high degree of contact makes it difficult for partners to form a stable routine and dyadic communication skills. Thus extended family involvement could interfere with marital dynamics.

Issues consistent with hindrances have also been raised in studies of interracial and gay/lesbian relationships. For example, Schoepflin (2009) reported that undergraduates who engaged in interracial relationships received more negative reactions from their family members (than when undergraduates engaged in same-race relationships). Similarly, Vaquera and Kao (2005) noted that interracial romantic couples were mindful that social network members might be uncomfortable with their displays of affection. In an effort to avoid the risk of rejection from network members, romantic couples sometimes inhibited or withheld affection. In a study of gay/lesbian individuals, Oswald (2000) found that they experienced multiple hindrances to involvement in family members' heterosexual weddings. As the weddings were public events, many community members would be aware of the gay/lesbian relationships. Thus gay/lesbian adults were encouraged to engage in multiple behaviors to hide their relationships. For example, individuals were asked to (1) not bring their partners to the weddings, (2) not be photographed in family pictures, and (3) falsify their relationship status (e.g., romantic partners are only friends). Although these actions might not actively destroy interracial or homosexual relationships, they clearly make it harder for romantic couples to feel accepted, respected, or safe.

Disapproval

In contrast to disruption and hindrance, disapproval is the least intense dimension of interference. Disapproval represents the efforts of family/friends to censure a romantic relationship. It is a judgment against the current status or future potential of that relationship. Parallel to approval, disapproval might be a singular event that does not require much effort or repetition. In addition, expression of disapproval does not require that network members engage in any additional actions (e.g., hinder or disrupt romances). Disapproval is reactive because a relationship might already have progressed to a certain level of development before most network members are aware of the relationship.

Family/friends do not have to be perpetually present to have an impact on romantic relationships. The power of their disapproval can occur beyond their presence. For example, Wildermuth (2004) found that young adults in online relationships felt greater stigma and less satisfaction when the adults thought that family/friends would disapprove of the relationships. In reference to stability, Lehmiller and Agnew (2007) reported that family/friend disapproval was predictive of romantic relationship dissolutions within a seven-month period.

Although disapproval is less intense than hindrance or disruption, disapproval still contains some risk. When family/friends disapprove of romances, it is possible that individuals might choose to discontinue contact with network members. Individuals might not dissolve network relationship completely, but they can reduce both psychological and behavioral commitments. This premise is consistent with Bryan et al.'s (2001) finding that individuals were less satisfied with friendships when friends provided low support and high interference for romances. However, friend support/interference had only a small effect on love for romantic partners. Thus family/friends take a chance that their expressions of disapproval could have a deleterious impact on their relationships with individuals and have little or no impact on the status of romantic relationships.

APATHY

The dimensions of support and interference raise some questions about apathy. Apathy is defined as an indifference, lack of motivation, or lack of interest/responsiveness (e.g., Faerden et al. 2009; Wink 2006) and is distinguished from affective or cognitive disorders, such as depression (Levy et al. 1998). Conceptually, family/friends could be apathetic about individuals' romances and still be mentally healthy. Thus apathy would simply represent an absence of (any dimension of) support or interference for romantic relationships. This is consistent with research on diminished motivation (Martin 1997).

It is possible that there are circumstances in which network members might be truly apathetic. For example, they might have no reaction to romances that they perceive are casual or temporary. Unless individuals are engaging in potentially risky behaviors with casual partners (e.g., Hughes, Morrison, and Asada 2005), network members might not see sufficient reason to engage in judgment (approval, disapproval) or actions (promotion, facilitation, disruption, hindrance) in response to such relationships. Thus judgment or action might only seem worthwhile if romances appear to progress to more serious stages of development or affect (positively or negatively) network members' relationships with individuals. If apathy is a true absence, it requires less effort than any dimension of support or interference (see table 1).

Alternatively, it is possible that network members can't be truly apathetic. An argument could be made that if they care about individuals, they care about all aspects of those individuals' lives. If this premise is true, family/friends could experience very low levels of support or interference, but they could not experience a complete absence. However, it is possible for network members to withhold information, and in this case, it might appear to individuals as though the

Table 1
Dimensions of support and interference categorized by valence
and degree of effort required for network members (family/friends).

	Valence		
Degree of Effort	**Positive**	**None**	**Negative**
High	Promotion		Disruption
Moderate	Facilitation		Hindrance
Low	Approval		Disapproval
None		Apathy	

members are apathetic. If individuals want to know how network members judge their romances, the withholding of such information could be annoying or distressing to individuals. If the annoyance or distress has a negative impact on the romances, the appearance of apathy could actually be a hindrance (a dimension of interference).

CONCLUDING COMMENTS

According to Sarason and Sarason (2009), the science of close relationships will be advanced when there is a clearer conceptualization of support processes. They recommended that researchers move toward a multilevel view of support. It seems logical, then, that a multilevel view of interference would be equally valuable. This chapter provides one way to conceptualize these leveled processes. Three support (promotion, facilitation, approval) and three interference (disruption, hindrance, disapproval) dimensions were described briefly, and the potential role of apathy (as a response to romances) was noted.

Although these conceptualizations might add to the discussion about network-romance linkages, this conceptualization is incomplete. This multidimensional framework does not capture all of the nuances that exist within the relationships among family, friends, and romantic partners. Due to space limitations, the nuances cannot be addressed fully in this chapter. Thus sample issues are listed for consideration for future theoretical and empirical (research) work.

First, it is understood that the support and interference dimensions are not static. If friends offer facilitation at one time for romances, they are not committed to continuing facilitation forever. As noted in prior research (e.g., Milardo, Johnson, and Huston 1983), friends can move through various dimensions of support, interference, and/or apathy as they perceive changes within romances or experience changes in their interactions with individuals. Such movement can occur across dimensions for families as well. Thus longitudinal studies would be helpful in tracking changes in the dimensions over time.

Second, it is understood that network members' responses (support, interference, apathy) can be affected by their motivations. In research on influence attempts, DePaulo et al. (2004) noted that attempts can be self- or other-motivated. Thus it is possible that family members might engage in disruption (an interference dimension) because they are angry or jealous that romances have become the most important relationships in individuals' lives. In this case, their disruptive actions would be self-motivated. Alternatively, it is possible that family members engage in disruption because they are worried that romances are harmful to individuals (e.g., abusive, stifling, neglectful). In this case, their actions would be other-motivated. This other-motivation is consistent with prior research, which revealed that network members were more reactive and disapproving when they imagined that relationship wounds were inflicted on individuals rather than on them (Green, Burnette, and Davis 2008). To further complicate matters, network members and individuals can differ in their interpretations of motives. For example, individuals might perceive that family members are engaging in self-motivated responses when they hinder romances, whereas family members perceive that their hindrance is other-motivated. Indeed, it is possible that network members might think that they are being supportive of individuals' well-being while they are attempting to interfere with romances. Thus there might be little or no consensus about who (if any) is acting altruistically.

Third, it is understood that network members can simultaneously engage in support and interference (Felmlee 2008; Ruehlman and Wolchik 1988). If family/friends are ambivalent about the romances, they might provide both supportive and interfering responses. For example, parents might approve of romances at specific stages (e.g., dating) but disapprove of the prospect of increased involvement (e.g., marriage). It is also possible that individuals want to continue their interactions with network members even if members don't support or interfere with romances. This continuation might reflect family loyalty (e.g., Falicov 1999) or reflect that individuals find other aspects of their interactions with network members sufficiently fulfilling. This is consistent with research that suggests individuals are willing to endure aversive interactions for the sake of network relationships (Clark and Grote 1998). This fits with the phenomenon of frenemies (friends who are also enemies) in young adulthood (Bushman and Holt-Lunstad 2009).

Fourth, it is understood that individuals in romantic relationships can reject the responses of network members. Individuals are not automatons. They can accept or reject the responses (support, interference, apathy) given to them. They have the power to choose the ways in which they allow network members to affect their lives (e.g., Sarason and Sarason 2009). Thus the fact that family/friends offer facilitation does not mean that individuals want, need, or will accept facilitation for their romances. Research on acceptance/rejection choices would clarify the actual impact of network members' actions.

Fifth, it is understood that there can be differences in anticipated and actualized responses. Individuals know their family/friends well, so it is possible that they can accurately anticipate the ways in which family/friends will respond to romances. This anticipation can be as powerful as actual responses (Sarason et al. 1987). For example, Hughes et al. (2005) found that individuals withheld information from network members if they anticipated that members would disapprove of their romantic choices. In a similar way, anticipated support might influence romantic choices. This premise is consistent with research that access to social support was negatively related to depression among adults (Dressler, Campos Balieiro, and Dos Santos 1997). Research that examines the differential effects of anticipated and actual responses (interference, support, apathy) would be illuminating.

Sixth, it is understood that family and friends are not singular entities. There can be variations in the dimension of support or interference offered by (1) mothers or fathers, (2) brothers or sisters, (3) same-sex friends or opposite-sex friends, (4) best or casual friends, and (5) other combinations of network members. Network members have unique histories with individuals prior to romances. Thus it makes sense that these members would respond differently to individuals (and their new partners) after romantic relationships have begun. Research that specifies each type of network member (e.g., mother, brother, best friend, opposite-sex friend) would clarify the network-romance linkages.

Clearly, there is much more to learn about support and interference processes. The linkages between social networks and romances are complex. The support-interference dimensions offered in this chapter can initially add to the dialogue about network-romance linkages. The scientific and practical (e.g., therapeutic) value of these dimensions can only be evaluated over time.

REFERENCES

Agnew, C., T. Loving, and S. Drigotas. 2001. Substituting the forest for the trees: Social networks and the prediction of romantic relationship state and fate. *Journal of Personality and Social Psychology* 81:1042–1057.

Aquino, K., and S. Thau. 2009. Workplace victimization: Aggression from the target's perspective. *Annual Review of Psychology* 60:717–741.

Barry, C., S. Madsen, L. Nelson, J. Carroll, and S. Badger. 2009. Friendship and romantic relationship qualities in emerging adulthood: Differential associations with identity development and achieved adulthood criteria. *Journal of Adult Development* 16:209–222.

Bercovici, J. 2006. Workplace romance and sexual favoritism: Creating a dialogue between social science and the sexual harassment law. *Southern California Interdisciplinary Law Journal* 16:183–203.

Blair, K., and D. Holmberg. 2008. Perceived social network support and well-being in same-sex versus mixed-sex romantic relationships. *Journal of Social and Personal Relationships* 25:769–791.

Brown, E., T. Orbuch, and A. Maharaj. 2010. Social networks and marital stability among black American and white American couples. In *Support processes in intimate relationships*, edited by K. Sullivan and J. Davila, 318–335. New York: Oxford University Press.

Bryan, L., J. Fitzpatrick, D. Crawford, and J. Fischer. 2001. The role of network support and interference in women's perceptions of romantic, friend, and parental relationships. *Sex Roles* 45:481–499.

Bushman, B., and J. Holt-Lunstad. 2009. Understanding social relationship maintenance among friends: Why we don't end those frustrating friendships. *Journal of Social and Clinical Psychology* 28:749–778.

Clark, M., and N. Grote. 1998. Why aren't relationship costs always negatively related to indices of relationship quality? *Personality and Social Psychology Review* 2:2–17.

Coffman, M. 2008. Effects of tangible social support and depression on diabetes self-efficacy: A study of Hispanic older adults. *Journal of Gerontological Nursing* 34:32–39.

Copeland, A., and S. Norell. 2002. Spousal adjustment on international assignments: The role of social support. *International Journal of Intercultural Relations* 26:255–272.

Cranford, J. 2004. Stress-buffering or stress-exacerbation? Social support and social undermining as moderators of the relationship between perceived stress and depressive symptoms among married people. *Personal Relationships* 11:23–40.

Cutrona, C., P. Shaffer, K. Wesner, and K. Gardner. 2007. Optimally matching support and perceived spousal sensitivity. *Journal of Family Psychology* 21:754–758.

DePaulo, B., M. Ansfield, S. Kirkendol, and J. Boden. 2004. Serious lies. *Basic and Applied Social Psychology* 26:147–167.

Dressler, W., M. Campos Balieiro, and J. Dos Santos. 1997. The cultural construction of social support in Brazil: Associations with health outcomes. *Culture, Medicine and Psychiatry* 21:303–335.

Driscoll, R., K. Davis, and M. Lipetz. 1972. Parental interference and romantic love: The Romeo and Juliet effect. *Journal of Personality and Social Psychology* 24:1–10.

Duffy, M., D. Ganster, and M. Pagon. 2002. Social undermining in the workplace. *Academy of Management Journal* 45:331–351.

Dunkel-Schetter, C., and L. Skokan. 1990. Determinants of social support provision in personal relationships. *Journal of Social and Personal Relationships* 7:437–450.

Faerden, A., S. Friis, L. Agartz, E. Barrett, R. Nesvåg, A. Finset, and I. Melle. 2009. Apathy and functioning in first-episode psychosis. *Psychiatric Services* 60:1495–1503.

Falicov, C. 1999. The Latino family life cycle. In *The expanded family life cycle: Individual, family and social perspectives*, edited by B. Carter and M. McGoldrick, 141–152. Boston: Allyn and Bacon.

Felmlee, D. 2006. Interaction in social networks. In *Handbook of social psychology*, edited by J. Delamater, 389–409. New York: Springer.

Felmlee, D. 2008. Differential dynamic duos. Paper presented at the 2008 International Association for Relationship Research Conference, Providence, RI, July.

Ferrin, D., K. Dirks, and P. Shah. 2006. Direct and indirect effects of third-party relationships on interpersonal trust. *Journal of Applied Psychology* 91:870–883.

Fingerman, K. 2009. Consequential strangers and peripheral ties: The importance of unimportant relationships. *Journal of Family Theory & Review* 1:69–86.

Fitzpatrick, J. 2009. An expanded view of social support processes. Keynote address at the first Brazilian Conference on Relationship Research, Vitória, Brazil, December.

Fitzpatrick, J., D. Feng, and D. Crawford. 2003. A contextual model analysis of women's social competence, affective characteristics and satisfaction in premarital relationships. *Journal of Family Communication* 3:107–122.

Gordon, P. 2003. The decision to remain single: Implications for women across cultures. *Journal of Mental Health Counseling* 25:33–44.

Green, J., J. Burnette, and J. Davis. 2008. Third-party forgiveness: (Not) forgiving your close other's betrayer. *Personality and Social Psychology Bulletin* 34:407–418.

Guerrero, L., and P. Mongeau. 2008. On becoming "more than friends": The transition from friendship to romantic relationships. In *Handbook of relationship initiation*, edited by S. Sprecher, A. Wenzel, and J. Harvey, 175–194. New York: Taylor and Francis.

Hughes, M., K. Morrison, and K. Asada. 2005. What's love got to do with it? Exploring the impact of maintenance rules, love attitudes, and network support on friends with benefits relationships. *Western Journal of Communication* 69:49–66.

Hunt, M. 2003. Shakespeare's Venetian paradigm: Stereotyping and sadism in the *Merchant of Venice* and *Othello*. *Papers on Language and Literature* 39:162–184.

Jankowiak, W., and E. Fischer. 1992. A cross-cultural perspective on romantic love. *Ethnology* 31:149–155.

Kim, H., D. Sherman, D. Ko, and S. Taylor. 2006. Pursuit of comfort and pursuit of harmony: Culture, relationships and social support seeking. *Personality and Social Psychology Bulletin* 32:1595–1607.

Klein, R., and R. Milardo. 2000. The social context of couple conflict: Support and criticism from informal third parties. *Journal of Social and Personal Relationships* 17:618–637.

Lehmiller, J., and C. Agnew. 2007. Perceived marginalization and the prediction of romantic relationship stability. *Journal of Marriage and the Family* 69:1036–1049.

Levy, M., J. Cummings, L. Fairbanks, D. Masterman, B. Miller, A. Craig, J. Paulsen, and I. Litvan. 1998. Apathy is not depression. *Journal of Neuropsychiatry and Clinical Neuroscience* 10:314–319.

Longwell-Grice, R. 2003. Get a job: Working class students discuss the purpose of college. *College Student Affairs Journal* 23:40–53.

Martin, R. 1997. Apathy: Who cares? An introduction to apathy and diminished motivation disorders. *Psychiatric Annals* 27:18–23.

Milardo, R., M. Johnson, and T. Huston. 1983. Developing close relationships: Changing patterns of interaction between pair members and social networks. *Journal of Personality and Social Psychology* 44:964–976.

Neyer, F., and D. Voigt. 2004. Personality and social network effects on romantic relationships: A dyadic approach. *European Journal of Psychology* 18:279–299.

Oswald, R. 2000. A member of the wedding? Heterosexism and family ritual. *Journal of Social and Personal Relationships* 17:349–368.

Overall, N., G. Fletcher, and J. Simpson. 2010. Helping each other grow: Romantic partner support, self-improvement and relationship quality. *Personality and Social Psychology Bulletin* 36:1496–1513.

Pierce, G., B. Sarason, L. Sarason, H. Joseph, and C. Henderson. 1996. Conceptualizing and assessing social support in the context of the family. In *Handbook of social support and the family*, edited by G. Pierce, B. Sarason and I. Sarason, 3–23. New York: Plenum Press.

Raley, R., S. Crissey, and C. Muller. 2007. Of sex and romance: Late adolescent relationships and young adult union formation. *Journal of Marriage and Family* 69:1210–1226.

Richardson, R., N. Barbour, and D. Bubenzer. 1991. Bittersweet connections: Informal social networks as sources of support and interference for adolescent mothers. *Family Relations* 40:430–434.

Ruehlman, L., and S. Wolchik. 1988. Personal goals and interpersonal support and hindrance as factors in psychological distress and well-being. *Journal of Personality and Social Psychology* 55:293–301.

Sarason, I., and B. Sarason. 2009. Social support: Mapping the construct. *Journal of Social and Personal Relationships* 26:113–120.

Sarason, I., B. Sarason, E. Shearin, and G. Pierce. 1987. A brief measure of social support: Practical and theoretical implications. *Journal of Social and Personal Relationships* 4:497–510.

Schoepflin, T. 2009. Perspectives of interracial dating at a predominantly white university. *Sociological Spectrum* 29:346–370.

Scott, D. 2002. Matchmaker, matchmaker, find me a mate: A cultural examination of a virtual community of single Mormons. *Journal of Media and Religion* 1:201–216.

Seegobin, W., and K. Tarquin. 2003. Mate selection in Trinidad and Tobago: A multireligious, multicultural perspective. In *Mate selection across cultures*, edited by R. Hamon and B. Ingoldsby, 61–75. Thousand Oaks, CA: Sage.

Shakespeare, W. 1993. *Othello*. New York: Washington Square Press.

Shulman, S., and O. Kipnis. 2001. Adolescent romantic relationships: A view from the future. *Journal of Adolescence* 24:337–351.

Simmonds, A. 2005. "Promises and pie crusts were made to be broke": Breach of promise of marriage and the regulation of courtship in early colonial Australia. *Australian Feminist Law Journal* 23:99–120.

Sinclair, C. 2008. Why source matters: The consequences of self-construal for source differences in the association between social network opinion and relational dynamics. Paper presented at the 2008 International Association for Relationship Research Conference, Providence, RI, July.

Sprecher, S., and D. Felmlee. 1992. The influence of parents and friends on the quality and stability of romantic relationships: A three-wave longitudinal investigation. *Journal of Marriage and the Family* 54:888–900.

Sprecher, S., D. Felmlee, T. Orbuch, and M. Willetts. 2002. Social networks and change in personal relationships. In *Stability and change in relationships*, edited by A. Vangelisti, H. Reis, and M. Fitzpatrick, 257–284. Cambridge: Cambridge University Press.

Taylor, J. 2004. Autonomy and informed consent: A much misunderstood relationship. *Journal of Value Inquiry* 38:383–391.

Vaquera, E., and G. Kao. 2005. Private and public displays of affection among interracial and intra-racial adolescent couples. *Social Science Quarterly* 86:484–508.

Venkataramani, V., and R. Dalal. 2007. Who helps and harms whom? Relational antecedents of interpersonal helping and harming in organizations. *Journal of Applied Psychology* 92:952–966.

Vinokur, A., and M. van Ryn. 1993. Social support and undermining in close relationships: Their independent effects on the mental health of unemployed persons. *Journal of Personality and Social Psychology* 65:350–359.

Walker, A., and R. Hirayama. 2010. Missing pieces of a positive relationship science: Comment on Fincham and Beach. *Journal of Family Theory & Review* 2:36–41.

Westman, M., D. Etzion, and E. Danon. 2001. Job insecurity and cross-over of burnout in married couples. *Journal of Organizational Behavior* 22:467–481.

Westman, M., and A. Vinokur. 1998. Unraveling the relationship of distress levels within couples: Common stressors, empathic reactions or cross-over via social interaction? *Human Relations* 51:137–156.

Wildermuth, S. 2004. The effects of stigmatizing discourse on the quality of on-line relationships. *Cyberpsychology and Behavior* 7:73–84.

Wink, K. 2006. A lesson from the Holocaust: From bystander to advocate in the classroom. *English Journal* 96:84–89.

Zaidi, A., and M. Shuraydi. 2002. Perceptions of arranged marriages by young Pakistani Muslim women living in a Western society. *Journal of Comparative Family Studies* 33:495–514.

Chapter 9

Media and Relationships:
An Emerging Research Area

Kimberly R. Johnson and Bjarne M. Holmes

Researchers have long argued that media can serve as a source of influence on a number of issues. Violence and aggressive acts, sex, risky behaviors such as smoking and drinking—all have been examined with regard to the prevalence and nature of portrayals within media content and to the potential effects such portrayals have on viewer cognitions and behaviors. An area of research to have emerged in recent years is that of media portrayals of romantic relationships and the beliefs and expectations of those who view them, with the evidence found thus far suggesting that viewers can indeed be drawn to and influenced by the messages inherent within such content.

MEDIA EFFECTS

In considering the potential for media influence on viewer cognitions, although several theoretical perspectives exist (see Escobar-Chaves et al. 2005 for review), much research is framed within one of three major theories, that of cultivation theory (Gerbner 1969; Gerbner and Gross 1976; Gerbner et al. 1980, 1994), social cognitive theory (Bandura 1986, 1999, 2002; Bandura and Huston 1961; Bandura, Ross, and Ross 1963), and priming theory (Berkowitz 1986; Jo and Berkowitz

1994). According to cultivation theory, individuals who are exposed over a pro-longed period of time to portrayals of reality as defined by television come to develop perceptions that are consistent with those portrayals. That is, television's themes and images serve to cultivate viewers' beliefs, attitudes, and expectations about their social environment that echo the cultural norms such themes prescribe. With its original focus on purely television as cultivator, Gerbner and colleagues (1994) emphasized that consistent and repetitive programming, in which similar-ity in presentation across content is mutually reinforcing, acts as a major source of socialization for the viewing public. Social cognitive theory, meanwhile, sug-gests the viewer takes a more active part in the internalization of media-presented themes and ideas. Here, through observing media characters' actions and behav-iors, as well as any ensuing consequences, individuals learn what is deemed to be typical or appropriate in society and integrate that knowledge into their own cognitions to be used to guide future behavior. Crucial in determining whether this act of modeling takes place is the nature of the consequences presented to individuals (Bandura 1994), such that if an observed behavior results in a desir-able outcome, then the appeal of achieving similar results and enjoying the same benefits serves as a potent motivator.

Lastly, priming theory offers insight into the immediate cognitive and behav-ioral effects of media exposure. Berkowitz (1986) and Jo and Berkowitz (1994) argue that the temporary after-effects of media exposure are brought about by the media portrayal priming cognitive schema that are semantically related to the portrayal being viewed, increasing their accessibility and likelihood of becom-ing activated. Furthermore, *affective* priming can occur, whereby the activation of emotion-related schema similar to those presented in the media brings about associated emotional responses, a typical example being violent media's portrayal of aggressive acts priming feelings of aggression within individuals exposed to such a presentation. Although the focus of the above speaks clearly of short-term processes, the potential long-term implications of repeated media priming are substantial: Similar in principle to cultivation theory, repeated priming of schema through prolonged media viewing may lead to chronic accessibility to media-congruent cognitions over time and ultimately may influence how individuals respond to and interact with others in their social environments (Bargh 1984; Hig-gins and King 1981; see Ward 2003).

The focus of early media effects research was primarily on the issue of vio-lence in the media and the potential negative cognitive, affective, and behavioral sequelae that viewing such media may produce (e.g., Eron et al. 1972; Gerbner et al.1979; Gerbner et al. 1980; Gross and Morgan 1985; Hansen and Hansen 1990; Josephson 1987; Signorielli, Gross, and Morgan 1982; Weaver and Wakshlag 1986). However, recent years have seen an additional focus of empirical attention emerge in the form of examination of media presentations of interpersonal rela-tionships. A primary concern driving empirical attention on media effects is that of the impact on children and teenagers, who, with their greater naïveté on more adult themes, are vulnerable to impression from the messages inherent within the media content that older viewers with greater experience are less susceptible to (Courtright and Baran 1980; Illouz 1998). Indeed, this concern exists as many researchers have argued and found evidence to suggest that adolescents look to the media as a source of information (Andre, Lund Frevert, and Schuchmann 1989; Angell, Gordon, and Begun 1999; Bachen and Illouz 1996; Brown 2002; Brown and Keller 2000; Committee on Public Education 2001; Jackson Harris 1994; Lowry and Shidler 1993; Signorielli 1991) due to the more discrete learning opportunities afforded in more private settings than discussion with family and friends would otherwise allow.

In instances in which learning is not a driving motivator behind media viewing, an additional concern then lies in the ubiquitous nature of mass media, with its repetitive and contextually consistent portrayals providing opportunity for inadvertent learning through the subconscious internalization encapsulated by cultivation processes. On this basis, then, it is unsurprising that the sexual aspects of romantic relationship experiences have been afforded a substantial proportion of the empirical attention within the relationship media literature.

SEXUAL MEDIA AND RELATIONSHIP PRESENTATIONS

Studies investigating media effects from a cultivation theoretical perspective have found evidence to suggest an association between sexual media consumption and viewers' beliefs and expectations. This focus on sexual media deviates from the generalized viewing described by Gerbner and colleagues (Gerbner 1969; Gerbner and Gross 1976; Gerbner et al. 1980, 1994), who originally argued that television comprises a centralized narrative with a uniform message across all genres and hence it is the overall exposure to television content that influences real-world perceptions. Perhaps a reflection of the more restricted and limited range of available programming when cultivation theory was originally conceptualized, more recent research has put forward that it is not overall exposure to television content but genre-specific viewing that has a more potent influence on audience cognitions (Holmes 2007; Rössler and Brosius 2001; Segrin and Nabi 2002; Shapiro and Kroeger 1991), such that, in this instance, it is viewers' exposure to *sexual media* content over time, rather than *general* content that has the potential for shaping viewers' sexual relationship attitudes, beliefs, and perceptions. Indeed, Potter and Chang (1990) highlight that research shows great variability in programming content across television channels and time of day (e.g., Greenberg 1980; Potter and Ware 1987) and, in testing differences in measurement of television exposure, found overall viewing to be a weak predictor of media effects compared to proportionate viewing focusing on program type.

Although not all research examining sexual media effects finds significant associations (e.g., Greenberg et al. 1982), viewing sexually oriented media has been identified as being associated with greater sexual expectations (Stevens Aubrey et al. 2003), dissatisfaction in one's own sexual activities (Baran 1976a, 1976b), overestimation of the sexual activity of peers, rates of pregnancies, sexually transmitted diseases, extramarital affairs (Buerkel-Rothfuss and Mayes 1981; Davis and Mares 1998; Martino et al. 2005; Olsen 1994; Ward and Rivadeneyra 1999), endorsement of more permissive attitudes (Bryant and Rockwell 1994; Strouse and Buerkel-Rothfuss 1987; Strouse, Buerkel-Rothfuss, and Long 1995; Taylor 2005), sexual-stereotypical beliefs (Ferris et al. 2007; Walsh-Childers and Brown 1993; Ward 2002; Ward and Friedman 2006), adversarial sexual beliefs (Zurbriggen and Morgan 2006), and greater acceptance of sexual harassment (Strouse, Goodwin, and Roscoe 1994). Interestingly, counter to Olsen's (1994) findings of increased estimates of pregnancies and sexually transmitted diseases, Martino et al. (2005) found an association between increased exposure to sexual media content and underestimation of the possibility of negative consequences of engaging in sexual activity, perhaps suggesting that while younger viewers might perceive increased possible negative outcomes for others, such risks may not be perceived as applicable to themselves.

Consistent with social cognitive theory are the studies demonstrating a relationship between greater media consumption and intentions to engage in sex, initiation of sexual activity (Martino et al. 2005), and general prevalence of sexual and risky behaviors. Lastly, studies using experimental methodologies to test priming processes have found sexual visual media to influence partner attractiveness ratings, with males reporting loving their wives less after exposure, and both males and females reporting less satisfaction in their partners' affection, appearance, and sexual interest and performance. In examining the effects of exposure to sexual content over an extended period of time, Zillman (1988b) exposed participants to pornographic media content over a period of six weeks and found a greater acceptance of sexual promiscuity and non-exclusivity in relationships, sex roles of male dominance and female servitude, and a lessening of the appeal of marriage and having children. Using the less sexually explicit medium of music videos (a media genre found to endorse sex-role stereotyping Hansen and Hansen (1990) found that participants who had been primed with a sex role–stereotypical music video judged a female interactant as more skilled and competent when she reciprocated a male interactant's sexual advances, suggesting more favorable general evaluations of females who appear more sexually responsive to others.

RELATIONSHIPS AND THE MEDIA

The above research provides strong evidence for an association between media viewing and sexual expectations, satisfaction, beliefs, behaviors, and perceptions of societal sexual norms and outcomes. While outnumbered by their sexually focused empirical counterparts, research has emerged in recent years extending its scope beyond examining purely the sexual aspects of relationships to exploring general interpersonal representations and their associations with viewer relationship beliefs and expectations.

In keeping with the revised cultivation theory of genre-specific viewing, Perse (1986) found regular soap opera viewers to report greater perceptions of divorce and individuals having illegitimate children. Perse (1986) found that perceptions of marriage as similar to those presented in soap operas were strongest for regular viewers of such programming. Signorielli (1991) found that adolescents who regularly viewed prime-time television programs, such as sitcoms, had greater aspirations to get married and start a family. However, also found was the tendency to believe that good marriages are rare and to question marriage as a way of life, suggesting a certain level of ambivalence in prime-time programming's presentation of married couples. Segrin and Nabi (2002) similarly found associations between media viewing and marriage expectations, reporting that individuals who more regularly viewed romantic media content (such as soap operas, daytime talk shows, and reality-based shows focusing on romantic relationships) held idealistic expectations about marital relations and indicated greater intentions to marry. Similar to marital expectations are the findings of research identifying associations with elevated partner and relationship expectations and standards: Eggermont (2004) found that adolescents' increased overall television viewing predicted placing greater importance on partner physical attractiveness and pleasant personality, while Holmes and Johnson (2009) found that for individuals not in relationships, greater television viewing predicted higher partner/relationship standards (as conceptualized by Fletcher and colleagues; see Campbell et al. 2001) than for individuals who viewed less media.

Further research has focused on the dysfunctional relationship beliefs outlined by Eidelson and Epstein (1982), who identified five dysfunctional beliefs that can be detrimental to interpersonal functioning and well-being: disagreement in relationships is destructive; mind reading should be expected; neither partner nor relationship quality can change (dismissing the potential for growth and development in either); sexual perfectionism; and the notion that men and women differ drastically with regard to their relationship needs and wants. Increased media viewing has been linked to each of the above beliefs (Haferkamp 1999; Holmes 2007; Holmes and Johnson 2009; Shapiro and Kroeger 1991), suggesting that messages inherent in such media content prescribe unhealthy ideals incongruent with healthy interpersonal functioning. Indeed, Holmes and Johnson (2009) argue that media's presentation of "ideal" as "typical" makes it a potentially detrimental influence on viewers' interpersonal cognitions, with further findings of media viewing and beliefs in soul mates and relationship destiny supporting this contention (Holmes 2007; Holmes and Johnson 2009).

Although no studies have examined romantic media effects from a social cognitive-theoretical perspective per se, research does exist to suggest that viewers do indeed look to media-presented relationships when formulating romantic relationship ideas. Drawing upon research by Granello (1997) in which television was

identified as a source of information on interpersonal relationships for younger people, Westman, Lynch, Lewandowski, and Hunt-Carter (2003) found that the more
sitcoms, dramas, magazine articles, and books were perceived as realistic or as an
ideal to strive for, the more they were used as sources of ideas on romantic relationships. In keeping with the notion of perceived realism, Punyanunt-Carter (2006)
found in her study that male participants were more likely to report perceiving sex
on television as more realistic than did female participants, but found the inverse
relationship for perceptions of realism of love. It is little surprising then that Morrison and Westman (2001) found that women were more likely than men to report
expecting their significant other to act similarly to those viewed on television, as
well as trying to model family life on those presented on sitcom television programs.

A further theoretical perspective hinted at but not directly tested for within
media effects research is that of social comparison (Festinger 1954), with evidence
suggesting that media viewing may induce (either consciously or subconsciously)
reflections on viewers' own situations relative to those suggested within media
presentations. Indeed, with prolonged television viewing comes increased viewer
involvement in storylines and the characters they comprise, with such characters
over time becoming as real to viewers as friends or neighbors (see Rose 1979).
In her naturalistic study examining college students' soap opera viewing, Lemish
(1985) found students to report experiences echoing social comparison processes,
for example, "It brings out the 'what could I do in that situation?' feeling of 'yeah,
that is a good, tender, loving scene and I probably would do the same thing'" (286).
Baran (1976a, 1976b) found individuals with greater media diets to feel dissatisfied in their sexual activity, while Holmes and Johnson (2009) and Shapiro and
Kroeger (1991) both found significant associations between exposure to romantic
media and relationship satisfaction, suggesting that ideals presented in the media
may indeed be subject to viewer comparison.

CONTENT ANALYSES

As suggested by the above research, it is apparent that the content of widely
viewed media is presented in such a way that research from cultivation, social
cognitive, and priming theoretical perspectives predicts adverse effects for viewers. Given their enormous popularity (e.g., Greenberg and Woods 1999; Katzman
1972; Whetmore and Kielwasser 1983), a focus of qualitative examination in early
content analysis work was that of daytime soap operas. Moral violations (Sutherland and Siniawksy 1982), physical and mental health problems (Cassata, Skill,
and Boadu 1979; Thompson et al. 2000), and risky behaviors (Diener 2007; Piepe
et al. 1986; Verma, Adams, and White 2007) have all been the focus of analysis; however, research examining the presentation of the nature and frequency of
sexual relationships and encounters predominates.

Greenberg, Abelman, and Neuendorf (1981), Lowry and Towles (1989) and
Lowry, Love, and Kirby (1981) all identified erotic touching to be the most

frequently occurring sexual activity, recorded as occurring nearly three times per hour in the latter study, and it was found to be most likely to happen between unmarried partners. Greenberg and D'Alessio (1985) found more controversial sexual references in their study, identifying references to prostitution and rape, whereas Heintz-Knowles (1996) reported more positive presentations of sexual experiences, identifying sexual relations between committed couples to be the most frequent, and finding such physical intimacy to be beneficial to relationship functioning.

Although limited in number, content analyses expanding their focus to include all relationship aspects paint a turbulent picture when it comes to soap opera characters' romantic experiences and histories. Relationships are of central importance but are complex, as characters' lives are intertwined within small, insular communities (Fine 1981). Relationship difficulties and tensions, divorce, and infidelity are rife (Barbatsis 1983; Goldsen 1975; Johnson and Holmes, in prep; Jones 1984; Katzman 1992; Liebes and Livingstone 1998; see Livingstone 1987, for a review) with couples at times separating, divorcing, rekindling their romance and remarrying all within a relatively confined time span (Johnson and Holmes, in prep).

Beyond soap opera programming, content analyses examining prime-time television identify similar sexual and interpersonal themes. Greenberg and Busselle (1996), Sprafkin and Silverman (1981) and Sapolsky (1982) all reported a high frequency of relationship behaviors such as hugging, kissing, and sexual acts, while Ward (1995) reported male sex-role themes (such as sex as central in defining masculinity and the adoption of unsavory tactics in attempting to bed women) and female sex-role themes (such as the importance of appearance in interpersonal success and responsibility for setting sexual limits) to predominate. Also identified were the messages of relationship maintenance as serious and often painful, as well as openness and intimacy as being key to interpersonal success. Kim et al. (2007) found that male characters were presented as open in pursuing female characters' affections, lavishing them with gifts or emphasizing their own strength, intelligence, or wealth to attract them. However, once in relationships, male characters were uncomfortable with commitment, needing to maintain independence from female partners who were typically presented as desiring emotional stability and intimacy. In keeping with this apparent fear of commitment, male infidelity was reported as commonplace, with television dramas' portrayals as negative but sitcoms using such relationship transgressions as a basis for humor. Lastly, in their content analysis of reality dating shows, Ferris et al. (2007) found that participants on such shows endorsed attitudes that see men as sex-driven, women as sex objects, and dating as a game. Furthermore, they found that endorsement of women as sex objects was rewarded (for example, through receiving praise or material gifts such as flowers or jewelry) more often than was punished (through condemnation from other participants).

As suggested by the small number of studies outlined above, there is limited research on the nature of presentations of romantic relationships across television programming. Fewer still are analyses examining the romantic content of film. Tanner et al. (2003) identified the theme of "love at first sight" as prevalent in Disney feature-length films, as well as the notion of relationships as easy to maintain with clearly identifiable sex roles. Johnson and Holmes (2009), meanwhile, found conflicting messages within romantic comedy films: Relationships were presented as having the qualities of both new (passion, excitement, and physical closeness) and long-term relationships (love, emotional support, and relationship and partner prioritization), were highly idealized (with downplaying of negative behaviors), and portrayed behaviors suggestive of the dysfunctional relationship beliefs outlined by Eidelson and Epstein (1982).

MOOD MANAGEMENT

The above-described research on media effects on romantic relationship cognitions (and indeed on effects outside this interpersonal focus) has provided a solid insight into how viewers respond to the images and ideas presented to them. However, such research generally appears to conceptualize the viewing audience as a passive victim of the messages inherent within such content with little regard for their role in media selection and interpretation. As such, this mechanistic approach to the media-viewer relationship has been criticized as overly simplistic and ignoring such factors as individual predispositions and selection processes (Klapper 1960; see Rubin 1994). Indeed, several researchers have argued that media effects research is too focused on what impact it has on viewers without empirical consideration of how viewers use media (e.g., Katz and Foulkes 1962) and as such more attention should be given to the viewer's roles in media selection (Hodgetts and Chamberlain 2006; see Chamberlain and Hodgetts 2008).

One line of research within the communications literature to address this weakness and concentrate more on viewer role is that of *uses and gratifications*, a paradigm that puts forward that individuals' psychological needs and expectations of media produce differential patterns of media exposure intended to address and gratify the needs prevalent at that time (Katz, Blumler, and Gurevitch 1974). Although there is some slight variation in the motives identified for media use and gratification (e.g., Bantz 1982; Palmgreen and Rayburn 1979; Perse 1986), researchers generally identify motives that can fall under two types of viewing: instrumental, in which media use is goal-directed and gratifies needs such as information seeking; and ritualized, in which media use is more habitual and gratifies needs for entertainment and diversion (Rubin 1981a, 1981b, 1983, 1984; Rubin and Rubin 1982; Windahl 1981). Although not directly tested within the uses and gratifications literature, certain viewing motives that are examined within this paradigm (such as escape, relaxation, and arousal) are suggestive of *mood management* as a determinant of media viewing behavior. Indeed, Finn and Gorr (1988) categorized the above viewing examples under the construct of "mood management," highlighting television viewing's applicability to managing mood states, and it is within this theoretical framework that media use within a romantic relationship context has recently been considered.

Having a basis in annoyance-alleviating effects research in which hedonically incompatible media was said to serve as a cognitive intervention for annoyed individuals' preoccupation with their negative affective state (Bryant and Zillman 1977; Zillman and Johnson 1973), Zillman's (1988a) mood management theory's basis conceptualizes the viewers as having hedonistic motivations in their media selections, such that they are driven to avoid and reduce the intensity of negative, aversive stimulation while being driven to seek out and maximize pleasurable and gratifying affective experiences. To this end, Zillman (2000) described media content that is excitatory, cognitively absorbing, positively valenced, and hedonically incongruent with the viewer's current mood state that is most effective for mood management.

General research testing mood management theory has found evidence to support its postulates. Showing evidence of preference for hedonically incongruent media content when current mood state is negative, Bryant and Zillman (1985) found individuals in bored states of mind more frequently selected exciting rather than relaxing programs, while stressed individuals selected both exciting and relaxing programs in similar amounts. In examining feelings of apprehension and media selection, Wakshlag, Vial, and Tamborini (1983) found individuals whose feelings of apprehension toward crime and victimization were primed through exposure to a crime documentary film selected films in which themes of less victimization and greater justice were predominant. Focusing on auditory media (i.e., music) selection, Knobloch and Zillman (2002) reported individuals in negative moods to select energetic-joyful music for longer periods of time (and to be more decisive in their music selection) than did individuals in positive moods.

However, evidence has also emerged to counter the notion of positive hedonic gratification through media use encapsulated by mood management theory, instead finding evidence of some individuals preferring media that is congruent with their current negative moods states (e.g., Anderson et al. 996; Knobloch-Westerwick and Alter 2006). Addressing this "counterhedonistic media selection" controversy, Zillman (2000) differentiated between spontaneous and telic hedonism, in which the former encapsulates immediate gratification and the latter delayed gratification for later benefit. Oliver (1993, 2003, 2008) provides further suggestions of maintaining a sad mood through negative media selection as allowing for greater reflection on a troubling issue (ultimately permitting a satisfactory resolution) as well as the notion that seeking negatively valenced media may allow for the experience of a negative mood state that in and of itself may be gratifying through promoting personal expressiveness.

Studies examining mood management practices via media use within a romantic relationship context indeed suggest there to be differences in individuals' selections. Gibson, Aust, and Zillman (2000) found that nonlonely males enjoyed love-celebrating music more than their highly lonely counterparts, whereas the inverse was found for females, with highly lonely females enjoying such positively themed music more than less lonely females. Examining the role of romantic satisfaction in music preferences, Knobloch and Zillman (2003) found that, for both males and females, participants who were satisfied showed a preference for love-celebrating music while those who were dissatisfied showed a preference for love-lamenting music. Providing support for the counterhedonistic media selection inclination described by Zillman (2000) and Oliver (1993, 2003, 2008), the above findings by Knobloch and Zillman suggest individuals' feelings concerning their relationships encourage media selections and preferences that may allow for the experience of affect that is congruent with their current relationship regard.

Focusing on visual media selections and preferences, in their study in which participants imagined themselves going through hypothetical relationship situations (for example, being in love and feeling optimistic about the future or breaking up and feeling pessimistic about the future), Kim and Oliver (2006) found differences in media selection preferences did indeed exist. Specifically, they found that individuals who had imagined themselves breaking up with a partner reported a greater avoidance of films containing romance themes than those who imagined they were in love or not in a relationship, suggesting a mood management approach in which avoidance of aversive relationship-related mood states is what governs media choices. Further found was that individuals who imagined themselves to be romantically pessimistic about their relationship future were significantly more likely to avoid romance films than nonromance films, again suggesting a viewing motive to protect against worsening mood states.

Taken together, the above research into the content and effects of relationship media portrayals, as well as how individuals use media in mood-regulation practices within a relationship context, highlights an interesting interaction between media and the viewers who use it. The reviewed studies suggest that media have the potential to serve as a source of information when forming ideas on relationship expectations and beliefs, as an influence on how viewers understand, interpret, and evaluate their romantic relationship experiences, and as a means of managing moods resulting from concurrent relationship feelings. While there is still much to be learned in this area, the studies reviewed have provided much insight into, as well offered direction for future studies on, the issue of relationships and the media.

REFERENCES

Anderson, D. R., P. A. Collins, K. L. Schmitt, and R. B. Jacobvitz. 1996. Stressful life events and television viewing. *Communication Research* 23:243–260.

Andre, T., R. Lund Frevert, and D. Schuchmann. 1989. From whom have college students learned what about sex? *Youth and Society* 20:241–268.

Angell, E., D. Gordon, and B. Begun. 1999. It's their world: A guide to who's hot. *Newsweek*, 66–67.

Bachen, C. M., and E. Illouz. 1996. Imagining romance: Young people's cultural models of romance and love. *Critical Studies in Mass Communication* 13:279–308.

Bandura, A. 1986. *Social foundations of thought and action: A social cognitive theory.* Upper Saddle River, NJ: Prentice-Hall.

Bandura, A. 1994. Self-efficacy. In *Encyclopedia of Psychology,* edited by R. Corsini, 368–369. New York: Wiley.

Bandura, A. 1999. A social cognitive theory of personality. In *Handbook of personality,* 2nd ed., edited by L. Pervin and O. John, 154–196. New York: Guilford Press.

Bandura, A. 2002. Social cognitive theory of mass communication. In *Media effects: Advances in theory and research,* 2nd ed., edited by J. Bryan and D. Zillman, 61–90. Hillsdale, NJ: Erlbaum.

Bandura, A., and A. C. Huston. 1961. Identification as a process of incidental learning. *Journal of Abnormal and Social Psychology* 63:311–318.

Bandura, A., D. Ross, and S. A. Ross. 1963. Imitation of film-mediated aggressive models. *Journal of Abnormal and Social Psychology* 66:3–11.

Bantz, C. R. 1982. Exploring uses and gratifications: A comparison of reported uses of television and reported uses of favorite program type. *Communication Research* 9:352–379.

Baran, S. J. 1976a. Sex on TV and the adolescent's self-image. *Journal of Broadcasting* 20:61–68.

Baran, S. J. 1976b. How TV and film portrayals affect sexual satisfaction in college students. *Journalism Quarterly* 53:468–473.

Barbatsis, G. 1983. Soap opera as etiquette book: Advice for interpersonal relationships. *Journal of American Culture* 6:88–91.

Bargh, J. A. 1984. Automatic and conscious processing of social information. In *Handbook of social cognition,* edited by R. S. Wyers and T. K. Srull, vol. 3, 1–44. Hillsdale, NJ: Erlbaum.

Berkowitz, L. 1986. Situational influences on reactions to observed violence. *Journal of Social Issues* 42:93–106.

Brown, J. D. 2002. Mass media influences on sexuality. *Journal of Sex Research* 3:42–45.

Brown, J. D., and S. N. Keller. 2000. Can the mass media be healthy sex educators? *Family Planning Perspectives* 32:255–256.

Bryant, J., and S. C. Rockwell. 1994. Effects of massive exposure to sexually oriented primetime television programming on adolescents' moral judgments. In *Media, children, and the family: Social scientific, psychodynamic, and clinical perspectives,* edited by J. Zillman, J. Bryant, and A. C. Huston, 183–195. Hillsdale, NJ: Erlbaum.

Bryant, J., and D. Zillman. 1977. The mediating effect of the intervention potential of communications on displaced aggressiveness and retaliatory behavior. In *Communication year 1,* edited by B. D. Ruben, 291–306. New Brunswick, NJ: ICA-Transaction Press.

Bryant, J., and D. Zillman. 1985. Using television to alleviate boredom and stress: Selective exposure as a function of induced excitational states. *Journal of Broadcasting and Electronic Media* 28:1–20.

Buerkel-Rothfuss, N. L., and S. Mayes. 1981. Soap opera viewing: The cultivation effect. *Journal of Communication* 31:108–115.

Campbell, L. J., J. A. Simpson, D. A. Kashy, and G. J. O. Fletcher. 2001. Ideal standards, the self, and flexibility of ideals in close relationships. *Personality and Social Psychology Bulletin* 27:447–462.

Cassata, M. B., T. D. Skill, and S. O. Boadu. 1979. In sickness and in health. *Journal of Communication* 29:73–80.

Chamberlain, K., and D. Hodgetts. 2008. Social psychology and media: Critical considerations. *Social and Personality Psychology Compass* 2(3):1109–1125.

Committee on Public Education. 2001. Sexuality, contraception, and the media. *Pediatrics* 107:191–194.

Courtright, J. A., and S. J. Baran. 1980. The acquisition of sexual information by young people. *Journalism Quarterly* 57:107–114.

Davis, S., and M-L Mares. 1998. Effects of talk show viewing on adolescents. *Journal of Communication* 48:69–86.

Diener, B. J. 2007. A longitudinal study of generic alcohol and tobacco cues in daytime soap opera programs: Fall 1986, 1991, and 2001. *Journal of Business and Economics Research* 5:41–48.

Eggermont, S. 2004. Television viewing, perceived similarity, and adolescents' expectations of a romantic partner. *Journal of Broadcasting and Electronic Media* 48:244–265.

Eidelson, R. J., and N. Epstein. 1982. Cognition and relationship maladjustment: Development on a measure of dysfunctional relationship beliefs. *Journal of Consulting and Clinical Psychology* 50:715–720.

Eron, L. D., L. R. Huesmann, M. M. Lefkowitz, and L. O. Walder. 1972. Does television violence cause aggression? *American Psychologist* 27:253–263.

Escobar-Chaves, S. L., S. R. Tortolero, C. M. Markham, B. J. Low, P. Eitel, and P. Thickstun. 2005. Impact of the media on adolescent sexual attitudes and behaviors. *Pediatrics* 116:303–326.

Ferris, A. L., S. W. Smith, B. S. Greenberg, and S. L. Smith. 2007. The content of reality dating shows and viewer perceptions of dating. *Journal of Communication* 57:490–510.

Festinger, L. 1954. A theory of social comparison processes. *Human Relations* 7:117–140.

Fine, M. G. 1981. Soap opera conversations: The talk that binds. *Journal of Communication* 31:97–107.

Finn, S., and M. B. Gorr. 1988. Social isolation and social support as correlates of television viewing motivations. *Communication Research* 15:135–158.

Gerbner, G. 1969. Toward "cultural indicators": The analysis of mass mediated messages. *AV Communication Review* 17:137–148.

Gerbner, G., and L. Gross. 1976. Living with television: The violence profile. *Journal of Communication* 26:173–199.

Gerbner, G., L. Gross, M. Morgan, and N. Signorielli. 1980. The mainstreaming of America: Violence profile no. 11. *Journal of Communication* 30:10–29.

Gerbner, G., L. Gross, M. Morgan, and N. Signorielli. 1994. Growing up with television: The cultivation perspective. In *Media effects: Advances in theory and research*, edited by J. Bryant and D. Zillman, 17–41. Hillsdale, NJ: Erlbaum.

Gerbner, G., L. Gross, M. Morgan, N. Signorielli, and M. Jackson-Beeck. 1979. The demonstration of power: Violence profile no. 10. *Journal of Communication* 29:177–196.

Gibson, R., C. F. Aust, and D. Zillman. 2000. Loneliness of adolescents and their choice and enjoyment of love-celebrating versus love-lamenting popular music. *Empirical Studies of the Arts* 18:43–48.

Goldsen, R. K. 1975. Throwaway husbands, wives and lovers. *Human Behavior* 4:64–69.

Granello, D. H. 1997. Using Beverly Hills 90210 to explore developmental issues in female adolescents. *Youth & Society* 29:24–53.

Greenberg, B. S. 1980. *Life on television: Content analyses of US TV drama.* Norwood, NJ: Ablex.

Greenberg, B. S., R. Abelman, and K. Neuendorf. 1981. Sex on the soap operas: Afternoon delight. *Journal of Communication* 31:83–89.

Greenberg, B. S., and R. W. Busselle. 1996. Soap operas and sexual activity: A decade later. *Communication Research* 46:153–160.

Greenberg, B. S., and D. D'Alessio. 1985. Quantity and quality of sex in the soaps. *Journal of Broadcasting and Electronic Media* 29:309–321.

Greenberg, B. S., K. Neuendorf, N. Buerkel-Rothfuss, and L. Henderson. 1982. The soaps: What's on and who cares? *Journal of Broadcasting and Electronic Media* 26:519–535.

Greenberg, B. S., and M. G. Woods. 1999. The soaps: Their sex, gratifications, and outcomes. *Journal of Sex Research* 36:250–257.

Gross, L., and M. Morgan. 1985. Television and enculturation. In *Broadcasting research methods*, edited by J. R. Dominick and J. E. Fletcher, 221–234. Boston: Allyn and Bacon.

Haferkamp, C. J. 1999. Beliefs about relationships in relation to television viewing, soap opera viewing, and self-monitoring. *Current Psychology: Developmental, Learning, Personality, Social* 18:193–204.

Hansen, C. H., and R. D. Hansen. 1990. Rock music videos and antisocial behavior. *Basic and Applied Social Psychology* 11:357–369.

Heintz-Knowles, K. E. 1996. *Sexual activity on daytime soap operas: A content analysis of five weeks of television programming.* Menlo Park, CA: Henry J. Kaiser Family Foundation.

Higgins, E. T., and G. King. 1981. Accessibility of social constructs: Information-processing consequences on individual and contextual variability. In *Personality, cognition, and social interaction*, edited by N. Cantor and J. F. Kihlstrom, 69–122. Hillsdale, NJ: Erlbaum.

Hodgetts, D., and K. Chamberlain. 2006. Developing a critical media research agenda for health psychology. *Journal of Health Psychology* 11:317–327.

Holmes, B. M. 2007. In search of my "one-and-only": Romance-oriented media and beliefs in romantic relationship destiny. *Electronic Journal of Communication* 17(3 and 4).

Holmes, B. M., and K. R. Johnson. 2009. Where fantasy meets reality: Media exposure, relationship beliefs and standards, and the moderating effect of a current relationship. In *Social psychology: New research*, edited by E. P. Lamont, 117–134. New York: Nova Science.

Illouz, E. 1998. The lost innocence of love: Romance as a postmodern condition. *Theory, Culture & Society* 15:161–186.

Jackson Harris, R. 1994. The impact of sexually explicit media. In *Media effects: Advances in theory and research*, edited by J. Bryant and D. Zillman, 247–272. Hillsdale, NJ: Erlbaum.

Jo, E., and L. Berkowitz. 1994. A priming effect analysis of media influences: An update. In *Media effects: Advances in theory and research*, edited by J. Bryant and D. Zillman, 43–60. Hillsdale, NJ: Erlbaum.

Johnson, K. R., and B. M. Holmes. 2009. Contradictory messages: A content analysis of Hollywood-produced romantic comedy feature films. *Communication Quarterly* 57:352–373.

Johnson, K. R., and B. M. Holmes. In preparation. A content analysis of soap opera romantic relationships.

Jones, M. 1984. The family on television: The portrayal of the family on British television. In *The family on television: A comparative study by content analysis of the way television portrays the family in Denmark, Great Britain, Hungary and Australia.* Munich: Stiftung Prix Jeunesse International.

Josephson, W. L. 1987. Television violence and children's aggression: Testing the priming, social script, and disinhibition predictions. *Journal of Personality and Social Psychology* 53:882–890.

Katz, E., J. G. Blumler, and M. Gurevitch. 1974. Utilization of mass communication by the individual. In *The uses of mass communications: Current perspectives on gratifications research*, edited by J. G. Blumler and E. Katz, 19–32. Beverly Hills, CA: Sage.

Katz, E., and D. Foulkes. 1962. On the use of the mass media as "escape": Clarification of a concept. *Public Opinion Quarterly* 26:377–388.

Katzman, N. 1972. Television soap operas: What's been going on anyway? *Public Opinion Quarterly* 36:200–212.

Kim, J., and M. B. Oliver. 2006. Exploring media selections and avoidances as a means of mood regulation in the context of romantic relationships. Paper presented at the annual meeting of the International Communication Association, Dresden, Germany, June. http://www.allacademic.com/meta/p92789_index.html. Accessed April 21, 2011.

Kim, J. L., A. L. Sorsoli, K. Collins, B. A. Zylbergold, D. Schooler, and D. Tolman. 2007. From sex to sexuality: Exposing the heterosexual script on primetime network television. *Journal of Sex Research* 44:145–157.

Klapper, J. T. 1960. *The effects of mass communication.* New York: Free Press.

Knobloch, S., and D. Zillman. 2002. Mood management via the digital jukebox. *Journal of Communication* 52:351–366.

Knobloch, S., and D. Zillman. 2003. Appeal of love themes in popular music. *Psychological Reports* 93:653–658.

Knobloch-Westerwick, S., and S. Alter. 2006. Mood adjustment to social situations through mass media use: How men ruminate and women dissipate angry moods. *Human Communication Research* 32:58–73.

Lemish, D. 1985. Soap opera viewing in college: A naturalistic study. *Journal of Broadcasting and Electronic Media* 29:275–293.

Liebes, T., and F. Livingstone. 1998. European soap operas: The diversification of a genre. *European Journal of Communication* 13:147–180.

Livingstone, S. M. 1987. The representation of personal relationships in television drama: Realism, convention and morality. In *Accounting for relationships: Explanation, representation and knowledge*, edited by R. Burnett, P. McGhee, and D. Clarke, 248–268. New York: Methuen.

Lowry, D., G. Love, and M. Kirby. 1981. Sex on the soap operas: Patterns of intimacy. *Journal of Communication* 31:90–96.

Lowry, D., and J. Shidler. 1993. Prime time TV portrayals of sex, "safe sex," and aids: A longitudinal analysis. *Journalism Quarterly* 70:628–637.

Lowry, D. T., and D. E. Towles. 1989. Soap opera portrayals of sex, contraception, and sexually transmitted diseases. *Journal of Communication* 39:76–83.

Martino, S. C., R. L. Collins, D. E. Kanouse, M. Elliott, and S. H. Berry. 2005. Social cognitive processes mediating the relationship between exposure to television's sexual content and adolescents' sexual behavior. *Journal of Personality and Social Psychology* 89:914–924.

Morrison, C., and A. S. Westman. 2001. Women report being more likely than men to model their relationships after what they have seen on TV. *Psychological Reports* 89:252–254.

Oliver, M. B. 1993. Exploring the paradox of the enjoyment of sad films. *Human Communication Research* 19:315–342.

Oliver, M. B. 2003. Mood management and selective exposure. In *Communication and emotion: Essays in honor of Dolf Zillman*, edited by J. Bryant, D. Rosskos-Ewoldsen, and J. Cantor, 85–106. Mahwah, NJ: Erlbaum.

Oliver, M. B. 2008. Tender affective states as predictors of entertainment preference. *Journal of Communication* 58:40–61.

Olsen, B. 1994. Soaps, sex and cultivation. *Mass Communication Review* 21:106–113.

Palmgreen, P., and J. D. Rayburn II. 1979. Uses and gratifications and exposure to public television: A discrepancy approach. *Communication Research* 6:155–179.

Perse, E. M. 1986. Soap opera viewing patterns of college students and cultivation. *Journal of Broadcasting and Electronic Media* 30:175–193.

Piepe, A., P. Charlton, J. Morey, C. White, and P. Yerrell. 1986. Smoke opera? A content analysis of the presentation of smoking in TV soap. *Health Education Journal* 45:199–203.

Potter, W. J., and I. C. Chang. 1990. Television exposure measures and the cultivation hypothesis. *Journal of Broadcasting and Electronic Media* 34:313–333.

Potter, W. J., and W. Ware. 1987. An analysis of the contexts of antisocial acts on prime-time television. *Communication Research* 14:664–686.

Punyanunt-Carter, N. M. 2006. Love on television: Reality perception differences between men and women. *North American Journal of Psychology* 8:269–276.

Rose, B. 1979. Thickening the plot. *Journal of Communication* 29:81–84.

Rössler, P., and G. Brosius. 2001. Do talk shows cultivate adolescents' views of the world? A prolonged-exposure experiment. *Journal of Communication* 51:143–163.

Rubin, A. M. 1981a. An examination of television viewing motivations. *Communication Research* 8:141–165.

Rubin, A. M. 1981b. A multivariate analysis of "60 Minutes" viewing motivations. *Journalism Quarterly* 58:529–534.

Rubin, A. M. 1983. Television uses and gratifications: The interactions of viewing patterns and motivations. *Journal of Broadcasting* 27:37–51.

Rubin, A. M. 1984. Ritualized and instrumental television viewing. *Journal of Communication* 34:67–77.

Rubin, A. M. 1994. Media uses and effects: A uses-and-gratifications perspective. In *Media effects: Advances in theory and research*, edited by J. Bryant and D. Zillman, 417–436. Hillsdale, NJ: Erlbaum.

Rubin, A. M., and R. B. Rubin. 1982. Contextual age and television use. *Human Communication Research* 8:228–244.

Sapolsky, B. 1982. Sexual acts and references on prime-time TV: A two-year look. *Southern Speech Communication Journal* 47:212–226.

Segrin, C., and R. L. Nabi. 2002. Does television viewing cultivate unrealistic expectations about marriage? *Journal of Communication* 52:247–263.

Shapiro, J., and L. Kroeger. 1991. Is life just a romantic novel? The relationship between attitudes about intimate relationships and the popular media. *American Journal of Family Therapy* 19:226–236.

Signorielli, N. 1991. Adolescents and ambivalence toward marriage: A cultivation analysis. *Youth & Society* 23:121–149.

Signorielli, N., L. Gross, and M. Morgan. 1982. Violence in television programs: Ten years later. In *Television and behavior: Ten years of scientific progress and implications for the eighties*, edited by D. Pearl, L. Bouthilet, and J. Lazar, vol. 2, 158–173, DHHS Publication ADM 82-1196. Washington, DC: U.S. Government Printing Office.

Sprafkin, J., and L. Silverman. 1981. Update: Physically intimate and sexual behavior on prime-time television, 1978–79. *Journal of Communication* 31:34–40.

Stevens Aubrey, J., K. Harrison, L. Kramer, and J. Yellin. 2003. Variety versus timing: Gender differences in college students' sexual expectations as predicted by exposure to sexually oriented television. *Communication Research* 30:432–460.

Strouse, J. S., and N. L. Buerkel-Rothfuss. 1987. Mass exposure and the sexual attitudes and behavior of college students. *Journal of Sex Education and Therapy* 13:43–51.

Strouse, J. S., N. L. Buerkel-Rothfuss, and E. C. Long. 1995. Gender and family as moderators of the relationship between music video exposure and adolescent sexual permissiveness. *Adolescence* 30:505–521.

Strouse, J. S., M. P. Goodwin, and B. Roscoe. 1994. Correlates of attitudes toward sexual harassment among early adolescents. *Sex Roles* 31:559–577.

Sutherland, J. C., and S. J. Siniawsky. 1982. The treatment and resolution of moral violations on soap operas. *Journal of Communication* 32:67–74.

Tanner, L. R., S. A. Haddock, T. S. Zimmerman, and L. K. Lund. 2003. Images of couples and families in Disney feature-length animated films. *American Journal of Family Therapy* 31:355–373.

Taylor, L. D. 2005. Effects of visual and verbal sexual television content and perceived realism on attitudes and beliefs. *Journal of Sex Research* 42:130–137.

Thompson, T. L., J. D. Robinson, L. P. Cusella, and S. Shellabarger. 2000. Women's health problems in soap operas: A content analysis. *Women's Health Issues* 10:202–209.

Verma, T., J. Adams, and M. White. 2007. Portrayal of health-related behaviours in popular UK television soap operas. *Journal of Epidemiol Community Health* 61:575–577.

Wakshlag, J., V. Vial, and R. Tamborini. 1983. Selecting crime drama and apprehension about crime. *Human Communication Research* 10:227–242.

Walsh-Childers, K., and J. D. Brown. 1993. Adolescents' acceptance of sex-role stereotypes and television viewing. In *Media, sex, and the adolescent*, edited by B. S. Greenberg, J. D. Brown, and N. L. Buerkel-Rothfuss, 117–133. Creskill, NJ: Hampton Press.

Ward, L. M. 1995. Talking about sex: Common themes about sexuality in the prime-time television programs children and adolescents view most. *Journal of Youth and Adolescence* 24:595–615.

Ward, L. M. 2002. Does television exposure affect emerging adults' attitudes and assumptions about sexual relationships? Correlational and experimental confirmation. *Journal of Youth and Adolescence* 31:1–15.

Ward, L. M. 2003. Understanding the role of entertainment media in the sexual socialization of American youth: A review of empirical research. *Developmental Review* 23:347–388.

Ward, L. M., and K. Friedman. 2006. Using TV as a guide: Associations between television viewing and adolescents' sexual attitudes and behavior. *Journal of Research on Adolescence* 16:133–156.

Ward, L. M., and R. Rivadeneyra. 1999. Contributions of entertainment television to adolescents' sexual attitudes and expectations: The role of viewing amount versus viewer involvement. *Journal of Sex Research* 36:237–249.

Weaver, J., and J. Wakshlag, 1986. Perceived vulnerability to crime, criminal victimization experience, and television viewing. *Journal of Broadcasting and Electronic Media* 30:141–158.

Westman, A. S., T. J. Lynch, L. Lewandowski, and E. Hunt-Carter. 2003. Students' use of mass media for ideas about romantic relationships was influenced by perceived realism of presentations and parental happiness. *Psychological Reports* 92:1116–1118.

Whetmore, E. J., and A. P. Kielwasser. 1983. The soap opera audience speaks: A preliminary report. *Journal of American Culture* 6:110–116.

Windahl, S. 1981. Uses and gratifications at the crossroads. *Mass Communication Review Yearbook* 2:174–185.

Zillman, D. 1988a. Mood management through communication choices. *American Behavioral Scientist* 31:327–340.

Zillman, D. 1988b. Mood management: Using entertainment to full advantage. In *Communication, social cognition, and affect*, edited by L. Donohew, H. E. Sypher, and E. T. Higgins, 147–171. Hillsdale, NJ: Erlbaum.

Zillman, D. 2000. Mood management in the context of selective exposure theory. In *Communication yearbook*, vol. 23, edited by M. E. Roloff, 103–123. Thousand Oaks, CA: Sage.

Zillman, D., and R. C. Johnson. 1973. Motivated aggressiveness perpetuated by exposure to aggressive films and reduced by exposure to nonaggressive films. *Journal of Research in Personality* 7:261–276.

Zurbriggen, E. L., and E. M. Morgan. 2006. Who wants to marry a millionaire? Reality dating television programs, attitudes toward sex, and sexual behaviors. *Sex Roles* 54:1–17.

Chapter 10

Breaking Up Is Hard to Do: The Impact of Relationship Dissolution on Psychological Distress

Laura J. Hunt and Man Cheung Chung

Humans are social beings and have a basic need for contact with others and to feel loved and accepted (Maslow 1943). Thus romantic relationships are common and have been considered a "testing ground" for marriage (Lloyd and Cate 1985). Prior research has investigated areas such as commitment (Surra 1987), power (Felmlee 1994), stability (Lloyd, Cate, and Henton 1984), and the dissolution process (Duck 1982; Baxter 1984; Felmlee, Sprecher, and Bassin 1990). Since the dissolution of a romantic relationship is one of the most "intense and painful social experiences" (Baxter 1982, 223), its effect on well-being merits further research. Compared to marriage and divorce, romantic relationships remain under-investigated. Brehm (1987) has described romantic relationships as "invisible" compared to marriage, as they do not involve the same documentation and social recognition. Due to such invisibility within society, the distress caused by the dissolution of a romantic relationship is often disenfranchised and not very well understood (Kaczmarek and Backlund 1991). Yet the breakup of a romantic relationship can be as distressing, if not more so, as the breakup of a marriage (Orbuch 1992).

Research has shown relationship dissolution to be a common factor in people seeking therapist support. With this phenomenon being identified as one of the most painful life experiences, it is not surprising that individuals report a range of negative consequences, including depression (Mearns 1991), grief (Kaczmarek and Backlund 1991), anger (Sbarra 2006), and negative cognitions (Boelen and Reijntjes 2009). Couple therapists have also identified relationship dissolution as the most difficult problem to treat (Whisman, Dixon, and Johnson 1997). That said, the degree to which individuals "suffer" and the length of time it takes to adjust to the dissolution has been shown to vary considerably between individuals. Much research has attempted to identify the factors that can have an impact on the degree and nature of the distress as well as how the dissolution of a romantic relationship is experienced. Thus the aim of this chapter is to identify and review the available literature investigating the impact of romantic dating relationships on psychological well-being and to gain a better understanding of the factors that may contribute to the variability in distress experienced as a result of the breakup.

REVIEW

Studies were identified by searching three main databases; PsycINFO, Swets-Wise, and PsycARTICLES. Further articles were obtained by searching the reference lists of published articles and by emailing a number of prolific authors in the area of relationship dissolution. A number of search terms were used. These included "(romantic/dating) relationship breakup," "(romantic/dating) relationship dissolution," "(romantic/dating) relationship termination," "(romantic/dating) relationship disengagement," and "(romantic/dating) relationship loss." To be included in the review, articles had to meet three main criteria. First, they had to include a sample of individuals who had experienced the dissolution of a romantic *dating* relationship. This excluded many studies that focused predominantly on the impact of divorce. Second, the study had to include an adult sample, which excluded papers focusing exclusively on an adolescent sample (under eighteen years of age). Third, the papers had to discuss the impact of relationship dissolution on well-being. This excluded papers that focused on any other aspect of romantic relationships or papers that focused on the *process* of disengagement.

A total of twenty-eight articles were identified using the above criteria, twenty-four employing a quantitative methodology and four employing mixed methods. The following section reviews these articles and identifies both the impact that dissolution had on an individual's well-being and the factors that might contribute to the extent of the impact.

DEMOGRAPHIC VARIABLES

Thirteen papers investigated whether demographic factors had an impact on the amount of distress that was experienced following the dissolution of a romantic relationship (see table 1). These studies suggested women experienced more distress, higher levels of despair, death anxiety, anger, hostility, loss of control, and

Table 1
The impact of demographic variables on distress following the dissolution of a romantic relationship.

Study	Design	Sample	Demographic variable	Findings
Boelen and Reijntjes (2009)	Cross-sectional	Undergraduate students (N = 79)	Age, gender, current dating status	Age and gender not related to distress; current dating status related to experience of grief, anxiety and depression
Choo, Levine, and Hatfield (1996)	Cross-sectional	Undergraduate students (N = 250); includes participants who were previously engaged (6%) or married (4%)	Gender	Men less likely to report joy or relief; women more likely to blame partner for dissolution
Chung et al. (2002a)	Cross-sectional	University students (N = 65); includes participants who were married and divorced (does not say if this was at time of questionnaire)	Gender	No significant gender differences reported regarding traumatic stress reactions following breakup
Davis, Shaver, and Vernon (2003)	Cross-sectional	Adults in community (N = 5,248); dating couples only	Gender, age	Gender unrelated to attachment anxiety following breakup; anxiety negatively related to age; avoidance positively related to age
Drew et al. (2004)	Cross-sectional	Undergraduate students (N = 107); includes heterosexual (97%), homosexual (1%), and bisexual (2%) participants	Gender	Women reported higher levels of dysphoria than men
Hill, Rubin, and Peplau (1976)	Longitudinal	University students (N =206); 103 couples	Gender	Men reported more depression, loneliness, unhappiness and guilt

(continued)

Table I (continued)

Study	Design	Sample	Demographic variable	Findings
Kaczmarek, Backlund, and Biemer (1990)	Cross-sectional	University students (N = 337)	Gender	No significant gender differences found regarding adjustment following breakup
Kurdek (1991)	Longitudinal	Adult couples (N = 26), including 6 gay and 7 lesbian couples	Sexuality	No significant differences between gay and lesbian participants regarding the emotional adjustment to the breakup
Robak and Weitzman (1998)	Cross-sectional	University psychology students (N = 148)	Gender	Women reported higher amounts of despair, death anxiety, anger/hostility, loss of control, and somatization
Ruvolo, Fabin, and Ruvulo (2001)	Longitudinal	University students: couples, 1st wave (N = 301); dating couples, 2nd wave (N = 312)	Gender	Women less secure following break-up; men were found to be more insecure after the breakup if they had been categorized as insecure before the breakup
Sprecher (1994)	Longitudinal	Heterosexual dating couples (N = 47)	Gender	No significant gender differences reported
Sprecher et al. (1998)	Cross-sectional	Young adults (N = 257)	Gender	Women reported more upset
Tashiro and Frazier (2003)	Cross-sectional	Undergraduate students (N = 92)	Gender	No significant gender differences found regarding distress experienced following dissolution; women reported significantly more stress-related growth

somatization (Robak and Weitzman 1998), dysphoria (Drew et al. 2004), and a decreased sense of security (Ruvolo, Fabin, and Ruvolo 2001). Although Sprecher et al. (1998) found women reported more distress than men, this was only associated with the initial distress following the breakup. Other studies suggested men experienced greater distress following breakup, reporting less joy and relief (Choo, Levine, and Hatfield 1996) and more depression, unhappiness, and guilt (Hill, Rubin, and Peplau 1976). Still other studies did not find any significant gender differences (Kaczmarek, Backlund, and Biemer 1990; Sprecher 1994; Chung et al. 2002a; Chung et al. 2003; Tashiro and Frazier 2003; Boelen and Reijntjes 2009).

The fact that gender has received the most attention among the demographic variables suggests that it has an important role to play in how dissolution is experienced. However, due to inconsistent results, it is not possible to ascertain whether men or women experience more distress following dissolution. The role of gender on the experience of distress following dissolution remains inconclusive. This implies that the common assumption that women will experience more distress following relationship dissolution than men is nothing more than an expectation possibly resulting from gender stereotypes. Similarly, no conclusions as to the effect age may have on distress can be drawn due to the limited number of studies. The majority of studies did not include age as a variable and focused mainly on student samples. It is possible such groups may react differently to dissolution than older samples, and this could make generalizing the results to nonstudent populations problematic.

Surprisingly, we found no papers focusing on other demographic variables, such as socioeconomic status, religious orientation, or educational achievement, and how these influence the amount of distress experienced following breakup. Rather, studies focusing on such variables were mainly concerned with relationship stability (see Felmlee, Sprecher, and Bassin 1990). Although it would be interesting to further explore the role that demographic variables may have on distress outcomes, in some respects, studies on demographic variables are largely atheoretical (Sprecher and Fehr 1998). They provide limited information on the psychological perspectives of those involved and on the interface between intrapersonal and interpersonal factors associated with the complexity of dissolution. More research on demographic variables and how these are associated with other psychological factors is required to further the field.

RELATIONSHIP VARIABLES

Eight studies investigated whether the variables pertaining to the relationship have an impact on distress following a breakup (see table 2). Research suggests variables that may be associated with distress following dissolution include closeness (Simpson 1987; Frazier and Cook 1993; Davis, Shaver, and Vernon 2003; Robak and Weitzman 1998; Kaczmarek, Backlund, and Biemer 1990), commitment (Sprecher et al. 1998; Boelen and Reijntjes 2009), suddenness of the breakup

Table 2
The impact of relationship variables on distress following the dissolution of a romantic relationship.

Study	Design	Sample	Relationship variable	Findings
Boelen and Reijntjes (2009)	See Table 1	See Table 1	Relationship duration; length of time elapsed since dissolution; commitment; suddenness of dissolution	Perceived commitment of relationship strongly associated with experience of complicated grief; the more sudden the breakup, the higher the score for complicated grief
Davis, Shaver, and Vernon (2003)	See Table 1	See Table 1	Emotional involvement	Emotional involvement significantly associated with all indices of emotional distress
Fine and Sacher (1997)	Longitudinal	University students (N = 38), including 10 ex-couples	Commitment; relationship satisfaction; alternative quality; relationship duration	Men reported higher levels of distress if they had been committed to the relationship and satisfied (distress was marginally related to alternative quality); women also reported more distress if they reported being committed to the relationship (distress marginally associated with alternative quality)
Frazier and Cook (1993)	Cross-sectional	University students (N = 85)	Commitment; relationship satisfaction; closeness; relationship duration; perceived alternatives	Greater satisfaction, closeness, and perceived alternatives all associated with initial retrospective ratings of distress but not current levels of distress or adjustment

Study	Design	Sample	Variables	Findings
Kaczmarek, Backlund, and Biemer (1990)	See Table I	See Table I	Suddenness of breakup; closeness; relationship duration; length of time elapsed since the dissolution	Greater percentage of participants reported feeling depressed if the dissolution was reported as sudden and the relationship was considered close and was of longer duration
Robak and Weitzman (1998)	See Table I	See Table I	Closeness (intimacy, whether marriage had been considered)	The closer the relationship, the more grief symptoms reported; the more marriage had been considered, the more grief symptoms reported and the longer the time to recover from breakup
Simpson (1987)	Longitudinal	University students (N = 234)	Relationship satisfaction; closeness; relationship duration; sexual nature of relationship; exclusivity of relationship; self-monitoring propensity; orientation to sexual relations; ease at which alternative partner could be found; the quality of best actual and imagined alternative dating partner	Results indicated relationship duration, closeness, and perceived alternatives were associated with distress following dissolution
Sprecher et al. (1998)	See Table I	See Table I	Who initiated the start of the relationship; relationship satisfaction; commitment; relationship duration	Those who reported putting more effort into initiating the relationship reported greater distress initially after breakup; satisfaction associated with greater initial distress; commitment was most strongly associated with distress; relationship duration had a strong positive effect on initial and current distress

(Boelen and Reijntjes 2009; Kaczmarek, Backlund, and Biemer 1990), perceived alternatives (Frazier and Cook 1993; Simpson 1987), and time since the breakup occurred (Boelen and Reijntjes 2009).

Regarding relationship satisfaction, results are inconsistent. There is evidence to suggest satisfaction can have an impact on the distress experienced (Sprecher et al. 1998; Frazier and Cook 1993). However, Fine and Sacher (1997) found satisfaction to be significantly associated with distress in men only, and Simpson (1987) did not find any significant association between satisfaction and distress. Similarly, results are inconsistent regarding duration, with some research indicating the factor is significantly related to the experience of distress following relationship dissolution (Sprecher et al. 1998; Simpson 1987; Boelen and Reijntjes 2009; Kaczmarek, Backlund, and Biemer 1990) and other studies not producing significant results (Fine and Sacher 1997; Frazier and Cook 1993).

INITIATOR STATUS

The perception of who initiated the breakup and the impact this has on well-being after the relationship loss is a fairly well researched area within the available literature. Twelve of the studies made reference to the impact of initiator status (see table 3). Overall, the findings have produced mixed results. A number of the studies suggest those perceiving the partner to have initiated the breakup experienced the event as more stressful (Frazier and Cook 1993; Sprecher et al. 1998), reported increased depression (Peterson, Rosenbaum, and Conn 1985), loss of self-esteem, rumination (Perilloux and Buss 2008), increased grief (Boelen and Reijntjes 2009; Robak and Weitzman 1998), intense feelings of loss, anger, loss of control, and an increased feeling of unreality (Robak and Weitzman 1998). Fine and Sacher (1997), however, found only males reported increased distress if they perceived their partner initiated the breakup, and Tashiro and Frazier (2003) did not find any significant difference between initiators and non-initiators.

There are a number of methodological issues that could have contributed to the inconsistency observed in results. First, the studies (other than Sprecher 1994 and Hill, Rubin, and Peplau 1976) used only one partner from the ex-couple. Research has found individuals employ a *systematic self-bias* (Hill, Rubin, and Peplau 1976) and are more likely to say they initiated a breakup in an attempt to protect their egos (Gray and Silver 1990). In other words, examining the account of only one ex-partner provides an incomplete understanding of the process of dissolution by providing an unbalanced and unfair perspective. One-sided samples will be self-selected and may have certain motivations for participating (Weber 1998). Only a few studies have attempted to examine both partners' perspectives (Hill, Rubin, and Peplau 1976; Sprecher 1994; Kurdek 1991), highlighting an area where further research will be useful.

Another issue to consider is the meaning of "initiator status." Perhaps a more helpful way to look at initiator status is to look at responsibility. It is possible that

Table 3
The impact of initiator status on distress following the dissolution of a romantic relationship.

Study	Design and data	Sample	Findings
Ayduk, Downey, and Kim (2001)	Longitudinal	Female students (N = 223)	Women high in rejection sensitivity[a] reported more depression in a partner-initiated breakup
Boelen and Reijntjes (2009)	See Table 1	See Table 1	Partner-initiated breakup associated with complicated grief, not anxiety or depression
Davis, Shaver, and Vernon (2003)	See Table 1	See Table 1	Those who initiated breakup reported less anxiety and emotional involvement and higher avoidance
Fine and Sacher (1997)	See Table 2	See Table 2	More distress experienced by males who perceived their partner initiated the breakup
Frazier and Cook (1993)	See Table 2	See Table 2	Controllability of breakup significantly associated with stressfulness, current adjustment, and recovery
Hill, Rubin, and Peplau (1976)	See Table 1	See Table 1	Participants felt less depressed and lonely, and more happy but more guilty, if they initiated the breakup
Peterson, Rosenbaum, and Conn (1985)	Cross-sectional	University students: Study 1 (N = 68), Study 2 (N = 80)	Higher depressed mood reported by participants who felt the breakup was uncontrollable
Perrilloux and Buss (2008)	Cross-sectional	University students (N = 199)	Participants who reported a partner-initiated breakup reported higher levels of depression and rumination and a loss of self-esteem

(continued)

Table 3 (*continued*)

Study	Design and data	Sample	Findings
Robak and Weitzman (1998)	See Table 1	See Table 1	Partner-initiated breakup associated with feelings of loss, grief at time of breakup, and, later, higher levels of anger, loss of control, increased rumination and increased unreality related to the event
Sprecher (1994)	See Table 1	See Table 1	Women more likely to be seen as initiators, but only by women themselves
Sprecher et al. (1998)	See Table 1	See Table 1	Participants who reported a partner-initiated breakup experienced more distress
Tashiro and Frazier (2003)	See Table 1	See Table 1	Found no significant difference between participants who reported either being left or having initiated the breakup

[a]Rejection sensitivity is defined as "the disposition to anxiously expect, readily perceive and overreact to rejection" (Ayduk et al. 2001, 868).

an individual who ends a relationship actually perceives his or her partner as holding responsibility for why the relationship ended. Considering individuals as either the "leaver" or the "left" may be oversimplifying a complicated process and could thus influence results.

ATTACHMENT

Seven articles investigated the association between attachment style and the experience of distress following relationship dissolution (see table 4). Hazen and Shaver (1987) were the first researchers to apply the attachment model to adult romantic relationships. The seven articles' findings suggested that there were marked differences in the responses to relationship dissolution between attachment styles. Respondents reporting higher attachment security demonstrated an increased probability of anger recovery (Sbarra 2006) and less negative affect, such as grief (Pistole 1995).

Meanwhile, participants endorsing preoccupied attachment styles were more likely to report that their partner had initiated the breakup due to being unhappy with the relationship, that they were having difficulty adjusting to the breakup, and that they felt the breakup had been a mistake (Barbara and Dion 2000). In addition, they reported more negative affect, including higher levels of tension, depression, and confusion (Pistole 1995). Fearful and dismissing attachment styles were also highly associated with distress following relationship breakup (Sprecher et al. 1998), although Pistole (1995) found that endorsing a dismissive attachment style could lead to increased energy and less confusion. Similarly, anxious-ambivalent participants reported a higher degree of upset after a breakup and reported more surprise and less relief than those with an avoidant attachment style (Feeney and Noller 1992).

The samples used in the above studies were fairly consistent, with six of them using a student population. Other than Davis, Shaver, and Vernon (2003) and Pistole (1995), sample sizes appeared fairly small, and as with the majority of studies conducted on romantic relationships, there was a misrepresentation of female participants. Davis, Shaver, and Vernon (2003) achieved a large sample by employing an Internet-survey methodology. Although this might have resulted in a more diverse sample, as they stated in their paper, the sample might also have been biased toward "young computer users" with an interest in relationship issues.

The studies employed a number of measures for identifying attachment styles. Feeney and Noller (1992), the earliest paper, employed a single-item measure for attachment that initially was used by Hazen and Shaver (1987). This measure involves participants choosing one paragraph from a possible three, which is then used to categorize the individual as secure, avoidant, or anxious-ambivalent. Although this measure has been used in a number of studies regarding attachment (see Keelan, Dion, and Dion 1994; Cooper, Shaver, and Collins 1998), it has been reported to only have moderate stability when reporting attachment styles. Furthermore, the measure only provides a single measure of avoidant attachment style, which could skew results (Barbara and Dion 2000).

A four-category measure (Bartholomew and Horowitz 1991) that allowed participants to be categorized as secure, fearful, preoccupied, or dismissing was developed. This measure has been employed in two of the above studies (Davis, Shaver, and Vernon 2003; Pistole 1995), both of which found that relationship dissolution was particularly distressing for those endorsing a fearful attachment style. This measure provides an extension of the original Hazen and Shaver (1987) tool and thus may provide a more reliable method for assessing attachment styles. However, category-based measures place participants in one exclusive category of attachment when they may be best described by a combination of two. It also does not allow for an evaluation of individual difference within these categories. Furthermore, with single-item measures, it can be difficult to establish reliability and the statistical analysis that can be performed is limited.

The research presented by Sbarra (2006) and Sbarra and Emery (2005) used the same sample for both papers and employed the Relationship Scales Questionnaire

Table 4
The impact of attachment on distress following the dissolution of a romantic relationship.

Study	Design	Sample	Measures	Findings
Barbara and Dion (2000)	Cross-sectional	Undergraduate students (N = 115)	Attachment Style Questionnaire (Feeney, Noller, and Hanrahan 1994)	Participants scoring high on the preoccupied attachment style reported feeling their partner was unhappy and had initiated the breakup, were having difficulty adjusting to the breakup, and were experiencing more negative emotion compared to participants endorsing other attachment styles
Boelen and Reijntjes (2009)	See Table 1	See Table 1	Experiences in Close Relationships—Revised Questionnaire (Fraley, Waller, and Brennan 2000)	Attachment anxiety was associated with complicated grief
Davis, Shaver, and Vernon (2003)	See Table 1	See Table 1	Experiences in Close Relationships (Brennan et al. 1998)	Attachment-related anxiety was related to preoccupation with the ex-partner, greater preservation of the loss, more extreme emotional and physical distress, attempts to restart the relationship, angry behavior, and dysfunctional coping

Study	Design	Sample	Measure	Findings
Feeney and Noller (1992)	Longitudinal	Undergraduate students (N = 193)	Forced-choice item (Hazen and Shaver 1987); 15-item Measure of Attachment Style	Avoidant attachment style experienced the most relief, anxious/ambivalent reported feeling the most surprised and most upset
Pistole (1995)	Cross-sectional	Undergraduate students (N = 118)	Single-item measure (Bartholomew and Horowitz 1991)	Securely attached individuals reported less negative grief following dissolution; fearful and preoccupied individuals reported the most distress
Sbarra (2006)	Longitudinal	Undergraduate students (N = 58)	Relationship Styles Questionnaire (Griffin and Bartholomew 1994)	Attachment security associated with an increased probability of recovery from anger; greater levels of attachment preoccupation associated with decreased probability of recovery from sadness
Sbarra and Emery (2005)	Longitudinal	Undergraduate students (N = 58)	Relationship Styles Questionnaire (Griffin and Bartholomew 1994)	Attachment security was negatively correlated with anger and positively correlated with relief; secure attachment also demonstrated a faster recovery from sadness

(Griffin and Bartholomew 1994), which provides continuous scores for the four attachment styles and has been found to have strong test-retest reliability and discriminant validity. However, other researchers have stated the reliabilities from this measure have been variable (Barbara and Dion 2000). Barbara and Dion (2000) have used the Attachment Style Questionnaire, which identifies five dimensions: confidence, discomfort with closeness, need for approval, preoccupation with relationships, and relationships as secondary, representing a combination of the styles highlighted in the above-discussed measures. Because all the papers use different measures, comparing results may be problematic, as it is likely they are all measuring slightly different concepts. Interestingly, none of the papers used the Adult Attachment Interview, the "gold standard" for assessing attachment style.

It is possible attachment styles were affected by the dissolution process. Research conducted by Ruvolo, Fabin, and Ruvolo (2001) found evidence that attachment style altered as a result of experiencing relationship dissolution. With the use of retrospective data, it is not possible to know the attachment characteristics of participants before dissolution. Furthermore, the studies that used a more prospective design (Sbarra 2006; Sbarra and Emery 2005) used a daily diary approach, which may have influenced results. It is possible that such a method acted as an "intervention" by providing participants with a space to reflect on the dissolution process.

COGNITIVE FACTORS

The association between cognitive factors and the impact of romantic relationship dissolution on well-being has also received attention. Five studies looked at schemas, negative cognitions, or attributions (see table 5). Overall, the evidence proposes that cognitive factors play a role in the degree of distress experienced following relationship dissolution. Female participants who reported interpersonal attributions tended to feel more negativity toward their ex-partner (Stephen 1987), perceiving the event as uncontrollable was associated with depression (Peterson, Rosenbaum, and Conn 1985), and those who attributed the dissolution to "other" (causal attributions referring to the partner) and "environmental" factors (the environment surrounding the relationship) experienced more distress (Tashiro and Frazier 2003).

Attributions have been found to change over the course of a relationship (Duck 1982), and they are likely to change over the course of dissolution (as investigated by Stephen 1987). Furthermore, environmental factors are important in relationships and are often "forgotten" by researchers and participants (Tashiro and Frazier 2003), and indeed Stephen (1987) "dropped" environmental attributions from analyses due to respondents highlighting them infrequently. How attributions change over time is an area requiring further exploration. It will be important to consider the length of time or the stage an individual is in regarding dissolution in future research.

Table 5
The impact of cognitive factors on distress following the dissolution of a romantic relationship.

Study	Design	Sample	Cognitive variable and measure employed	Findings
Boelen and Reijntjes (2009)	See Table I	See Table I	Negative cognitions; Grief Cognitions Questionnaire (GCQ)	Negative cognitions that were taped by the Complicated Grief Questionnaire associated with complicated grief; negative cognitions associated with depression and anxiety
Choo, Levine, and Hatfield (1996)	See Table I	See Table I	Love schemas; Love Schema Scale (Hatfield and Rapson 1996)	Participants with different love schemas reacted differently to breakup; participants reporting secure, skittish, and uninterested schemas reported more joy; participants with a clingy schema reported more anxiety, anger, and sadness
Peterson, Rosenbaum, and Conn (1985)	Cross-sectional	University students: Study 1 (N = 68), Study 2 (N = 80)	Causal attributions; no specific measure (asked questions such as how much control they had), rated on a scale of 1 = none, 3 = total	Causal attributions related to the breakup did not predict the degree of depressed mood; viewing event as uncontrollable related to higher amounts of depression
Stephen (1987)	Longitudinal	Mainly university students (N = 93 ex-partners)	Attributions derived from qualitative data	Females who reported more interpersonal attributions tended to feel more negatively toward their ex-partner; type of attribution found to be related to impact of dissolution
Tashiro and Frazier (2003)	See Table I	See Table I	Attributions; 40-item scale (items derived from previous qualitative research)	Participants who attributed dissolution to "other" and environmental factors reported more distress

Individuals endorsing different "love schemas" reacted differently to relationship dissolution. Individuals who reported secure, skittish, and uninterested schemas experienced higher levels of joy and relief, whereas individuals reporting a clingy schema reported more anxiety, sadness, and anger (Choo, Levine, and Hatfield 1996). Catastrophic misinterpretations regarding the individual's personal reaction to the breakup were the most strongly associated with the experience of complicated grief, depression and anxiety (Boelen and Reijntjes 2009).

Overall, the research suggests the way an individual appraises the situation is associated with their emotional reaction following relationship dissolution. It must be noted that a limited amount of research has focused specifically on the impact of cognitive factors on distress following dissolution, and thus it is difficult to draw any concrete conclusions from the studies identified.

PERSONALITY FACTORS

Three of the articles focused on the impact personality factors can have on the degree of distress experienced following romantic relationship dissolution (see table 6). The studies found neuroticism to be related to higher amounts of distress

Table 6
The impact of personality factors on distress following the dissolution of a romantic relationship.

Study	Design	Sample	Personality measure	Findings
Boelen and Reijntjes (2009)	See Table 1	See Table 1	Neuroticism scale from Eysenck Personality Questionnaire-R short scale (Eysenck and Eysenck 1991)	Neuroticism associated with depression and anxiety
Chung et al. (2002b)	Cross-sectional	University students (N = 60)	Eysenck Personality Questionnaire-R short scale (Eysenck and Eysenck 1991)	Neuroticism significantly predicted the total impact of the dissolution; neuroticism not associated with general health
Tashiro and Frazier (2003)	See Table 1	See Table 1	Mini-Markers (Saucier 1994)	Neuroticism associated with increased distress; agreeableness associated with more personal growth

following relationship dissolution (Tashiro and Frazier 2003), including high levels of depression and anxiety (Boelen and Reijntjes 2009) and the total impact of the breakup (Chung et al. 2002b). These findings are consistent with previous research, which has found individuals high in neuroticism are likely to display more distress following a stressful incident due to a tendency to overreact and interpret events negatively (Watson, Clark, and Harkness 1994).

However, the available literature is still limited. Although neuroticism was found to be significant, Boelen and Reijntjes (2009) *only* investigated neuroticism. Other personality traits thus remain under-investigated. Further research is required investigating traits such as openness or alexithymia. Furthermore, as the studies are retrospective, it is not possible to determine whether participants' neuroticism scores were affected by the event of dissolution.

COPING

The mechanisms an individual employs to cope with stressful situations have been found to have an impact on the level of distress reported and the amount of time it takes to adjust. Three studies directly investigated the association between coping and emotional distress (see table 7). "Coping" is a wide area of research, and studies included in other sections of this chapter could be considered as investigating ways of coping. For example, developing accounts regarding initiator status can be viewed as a way of protecting the ego and thus a coping strategy, as could the attributions individuals make about any given situation.

Overall, the studies suggest coping does have an impact on the distress experienced following dissolution. Regarding social support, Chung et al. (2003) found the more distressing the dissolution, the more participants tried to seek social support. Frazier and Cook (1993) found participants with more social support reported feeling more adjusted, although such support was not associated with initial distress. Again, methodological issues may explain the slight difference in findings. Frazier and Cook (1993) studied participants who had broken up within six months, whereas Chung et al. (2003) studied participants who had experienced a breakup within twenty-four months. Current feelings or behaviors may have had an impact on retrospective accounts. Furthermore, all the samples used in the above studies used a student population. Coping mechanisms employed by student samples may differ from other social groups, and obviously the dissolution of dating relationships is not unique to this group.

Further research that investigates specific coping strategies employed and how these are associated with the distress experienced following dissolution and subsequent adjustment is required. It is possible coping mechanisms employed are associated with the appraisal of the situation. As attributions regarding the event alter (which has been shown to be the case regarding the process of dissolution), coping mechanisms may also modify. Research that starts to link these processes is required in order to provide a detailed and integrated view of dissolution.

Table 7
The impact of coping on distress following the dissolution of a romantic relationship.

Study	Design and data	Sample	Measures	Findings
Chung et al. 2003	Cross-sectional	Under-graduate students (N = 88)	Ways of Coping Questionnaire (Folkman and Lazarus 1980)	Seeking support, escape avoidance, and accepting responsibility associated with traumatic stress reaction following relationship dissolution
Frazier and Cook 1993	See Table 2	See Table 2	Perceived Social Support Inventory (Procidano and Heller 1983)	Social support was not related to distress, but participants with more social support reported feeling more recovered
McCarthy, Lambert, and Brack 1997	Longitudinal	University students (N = 231)	Coping Resources Inventory for Stress (Matheny et al. 1986)	Preventative coping influenced the evaluation of the desirability of the breakup and the initial experience of negative emotion; combative coping strategies were found to impact subsequent emotional response

GENERAL COMMENTS

This chapter provided a review of the current literature regarding the impact of romantic dating relationship dissolution on psychological well-being and sought to gain some understanding of the factors associated with psychological distress following the breakup. As a result of a breakup, one can experience emotional distress such as anger, depression, grief, traumatic stress symptoms, and confusion, as well as threats to one's internal security. Research also has demonstrated that there are a range of factors that can influence the distress an individual experiences, including demographic variables (gender, in particular), variables associated with the ex-relationship, who initiated the breakup, attachment style, cognitions, personality, and coping mechanisms.

While the effect of gender on psychological distress following relationship dissolution remains inconclusive, there seems to be evidence suggesting an association between the variables pertaining to the ex-relationship, such as the degree of closeness, commitment, suddenness of the breakup, perceived alternatives, and time since the breakup occurred and distress. Those who initiated the breakup also were related to distress, with the initiator experiencing less distress. Regarding the role of attachment, findings were fairly consistent, suggesting that individuals endorsing secure attachment styles coped better following dissolution. Those categorized as preoccupied and fearful were found to experience greater distress.

The areas of cognition, personality, and coping have received less attention. In terms of cognition, people's attributions seemed to be related to distress in that, for example, people who attributed the dissolution to other people or the environment tended to experience more distress. People who endorsed the secure, skittish, and uninterested love schemas experienced higher levels of joy and relief, whereas people with a clingy schema tended to report more anxiety, sadness, and anger. People's catastrophic misinterpretations regarding their personal reaction to the breakup also were associated with complicated grief, depression, and anxiety. In terms of personality, those with high neuroticism experienced more distress. Social support, as a way of coping, seemed to buffer against distress following relationship dissolution.

METHODOLOGICAL ISSUES

The above findings could have been influenced by the methods researchers used. A vast majority of studies employed a cross-sectional design, which can be problematic because it is a mistake to consider relationship dissolution as an *event* (Duck 1982). Rather, dissolution should be viewed as a process involving a number of stages. It is unlikely such methodology will capture the complexities of this process, and the stage of dissolution may have influenced results. Various criteria regarding when the breakup occurred have been employed, some stating the dissolution must have been within six months, twelve months, twenty-four months, or seven years of participation in the study, whereas some researchers did not outline any such criteria. If dissolution is thought of as a process, one could assume that people who experienced breakup six months previously may be at a different stage compared to people who broke up twenty-four months ago. This could make comparing results problematic, because processes, such as attributions and coping, may alter over time and could be affected by autobiographical memory. Furthermore, authors did not provide reasons for the time spans they selected. Studies conducted by Hill, Rubin, and Peplau (1976) and Sprecher (1994) stand out regarding their contribution to the field by offering longitudinal data and including both partners where possible, as does the research provided by Stephen (1987).

Although the studies reviewed in this chapter mainly focused on the distress resulting from the dissolution of romantic dating relationships, a number of the studies, in fact, included divorced, cohabiting, and married individuals, which may have influenced results. Combining such samples is likely to compromise results as it hinders the researcher's ability to investigate the unique nature of the process of dissolution in dating relationships (Barry, Lawrence, and Langer 2008). Furthermore, the majority of the research accessed student populations. Although this is not necessarily an inappropriate sample due to the high number of relationship dissolutions that are thought to occur among this social group, it does raise questions regarding how applicable the results are to a wider population. It is likely university samples have different characteristics compared to other social groups or other age groups. Using these results to think about dissolution in other populations could raise questions regarding generalizability.

The samples also were inconsistent as to whether they focused on heterosexual dating couples only or included gay, lesbian, and bisexual relationships. Those who focused purely on heterosexual couples did not provide a reason for doing so. Research by Kurdek (1991) suggests similarities among gay, lesbian, and heterosexual couples regarding dissolution. Excluding such samples from research exemplifies inequality in the literature, and indeed, research focusing on such social groups is limited. It should also be noted that samples included a high proportion of female participants and, in some cases, the sample sizes were small, which may have limited power in detecting smaller effects in the data. Davis, Shaver, and Vernon (2003) based their findings on an impressive sample of 5,248 nonstudents ranging in age from fifteen to fifty, which could provide a more diverse picture (although the sample is biased toward computer users).

AN INTEGRATIVE MODEL

Given what we have reviewed, the question remains: How do we integrate all the factors we have identified thus far, regardless of the varying degrees of conclusiveness, to form a coherent understanding of the psychology of romantic dating relationship dissolution? One way to do this is to draw on a theoretical model on the basis of which we integrate the findings from literature, such as the integrative model of posttraumatic stress disorder (PTSD) (Joseph et al. 1995). It is reasonable to draw on a PTSD model for different reasons. First, relationship dissolution is a traumatic experience, as was demonstrated in the literature. Second, as we mentioned in the literature review, studies have been conducted to show that following dissolution, people can experience reactions similar to posttraumatic stress reactions. For example, participants reported intrusive thoughts, which is one of the classic symptoms of PTSD. They reported that pictures about the dissolution often popped into their minds, that other things kept making them think about it, and that any reminder could bring back feelings about it. They often thought about the dissolution when they did not mean to, and they often had waves of strong feeling about it. Some even had nightmares and trouble falling asleep or staying asleep.

They also displayed avoidance behavior, another classic symptom of PTSD, in that they found themselves having to remove the dissolution from memory and often avoided letting themselves get upset when they thought about it or were reminded of it. They often found themselves having to stay away from reminders of the dissolution, and trying not to think about it or talk about it. They were aware of the fact that they still had strong feelings about it that they had not dealt with. They also often felt as if the dissolution had not happened or was not real. They felt somewhat numb toward the dissolution (Chung et al. 2002a, 2002b, 2003).

Third, it is intriguing to notice that the factors identified in the studies reviewed in this chapter in fact bear similarities to the factors described in this integrative model of posttraumatic stress. Sharing these similarities could reflect the fact that the psychological reactions of romantic dating dissolution mirror posttraumatic stress reactions.

By drawing on a posttraumatic stress model, however, we are not trying to establish whether or not people, following the dissolution of a dating relationship, would suffer from posttraumatic stress disorder. In order for people to be diagnosed as suffering from PTSD, they need to have experienced an event or events that involved actual or threatened death or serious injury or a threat to the physical integrity of oneself or others. Responses to such experiences could involve intense fear, helplessness, or horror (American Psychiatric Association 1994). Although relationship dissolution is a traumatic experience, in most cases, it does not threaten the physical integrity of the individual. An exception to this, of course, would be relationship dissolution with physical abuse and violence as the major cause (Lloyd 1991; Riggs 1993; Riggs, O'Leary, and Breslin 1990). Furthermore, responses to relationship dissolution do not usually involve intense fear and horror, although people might feel helpless about the dissolution. Nevertheless, the traumatic reactions of relationship dissolution, such as intrusive thoughts and avoidance behavior, resemble classic posttraumatic symptoms.

In short, this integrative model aims to examine the interface between the effect of trauma, cognition, personality, coping, and distress. On the basis of this model, one could integrate the factors we have identified in the literature review as follows. A traumatic event, in this case a relationship dissolution, presents people with stimuli (i.e., event stimuli) that generate extreme emotional arousal but cannot be immediately processed at that time. These event stimuli could be conceptualized in terms of the variables pertaining to the ex-relationship and who initiated the breakup. These event stimuli are then stored in memory but cannot easily be assimilated with other stored memories. These are called "event cognitions," and they in turn generate further cognitive activity whereby people appraise the information and, indeed, meaning associated with the breakup. Such appraisals, in turn, affect the degree of emotional distress, including anger, depression, grief, or posttraumatic stress symptoms as was demonstrated in the literature review. In other words, there is a mediational process in that the occurrence of the relationship dissolution gives rise to emotional distress via an appraisal mechanism.

Due to such emotional distress, people will use different coping strategies, one of which is seeking social support, also echoed by our review. The model goes on to point out that the way in which people develop these event cognitions and appraise the information and meaning presented by the dissolution is influenced by their own personality, prior experience, schema, and early life experience. Personality is also a factor considered in the literature review, and this could include personal characteristics such as age and gender. Arguably, attachment constitutes the prior or early life experience in this model, and cognition factors such as the love schema constitute the schema domain in the model. In the light of this model, one can now redraw the diagram and arrive at an integrative model for the factors involved in the dissolution of romantic dating relationship. Of course, this is by no means the ultimate model describing the psychology of relationship dissolution. On the contrary, it is simply an attempt to understand the complexity of relationship dissolution in a coherent and integrative manner. The robustness of this theoretical model awaits future empirical examination.

REFERENCES

Aitken-Harris, J. 1994. Perceptions of engineering, nursing and psychology students' personalities. *Canadian Journal of Behavioural Science* 26:484–491.

American Psychiatric Association. 1994. *Diagnostic and statistical manual of mental disorders.* 4th ed. Washington, D.C.: American Psychiatric Association.

Ayduk, O., G. Downey, and M. Kim. 2001. Rejection sensitivity and depressive symptoms in women. *Personality and Social Psychology Bulletin* 27:868–877.

Barbara, A. M., and K. L. Dion. 2000. Breaking up is hard to do, especially for strongly preoccupied lovers. *Journal of Personal and Interpersonal Loss* 5:315–342.

Barry, R., E. Lawrence, and A. Langer. 2008. Conceptualization and assessment of disengagement in romantic relationships. *Personal Relationships* 15:297–315.

Bartholomew, K., and L. M. Horowitz. 1991. Attachment styles among young adults: A test of a four-category model. *Journal of Personality and Social Psychology* 61:226–244.

Baxter, L. A. 1982. Strategies for ending relationships: Two sides. *Western Journal of Speech Communication* 46:223–241.

Baxter, L. A. 1984. Trajectories of relationship disengagement. *Journal of Social and Personal Relationships* 1:29–48.

Boelen, P. A., and A. Reijntjes. 2009. Negative cognitions in emotional problems following romantic relationship break-ups. *Stress and Health* 25:11–19.

Brehm, S. 1987. Coping after a relationship ends. In *Coping with negative life events*, edited by C. R. Snyder and C. E. Ford, 191–212. New York: Plenum.

Brennan, K. A., C. L. Clark, and P. R. Shaver. 1998. Self-report measurement of adult romantic attachment: An integrative overview. In *Attachment theory and close relationships*, edited by J. A. Simpson & W. S. Rholes, pp. 46–76. New York: Guilford Press.

Choo, P., T. Levine, and E. Hatfield. 1996. Gender, love schemas, and reactions to romantic break-ups. *Journal of Social Behavior and Personality* 11:143–160.

Chung, M. C., S. Farmer, K. Grant, R. Newton, S. Payne, M. Perry, J. Saunders, C. Smith, and N. Stone. 2002a. Gender differences in love styles and post traumatic stress reactions following relationship dissolution. *European Journal of Psychiatry* 16:210–220.

Chung, M. C., S. Farmer, K. Grant, R. Newton, S. Payne, M. Perry, J. Saunders, C. Smith, and N. Stone. 2002b. Self-esteem, personality and post traumatic stress symptoms following the dissolution of a dating relationship. *Stress and Health* 18:83–90.

Chung, M. C., S. Farmer, K. Grant, R. Newton, S. Payne, M. Perry, J. Saunders, C. Smith, and N. Stone. 2003. Coping with post-traumatic stress symptoms following relationship dissolution. *Stress and Health* 19:27–36.

Cooper, M. L., P. R. Shaver, and N. L. Collins. 1998. Attachment styles, emotional regulation and adjustment in adolescence. *Journal of Personality and Social Psychology* 74:1380–1387.

Davis, D., P. R. Shaver, and M. L. Vernon. 2003. Physical, emotional and behavioral reactions to breaking-up: The roles of gender, age, emotional involvement, and attachment style. *Personality and Social Psychology Bulletin* 29:871–884.

Drew, S. S., M. Heesacker, H. M. Frost, and L. E. Oelke. 2004. The role of relationship loss and self-loss in women's and men's dysphoria. *Journal of Social and Personal Relationships* 21:381–397.

Duck, S. W. 1982. A topography of relationship disengagement and dissolution. In *Personal relationships 4: Dissolving personal relationships*, edited by S. W. Duck, 1–30. Academic Press: New York.

Eysenck, H., and S. Eysenck. 1991. *Eysenck personality scales*. London: Hodder & Stoughton.

Feeney, J. A., and P. Noller. 1992. Attachment style and romantic love: Relationship dissolution. *Australian Journal of Psychology* 44:69–74.

Feeney, J., P. Noller, and M. Hanrahan. 1994. Assessing adult attachment. In *Attachment in adults: Clinical and developmental perspectives,* edited by M. Sperlin and W. Berman, 122–158. New York: Guilford.

Felmlee, D. H. 1994. Who's on top? Power in romantic relationships. *Sex Roles* 31:275–295.

Felmlee, D., S. Sprecher, and E. Bassin. 1990. The dissolution of intimate relationships: A hazard model. *Social Psychology Quarterly* 53:13–30.

Fine, M. A., and J. A. Sacher. 1997. Predictors of distress following relationship termination among dating couples. *Journal of Social and Clinical Psychology* 16:381–388.

Folkman, S., and R. Lazarus. 1980. An analysis of coping in a middle-aged community sample. *Journal of Health and Social Behavior* 21:219–239.

Fraley, R. C., N. G. Waller, and K. A. Brennan. 2000. An item-response theory analysis of self-report measures of adult attachment. *Journal of Personality and Social Psychology* 78:350–365.

Frazier, P. A., and S. W. Cook. 1993. Correlates of distress following heterosexual relationship dissolution. *Journal of Social and Personal Relationships* 10:55–67.

Gray, J. D., and R. C. Silver. 1990. Opposite sides of the same coin: Former spouses' divergent perspectives in coping with their divorce. *Journal of Personality and Social Psychology* 59:1180–1191.

Griffin, D. W., and K. Bartholomew. 1994. The metaphysics of measurement: The case of adult attachment. In *Advances in Personal Relationships*, vol. 5, edited by K. Bartholomew and D. Perlman, 17–52. London: Kingsley.

Hatfield, E., and R. Rapson. 1996. Stress and passionate love. In *Stress and emotion: Anxiety, anger and curiosity,* edited by C. Spielberger and I. Sarason, 16, 29–50. Boca Raton, FL: CRC Press, 2005.

Hazen, C., and P. R. Shaver. 1987. Romantic love conceptualised as an attachment process. *Journal of Personality and Social Psychology* 52:511–524.

Hill, C. T., Z. Rubin, and L. A. Peplau. 1976. Breakups before marriage: The end of 103 affairs. *Journal of Social Issues* 32:147–168.

Joseph, S., R. Williams, and W. Yule. 1995. Psychosocial perspective on posttraumatic stress. *Clinical Psychology Review* 15:515–544.

Kaczmarek, M. G., and B. A. Backlund. 1991. Disenfranchised grief: The loss of an adolescent romantic relationship. *Adolescence* 26:253–259.

Kaczmarek, M. G., B. A. Backlund, and P. Biemer. 1990. The dynamics of ending a romantic relationship: An empirical assessment of grief. *Journal of College Student Development* 31:319–324.

Keelan, J. P. R., K. K. Dion, and K. L. Dion. 1994. Attachment style and relationship satisfaction: Test of a self-disclosure explanation. *Canadian Journal of Behavioural Science* 30:24–35.

Kubler-Ross, E. 1973. *On death and dying*. New York: Routledge.

Kurdek, L. A. 1991. The dissolution of gay and lesbian couples. *Journal of Social and Personal Relationships* 8:265–278.

Lewandowski, G. W. 2009. Promoting positive emotions following relationship dissolution through writing. *Journal of Positive Psychology* 4:21–31.

Lloyd, S. A. 1991. The dark side of courtship: Violence and sexual exploitation. *Family Relations* 40:14–20.

Lloyd, S. A., and R. M. Cate. 1985. The developmental course of conflict in dissolution of premarital relationships. *Journal of Social and Personal Relationships* 2:179–94.

Lloyd, S. A., R. M. Cate, and J. M. Henton. 1984. Predicting premarital relationship stability: A methodological refinement. *Journal of Marriage and the Family* 46:71–76.

Maslow, A. H. 1943. A theory of human motivation. *Psychological Review* 50:370–396.

Matheny, K., D. Aycock, J. Pugh, W. Curlette, and K. Cannella Silva. 1986. Stress coping: A qualitative and quantitative synthesis with implications for treatment. *Counseling Psychology* 14:499–549.

McCarthy, C. J., R. G. Lambert, and G. Brack. 1997. Structural model of coping, appraisals and emotions after relationship breakup. *Journal of Counselling and Development* 76:53–64.

Mearns, J. 1991. Coping with a breakup: Negative mood regulation expectancies and depression following the end of a romantic relationship. *Journal of Personality and Social Psychology* 60:327–334.

Orbuch, T. L. 1992. A symbolic interactionist approach to the study of relationship loss. In *Close relationship loss: Theoretical approaches*, edited by T. L. Orbuch, 192–204. New York: Springer.

Perilloux, C., and D. M. Buss. 2008. Breaking up romantic relationships: Costs experienced and coping strategies deployed. *Evolutionary Psychology* 61:164–181.

Peterson, C., A. C. Rosenbaum, and M. K. Conn. 1985. Depressive mood reactions to breaking up: Testing the learned helplessness model of depression. *Journal of Social and Clinical Psychology* 3:161–169.

Pistole, M. C. 1995. College student's ended love relationships: Attachment style and emotion. *Journal of College and Student Development* 36:53–60.

Procidano, M., and K. Heller. 1983. Measures of perceived social support from friends and from family: Three validation studies. *American Journal of Community Psychology* 11:1–24.

Riggs, D. S. 1993. Relationship problems and dating aggression: A potential treatment target. *Journal of Interpersonal Violence* 8:18–35.

Riggs, D. S., K. D. O'Leary, and F. C. Breslin. 1990. Multiple correlates of physical aggression in dating couples. *Journal of Interpersonal Violence* 5:61–73.

Robak, R. W., and S. P. Weitzman. 1998. The nature of grief: Loss of love relationships in young adulthood. *Journal of Personal and Interpersonal Loss* 3:205–216.

Ruvolo, A. P., L. A. Fabin, and C. M. Ruvolo. 2001. Relationship experiences and change in attachment characteristics of young adults: The role of relationship breakups on conflict avoidance. *Personal Relationships* 8:265–281.

Saucier, G. 1994. Separating description and evaluation in the structure of personality attributes. *Journal of Personality and Social Psychology* 66:131–154.

Sbarra, D. A. 2006. Predicting the onset of emotional recovery following non-marital relationship dissolution: Survival analysis of sadness and anger. *Personality and Social Psychology Bulletin* 32:298–312.

Sbarra, D. A., and R. E. Emery. 2005. The emotional sequelae of non-marital relationship dissolution: Analysis of change and intra-individual variability over time. *Personal Relationships* 12:213–232.

Simpson, J. A. 1987. The dissolution of romantic relationships: Factors involved in relationship stability and emotional distress. *Journal of Personality and Social Psychology* 53:683–692.

Sprecher, S. 1994. Two sides to break-up of dating relationships. *Personal Relationships* 1:199–222.

Sprecher, S., and B. Fehr. 1998. The dissolution of close relationships. In *Perspectives on loss*, edited by J. H. Harvey, 99–112. New York: Routledge.

Sprecher, S., D. Felmlee, S. Metts, B. Fehr, and D. Vanni. 1998. Factors associated with distress following the breakup of a close relationship. *Journal of Social and Personal Relationships* 15:791–809.

Stephen, T. 1987. Attribution and Adjustment to Relationship Termination. *Journal of Social and Personal Relationships* 4:47–61.

Surra, C. A. 1987. Reasons for changes in commitment: Variations by courtship type. *Journal of Social and Personal Relationships* 4:17–33.

Tashiro, T., and P. Frazier. 2003. "I'll never be in a relationship like that again": Personal growth following romantic relationship break-ups. *Personal Relationships* 10:113–128.

Watson, D., L. A. Clark, and A. R. Harkness. 1994. Structures of personality and their relevance to psychopathology. *Journal of Abnormal Psychology* 103:18–31.

Weber, A. L. 1998. Losing, leaving and letting go: Coping with nonmarital breakups. In *The dark side of close relationships*, edited by B. H. Spitzberg and W. R. Cupach, 267–304. Mahway, NJ: Erlbaum.

Whisman, M. A., A. E. Dixon, and B. Johnson. 1997. Therapist's perspectives on couple problems and treatment issues in couple therapy. *Journal of Family Psychology* 11:361–366.

Chapter 11

Attachment and Romantic Relationships: The Roles of Working Models of Self and Other

Erica G. Hepper and Katherine B. Carnelley

Romantic love relationships are among the most endlessly fascinating yet frustratingly complex parts of life, inspiring more art, literature, and music than any other topic. Making sense of how and why romantic relationships function the way they do is, therefore, a research endeavor at once most rewarding and neverending. Why do some relationships sail through everything that life throws at them while others flounder at the first hiccup? Why does one friend experience drama after tumultuous drama with each new boyfriend while another can't trust or open up to anyone enough to get beyond a second date? Attachment theory (Bowlby 1969, 1973, 1980) draws on clinical, developmental, social, personality, and cognitive psychology and provides a rich theoretical framework for examining and answering such perennial questions. Although it was developed originally in the context of infants and their caregivers, in recent decades the theory has also provided insight into the development and functioning of romantic relationships. This chapter describes romantic relationship processes from an attachment perspective. We highlight in particular the cognitive models of self and others that form a person's attachment pattern or orientation. These models color the lens with which he or she views the self and the social world, and in turn underlie individual differences in romantic relationship functioning.

ATTACHMENT THEORY

Bowlby's (1969) attachment theory rests on the idea that attaching to close others is a fundamental human need. Bowlby argued that humans are born with a behavioral system dedicated to forming these attachment bonds—a program of goals and strategies based in the central nervous system that evolved to help infants maintain proximity to caregivers and thus ensure protection and survival. This attachment system is activated whenever the infant senses threat or danger, triggering feelings of distress and motivating behaviors to restore feelings of safety. Thus the function of the attachment system is protection, but the more immediate goal experienced by the person him- or herself is to reduce negative affect or emotions (Sroufe and Waters 1977). The normative strategy to achieve this is to display attachment behaviors (e.g., cry) and seek proximity to a caregiver or *attachment figure*. However, this strategy is adaptive only to the extent that a caregiver responds sensitively and predictably to these behaviors. Over time, an infant builds mental representations of the social world known as *internal working models*, based on the nature of his or her particular experiences with caregivers (Main, Kaplan, and Cassidy 1985). At their core lies the person's view of him- or herself (How worthy am I of affection?) and close others (How reliable and responsive are others to my needs?). These working models of self and other provide the lens through which a person understands the world as well as the compass guiding the strategies he or she uses to regulate affect and to navigate the rocky terrain of close relationships. Depending on their nature, one's working models are seen as more or less secure.

Although research into attachment processes began with infancy, Bowlby viewed attachment as relevant "from the cradle to the grave" (1979, 129). He argued that adult love relationships function as reciprocal attachment bonds in which each partner serves as an attachment figure for the other. Indeed, as reviewed by Zeifman and Hazan (2008), there are many striking similarities in the nature of adult pair-bond and parent-infant relationships, including the types of physical contact they feature and the release of the hormone oxytocin, which is thought to promote bonding. Crucially, adult pair bonds serve the key functions of attachment bonds: proximity maintenance, a safe haven in times of need, separation distress, and a secure base from which to explore in times of safety. Among coupled adults, the partner generally supersedes parents in fulfilling these functions (Zeifman and Hazan 2008). In adult romantic relationships the attachment system operates alongside (and interacts with) other behavioral systems such as care giving and sex.

As well as the normative processes outlined above, individual differences in attachment working models also characterize infant and adult attachment relationships in similar ways. The three attachment "styles" first observed by Mary Ainsworth and colleagues when studying infants in the Strange Situation lab paradigm (Ainsworth et al. 1978) were adopted by Hazan and Shaver (1987) in the first study of adult attachment and were shown not only to apply to adult love relationships but also to exist in similar proportions. More recently, research has demonstrated that individual differences in adult attachment are most accurately described in terms of two independent continuous dimensions: *anxiety* and *avoidance* (Brennan, Clark, and Shaver 1998; Fraley and Waller 1998).

Attachment anxiety refers to the extent to which a person worries about being rejected, fears abandonment, and doubts his or her worth in relationships (i.e., a more negative vs. positive working model of the self). High anxiety is thought to reflect a hyperactivated attachment system resulting from a history of relatively inconsistent or overprotective care giving (Ainsworth et al. 1978; Shaver and Mikulincer 2002). That is, in terms of survival it is adaptive to maintain proximity to such a caregiver, monitor the environment for threat, and readily display distress in the hope that it gains protection. Attachment avoidance refers to the extent to which a person avoids intimacy, dislikes depending on others, and downplays the importance of relationships (i.e., a more negative vs. positive working model of close others). Avoidance is thought to reflect a deactivated attachment system resulting from a history of relatively rejecting or cold care giving (Ainsworth et al. 1978; Shaver and Mikulincer 2002). That is, it is adaptive to maintain a safe distance from the caregiver, not show distress, and not to process signs of rejection. Bowlby (1973) referred to this strategy as "compulsive self-reliance." Attachment security is characterized by low levels of both anxiety and avoidance, and positive models of both self and others. Security is thought to reflect a flexibly functioning attachment system resulting from consistently responsive care-giving experiences. That is, it activates in response to threatening situations but is readily calmed by thoughts of or contact with attachment figures.

Levels of attachment anxiety and avoidance can be assessed in adulthood with reliable and valid self-report scales (Brennan, Clark, and Shaver 1998; Shaver and Mikulincer 2002). For example, secure people tend to agree with statements like "It helps to turn to my romantic partner in times of need," whereas highly anxious people agree with statements like "I need a lot of reassurance that I am loved by my partner" and highly avoidant people with statements like "I am nervous when partners get too close to me." (An online version of such a measure, which gives feedback on respondents' attachment style, is available at http://www.web-research-design.net/cgi-bin/crq/crq.pl/; see Fraley n.d.) Consistent with the idea that secure attachment is normative, and with Ainsworth et al.'s (1978) finding that about 60 percent of infants were classified secure, mean levels of anxiety and avoidance in adult samples tend to be below the scale midpoint. And supporting the idea that the two dimensions are independent, correlations between them are usually positive but weak (Mikulincer and Shaver 2007). A person's level of anxiety and avoidance heavily influences his or her approach to close relationships and interactions with potential, current, and past romantic partners, as we will discuss below.

It is important to note that attachment working models are not set in stone: One person will not necessarily display the same levels of anxiety and avoidance over time or across different relationships. Over time, the handful of longitudinal studies suggest that working models tend toward stability from infancy to adulthood and adjust but are not overwritten in response to life experiences (Fraley 2002; Waters et al. 2000). Across relationships, people hold multiple working models that are thought to be organized as a hierarchy (Collins and Read 1994). A general, global model is most chronically accessible and is applied when interacting with new people, whereas more specific models concerning types of relationship (e.g., friends) and particular relationships (e.g., my husband) are activated and applied when interacting with relevant others. In fact, global ratings of attachment style correlate only moderately with ratings in specific relationships (Ross and Spinner 2001). Most research has assessed attachment styles at a global or general-romantic level and has linked them to individual differences in the ways that people approach, experience, and cope with romantic relationships. In this chapter we aim to demonstrate that many such consequences can be explained by the views of self and others contained in attachment working models.

ATTACHMENT ORIENTATION AND ROMANTIC RELATIONSHIP FUNCTIONING

A vast body of research has examined the correlates of attachment orientation in romantic relationships. This research shows that, overall, secure attachment is linked to more intimate, satisfied, and balanced relationships than insecure attachment (see J. Feeney 2008; Mikulincer et al. 2002; Mikulincer and Shaver 2007, for reviews). In general, the partners of secure people tend to be more satisfied with their relationship than those of insecure people (Carnelley, Pietromonaco, and Jaffe 1996; Kane et al. 2007; Mikulincer et al. 2002). It is easier to be in a close relationship with someone who doesn't constantly fear abandonment like an anxious person, or with someone who doesn't feel uncomfortable self-disclosing or being intimate like an avoidant person. Unsurprisingly, insecure people's relationships are more likely to break up (Kirkpatrick and Hazan 1994). The relationships of people with high anxiety as opposed to high avoidance are characterized by different major issues, reflecting the distinct strategies that underlie anxiety (i.e., clinging to maintain intimacy) versus avoidance (i.e., distancing to protect from rejection).

Compared to secure people, the relationships of highly anxious people tend to be fraught with insecurity, jealousy, and conflict (Campbell et al. 2005; Collins and Read 1990; Hazan and Shaver 1987; Levy and Davis 1988; Simpson, Rholes, and Phillips 1996). Those with high anxiety also report a compulsive but insensitive style of care giving (Kunce and Shaver 1994) and may overcommit to a relationship early on, which leads to frustration when the partner doesn't reciprocate (Morgan and Shaver 1999). Anxious people's sex lives are similarly tumultuous: They report feeling ambivalent about their sexual experiences, using contraception rarely and consenting to unwanted sex (Birnbaum et al. 2006; Bogaert and Sadava 2002; Impett and Peplau 2002). A high need for intimacy underlies many of these patterns and causes conflict in anxious people's relationships (Feeney 1999; Feeney and Noller 1991).

The relationships of highly avoidant people tend to be low in satisfaction, commitment, and trust (Collins and Read 1990; Levy and Davis 1988), and avoidant individuals are less likely to either seek or provide care giving or support when their partner needs it (B. Feeney and Collins 2001; Simpson, Rholes, and Nelligan 1992). Avoidant people's sex lives are similarly distant: They report negative views of sex and low sexual satisfaction in marriage (Birnbaum 2007; Butzer and Campbell 2008) but are more likely to have unemotional or casual sex than those with low avoidance (Cooper et al. 2004; Stephan and Bachman 1999). A high need for self-reliance and distance underlies many of these patterns and can cause relationship problems (Feeney 1999).

Overall, both anxious and avoidant attachment strategies, though they may initially develop to gain protection from a caregiver, can impede involvement in smooth and satisfying relationships in adulthood. We argue that this impedance can be both understood, and potentially reduced, by considering the processes involved in insecure people's working models of self and others. In the following sections we outline how these processes may underlie a whole host of consequences of insecure attachment for romantic relationships.

MODEL OF SELF

The working model of self contains beliefs about how loveable and worthy one is in the context of close relationships as well as dynamic goals and strategies about how to be or become loveable and worthy. A wealth of social-psychological literature on the self (for reviews, see Baumeister 1998; Leary and Tangney 2003) provides a rich backdrop for studying attachment-related models of self. This literature has examined a range of ways in which people's self-concepts and self-processes can vary. These include valence (e.g., level of self-esteem; Leary et al. 1995), stability (e.g., fluctuation in self-esteem; Kernis and Goldman 2003), and regulation (e.g., contingencies of self-worth; Crocker and Wolfe 2001). Congruent with the theoretical development of working models of the self, individual differences in attachment are linked to each of these constructs. In particular, we propose that the sources on which self-esteem is based (Brennan and Morris 1997; Hepper and Carnelley 2010) underlie many attachment differences in romantic relationship functioning.

ATTACHMENT DIFFERENCES IN THE SELF SYSTEM

Security

Secure attachment emerges in infancy when a caregiver is consistently responsive in times of need. This allows the infant to explore the environment in times of
safety and develop the confidence and skills to deal with the world autonomously,
cope with challenges, and regulate his or her own emotions (Mikulincer and Shaver
2004; Mikulincer, Shaver, and Pereg 2003). Thus a secure working model of the self
is not only positive ("I am worthy of love and capable of mastering skills") but also
serves as a resource ("If things go wrong I can deal with them without falling to
pieces"). According to Deci and Ryan (1995), a sense of self developed in this way
fosters "true" self-esteem, as opposed to self-esteem contingent on fulfilling certain
conditions. Similarly, sociometer theory (Leary et al. 1995) suggests that the trait
self-esteem partly reflects chronic perceptions of social acceptance and can become
"functionally autonomous." Thus we would expect securely attached adults to possess
high and stable self-esteem that can be regulated internally rather than by depending
on external input such as feedback, affection, or proving themselves to others.

Indeed, evidence links attachment security to high self-esteem and positive
self-views (Brennan and Morris 1997; Collins and Read 1990; Luke, Maio, and
Carnelley 2004; Mikulincer 1995), as well as self-esteem stability (Foster, Kernis, and Goldman 2007), self-concept clarity (Alfasi et al. 2011), and capacity
for self-reinforcement (encouraging, supporting, and valuing oneself; Wei et al.
2005). Moreover, secure adults report having relatively noncontingent self-esteem
(Brandt and Vonk 2005; Park, Crocker, and Mickelson 2004), and their self-esteem
does not fluctuate much in response to daily feedback reported in a diary (Hepper
and Carnelley, in press) or manipulated feedback from romantic partners (Carnelley, Israel, and Brennan 2007). Thus evidence supports the notion that secure
attachment involves a stable, internally regulated self-concept: "To be worthy, I
just have to be myself."

Anxiety

Attachment anxiety emerges in an environment in which constantly maintaining closeness to an inconsistent caregiver prevents the infant from exploring and
thus developing a sense of efficacy or autonomous self-esteem (Mikulincer and
Shaver 2004). Obtaining intimacy and approval from others continues to serve as
a primary source of feelings of worth, but chronic fear of rejection means that no
amount of intimacy is ever enough. Thus we would expect highly anxious adults to
possess low self-esteem ("I don't deserve to be loved and can't cope without relying
on others"), which is also unstable because it is contingent on and hypersensitive
to signs of intimacy and approval. Self-esteem is boosted temporarily by acceptance but is crushed again when those feelings wane or new signs of rejection are
(repeatedly) perceived.

Indeed, evidence links the dimension of anxiety to low and unstable self-esteem (Brennan and Morris 1997; Foster, Kernis, and Goldman 2007; Luke, Maio, and Carnelley 2004; Mikulincer 1995; Schmitt and Allik 2005), uncertainty about the self (Pietromonaco and Feldman Barrett 1997), and poor capacity for self-reinforcement (Wei et al. 2005). Anxiety also predicts depression, which is mediated by overreliance on others for emotion regulation (Carnelley, Pietromonaco, and Jaffe 1994; Wei et al. 2005; Zuroff and Fitzpatrick 1995). Anxious people endorse external contingencies of self-worth; that is, they base their self-esteem on external sources such as physical appearance, others' approval, and romantic relationship success (Knee et al. 2008; Park, Crocker, and Mickelson 2004) and report wanting to gain liking and approval in everyday interactions (Pietromonaco and Feldman Barrett 2006). High-anxious adults also are very keen to receive feedback from others (Hepper and Carnelley 2010) but then exaggerate its importance and show greater fluctuation of self-esteem in response to feedback, especially when the feedback is negative (Carnelley, Israel, and Brennan 2007; Hepper and Carnelley, in press). Further, they report negative self-perceptions and lower self-esteem after negative relationship events (J. Feeney 2004). Thus evidence supports the idea that the anxious self-concept is over-invested in and dependent on constant love and approval: "I am not worthy unless someone loves me (and always tells me so)."

Avoidance

Avoidance emerges in an environment in which distance and self-reliance are prioritized in order to protect the infant from experiencing rejection; thus he or she lacks a true secure base and instead focuses on efficacy (Brennan and Morris 1997; Mikulincer and Shaver 2004). Feelings of worth are disengaged from interpersonal approval and cannot be regulated internally but may become invested in independent exploration. We would therefore expect high-avoidant adults to possess self-esteem that is not necessarily low but contingent on maintaining distance and self-reliance. Evidence suggests that avoidance does not relate consistently to self-esteem level or stability (Foster, Kernis, and Goldman 2007; Luke, Maio, and Carnelley 2004; Schmitt and Allik 2005) and that dismissing-avoidance is positively related to self-competence (but not self-liking; Brennan and Morris 1997), implying that feelings of worth can be maintained.

However, some studies have linked avoidance to poorly integrated self-concepts, low self-clarity, and poor self-understanding, suggesting that their positive self-reports are defensive (Davila and Cobb 2003; Kim 2005; Mikulincer 1995). Mikulincer (1998) further found that avoidant people's reports of positive self-views were increased by threat to self-reliance and reduced by the instruction that self-reliance is shown by balanced self-views, directly implicating self-reliance in their high self-esteem. They are also more likely than low-avoidant people to self-enhance after attachment threat by inflating independent, not interdependent,

self-views (Hart, Shaver, and Goldenberg 2005). Dismissing-avoidance is negatively related to self-reported contingencies of self-worth (Park, Crocker, and
Mickelson 2004) and linked to self-reported aversion and indifference to partner feedback (Carnelley, Israel, and Brennan 2007), which may reflect attempts to
prove self-reliance. Further, avoidant adults report being eager for agentic feedback
(Rholes et al. 2007), and dismissing-avoidants seek positive feedback about self-
reliance but not about relationships (Hepper and Carnelley 2010), implying that
they are motivated to enhance self-esteem in this domain. Interestingly, although
avoidant people fail to gain normative boosts to self-esteem after positive feedback
from others, when they notice everyday rejection, it dents their daily self-esteem
more than that of low-avoidants (Hepper and Carnelley, in press), implying that
when their defenses are broken, they suffer. Thus evidence supports the idea that
the avoidant self-concept is defensively disengaged from love and invested instead
in distance and self-reliance: "I don't need anyone else, and I am worthwhile as
long as that's the case."

CONSEQUENCES FOR ROMANTIC RELATIONSHIPS

Anxiety

Over and above fear of rejection, the investment of self-esteem in intimacy and
approval for anxious individuals can exacerbate problematic relationship behavior. One example is excessive reassurance-seeking: asking persistently for assur-
ance of affection regardless of whether it has already been provided (Joiner et al.
1999). As well as the general feedback-seeking mentioned above, highly anxious
people are more likely to engage in excessive reassurance-seeking (Brennan and
Carnelley 1999; Shaver, Schachner, and Mikulincer 2005). This behavior has an
impact on relationship partners, eliciting rejection and even feelings of depression
in the partner (Joiner et al. 1999), and decreases the perceived relationship quality,
at least for female partners (Shaver, Schachner, and Mikulincer 2005). Thus the
behavior motivated by contingent self-esteem is bad for the relationship.

Contingent self-esteem can also explain anxious people's reactions to a partner's
behavior. Consistent with the overreactions to negative feedback described above,
Collins et al. (2006) showed that anxious people made threatening attributions for
hypothetical partner transgressions (e.g., if a partner wanted to spend an evening
alone, they believed that the partner was losing interest in the relationship) and
reported behavioral intentions that would lead to conflict. In turn, Campbell et al.
(2005) found that participants higher in attachment anxiety perceived everyday
real conflict interactions to be more hurtful, to have escalated, and to have longer-
term consequences. Together, these findings illustrate how having self-esteem that
is so highly invested in romantic relationships can lead to tumultuous interactions.
Interestingly, although attachment-anxious people perceive more conflict in their

daily interactions (Campbell et al. 2005), other data suggest that for anxious people, daily conflict does not dent self-esteem to the same extent as rejection (Hepper and Carnelley, in press; Pietromonaco and Feldman Barrett 1997), suggesting that conflict can counter-intuitively satisfy a need for attention or intimacy.

Anxious people fluctuate strongly not only in their self-perceptions but also in perceptions of their partner and the relationship in response to feedback and other events. Pietromonaco and Feldman Barrett (2006) found that for those high in attachment anxiety, esteem for an interaction partner was most strongly determined by how the interaction made them feel about themselves. So they valued partners more when they obtained approval from those partners, and they did this to a greater extent than did secure individuals. Moreover, Campbell et al. (2005) found that high-anxious (compared to low-anxious) people's daily perceptions and future expectations of their relationship were most strongly affected by both their perceptions of conflict with and support from their romantic partners. Similar results showing anxious people's reactivity were found by J. Feeney (2002) regarding reactions to spouse behaviors and by Hepper and Carnelley (2008) regarding reactions to daily positive feedback from romantic partners. This serves as another mechanism by which investing self-esteem in continued shows of affection can have an impact on the relationship. If anxious people only value their partner or relationship when that partner feeds their need for self-esteem (Murray, Holmes, and Griffin 2000), this ego-involved attitude will be perceptible to the partner and undermine true affection.

Finally, contingent self-esteem may account for highly anxious people's risky sexual behavior in new and ongoing relationships (Bogaert and Sadava 2002; Cooper et al. 2004). That is, anxious individuals likely prioritize gaining approval and affection via sex, over sexual health and asserting their own preferences. Indeed, anxious people report having sex to gain intimacy, reassurance, nurturance, and love (Davis, Shaver, and Vernon 2004; Schachner and Shaver 2004). They may therefore defer to a partner's desires, in order to gain or maintain affections, rather than asserting their own. Consistent with this suggestion, attachment anxiety relates to low sexual self-esteem and self-efficacy about sexual encounters, initiating condom use, and resisting sexual pressure (Feeney et al. 2000; Hepper, Hogarth, and Carnelley 2006; Kershaw et al. 2007). Even clearer, Impett and Peplau (2002) found that anxious young women consented to unwanted sex to prevent their partner from losing interest. Basing one's self-esteem on approval from others can lead to poor health for oneself and one's close relationships.

Avoidance

The investment of self-esteem in distance from others and self-reliance may explain and exacerbate relationship issues for avoidant people. Efforts to maintain independence may prevent them from developing close relationships in the first place (Hazan and Shaver 1987). In ongoing relationships, Feeney (1999) found that avoidant men's self-reliance concerns caused struggles in their relationships regarding balancing closeness and distance. An issue stemming from avoidant people's aversion to and dismissiveness of feedback from their partner (Carnelley, Israel, and Brennan 2007) is that they are unlikely to take on board the partner's feelings and preferences and thus improve their relationship in future.

Finally, avoidants' self-reliance–contingent self-esteem may foster risky sexual behavior. Consistent with their self-esteem regulation, avoidant people report having sex to avoid intimacy and nurturance, gain emotional distance, and manipulate a partner (Davis, Shaver, and Vernon 2004; Schachner and Shaver 2004). Cooper et al. (2006) reported that avoidant young women engaged in extrarelationship sexual encounters in order to bolster their egos. Moreover, Hepper, Hogarth, and Carnelley (2006) found that for high-avoidant but not low-avoidant young women, more frequent casual sexual activity was linked to higher subsequent sexual self-esteem and self-efficacy for sexual encounters. We know from past research that avoidance relates to sex with strangers and low condom use, both of which put the individual at risk (e.g., Bogaert and Sadava 2002). Thus deriving sexual self-worth from such casual encounters is potentially dangerous, and if such encounters are conducted alongside an existing romantic relationship, it puts the relationship at risk if discovered.

MODEL OF OTHERS

The working model of others contains beliefs about close-relationship partners' availability, supportiveness, and reliability. Again, although initial working models develop in the context of primary caregiver relationships, they generalize to an extent across different relationship partners, and only after a specific relationship has developed over time does the working model of that partner diverge from more global models. One's attachment history strongly colors the content and structure of one's working model of close others, with dramatic consequences for the development, maintenance, and functioning of romantic relationships. According to research on significant-other concepts (Steiner-Pappalardo and Gurung 2002), models of the other can vary in valence, clarity (including stability), and connectedness to the self (e.g., differentiation: Pietromonaco and Feldman Barrett 1997; projection: Mikulincer and Horesh 1999). Working models that are relatively positive, clear, stable, and connected tend to characterize higher quality relationships (Murray 1999).

ATTACHMENT DIFFERENCES IN VIEWS OF OTHERS

Secure attachment develops in a context in which caregivers are predictable and responsive to one's needs, so contained within secure models of others are positive expectations such as "When I am in need, others will be there for me."

Accordingly, secure adults report positive views of others in general, have a benign view of human nature, and readily socialize and self-disclose to new people (Bartholomew and Horowitz 1991; Collins and Read 1990; Luke, Maio, and Carnelley 2004). They describe parents in benevolent and textured ways (Levy, Blatt, and Shaver 1998), and their beliefs and expectations of romantic partners are positive, coherent, and stable over multiple assessments (Alfasi, Gramzow, and Carnelley 2010; Alfasi et al. 2011; Steiner-Pappalardo and Gurung 2002). Secure adults are able to experience empathy, express gratitude and respect for their partners, and generously forgive transgressions (Frei and Shaver 2002; Joireman, Needham, and Cummings 2002; Mikulincer, Shaver, and Slav 2006). In short, secure people are able to hold balanced and kind views of their partner and treat them accordingly.

Attachment anxiety emerges in an environment in which caregivers are confusing and unpredictable and seeking affection sometimes pays off and sometimes does not. Thus anxious models of others reflect this ("When I am in need, I don't know whether others will be there for me") and create ambivalent, unstable, and incoherent views of others (Mikulincer and Shaver 2007). Indeed, evidence shows that highly anxious people describe parents in ambivalent ways (Levy, Blatt, and Shaver 1998), show attitudinal ambivalence toward partners (Mikulincer et al. 2010), and find other people difficult to understand (Collins and Read 1990). Anxious people's views of romantic partners are low in clarity (Alfasi et al. 2011; Steiner-Pappalardo and Gurung 2002) and fluctuate in valence over time (Alfasi, Gramzow, and Carnelley 2010; Graham and Clark 2006). Specifically, they may become more negative during the course of a relationship (Feeney 2002) or after discussing a problem (Simpson, Rholes, and Phillips 1996), but—consistent with the findings reviewed earlier on conflict interactions—they become more positive and complex after a conflict (Fishtein, Pietromonaco, and Feldman Barrett 1999). Also consistent with their intimacy goals, anxious people represent others in ways that minimize distance and differentiation from the self. For example, they report low uniqueness and high desire to merge with close others (Hazan and Shaver 1987; Pietromonaco and Feldman Barrett 1997), and under threat, they increase perceived similarity by projecting their own traits onto others (Mikulincer and Horesh 1999; Mikulincer, Orbach, and Iavnieli 1998). Overall, then, it seems that anxious people have generally hopeful expectations about other people but these are confused and easily malleable depending on recent events.

Attachment avoidance emerges in an environment in which caregivers are predictably rejecting, cold, or absent. As such, we would expect individuals high in avoidance to hold consistently negative working models of others ("When I am in need, others will not be there for me"), which help maintain their deactivating strategies and thus further protect from potential rejection (Mikulincer, Shaver, and Pereg 2003). At a global level, avoidance correlates negatively with evaluations of humanity (Luke, Maio, and Carnelley 2004), empathy for others, including outgroups (Boag and Carnelley 2011; Joireman, Needham, and Cummings 2002), and overall sociability and warmth (Griffin and Bartholomew 1994). Avoidant people describe their parents in simplistic punitive ways (Levy, Blatt, and Shaver 1998), and their models of romantic partners are low in clarity (Alfasi et al. 2011), unaccepting (Steiner-Pappalardo and Gurung 2002), and consistently negative over multiple occasions (Alfasi, Gramzow, and Carnelley 2010) and at an implicit level (Zayas and Shoda 2005). Interestingly, it has been suggested that avoidant people may try to cope with all this negativity by defensively idealizing some people, such as a parent (Main, Kaplan, and Cassidy 1985; Mikulincer and Shaver 2007). Consistent with a generally negative attitude, avoidance correlates negatively with respect for one's romantic partner and views of his or her moral qualities (Frei and Shaver 2002), trust (see Mikulincer and Shaver 2007), gratitude, and forgiveness (Mikulincer, Shaver, and Slav 2006). In terms of connectedness, avoidant individuals achieve further distance by placing significant others further from the self in a bull's-eye diagram representing their attachment network (Rowe and Carnelley 2005), perceiving greater differentiation between the self and others, and projecting their own unwanted traits onto others (Mikulincer and Horesh 1999; Mikulincer, Orbach, and Iavnieli 1998). Overall, avoidant people have stubbornly negative and/or defensively distant views of others.

CONSEQUENCES FOR ROMANTIC RELATIONSHIPS

Having positive, appreciative, and generous views of each other allows a romantic relationship to flourish and is key to long-term success (Mikulincer and Shaver 2007; Murray, Holmes, and Griffin 1996). Thus the negative or ambivalent models of others held by insecure individuals have consequences for their relationship functioning. These consequences are particularly widespread for avoidant people, whose negativity toward others, and subsequent drive for distance, pervade every stage of a romantic relationship from initial flirting to marriage (Mikulincer and Shaver 2007). Several of the characteristics linked to avoidance have been implicated as mediators of low relationship quality, including low self-disclosure and intimacy, lack of emotional expressiveness, and lack of forgiveness (Feeney 2008). Perhaps due to their low empathy and poor attention to emotional cues, avoidant people are also relatively insensitive caregivers, which has a huge impact on relationship quality (Feeney and Collins 2001). Avoidants' aversion to interpersonal closeness and touch (Brennan, Clark, and Shaver 1998) may further account for their lack of sexual satisfaction within a relationship (Butzer and Campbell 2008).

Insecure working models of others lead to less-than-optimal reactions to partners' behaviors. For example, high-avoidant people are likely to make pessimistic attributions for positive behaviors such as bringing dinner when one was sick (Collins et al. 2006) and are less likely to forgive negative behaviors but more likely to plot revenge than low-avoidants (Mikulincer, Shaver, and Slav 2006). Moreover, Feeney (2004) found that after hurtful events, avoidants' perceptions that the partner is not remorseful and engagement in destructive behaviors (e.g., anger, sarcasm) account for long-term negative effects on the relationship. Avoidant people also use less constructive conflict resolution strategies (i.e., less collaborating and compromising and more contentious behavior; Carnelley, Pietromonaco, and Jaffe 1994). Together, these findings illustrate the important role of negative models of others in exacerbating relationship problems.

As we saw in the previous section, the consequences of attachment anxiety for responses to stress and negative events tend to derive from negative views of the self rather than the partner. Nevertheless, anxious people's ambivalent models of others can also bias perceptions of a partner's intentions; for example, they perceive an ambiguously supportive message from their partner as being less supportive than if perceived by secure people or by independent observers (Collins and Feeney 2004). They also believe that positive partner behaviors may be motivated by selfish reasons (Collins et al. 2006). Because perceptions of social support are more influential than actual received support in predicting coping (Wethington and Kessler 1986), these biases have implications for long-term personal and relational well-being. Indeed, those high in attachment anxiety are the least optimistic about the future success of their romantic relationships (Carnelley and Janoff-Bulman 1992).

Further issues arise in times of stress, when the attachment system is activated and, generally speaking, support from close others is most important (Cohen and Wills 1985). For example, two behavioral studies have shown that as stress increases, secure people seek support from a romantic partner but avoidant people pull away and avoid physical contact (Fraley and Shaver 1998; Simpson, Rholes, and Nelligan 1992). Moreover, avoidant people do not find it physically comforting to have a partner with them in a stressful situation (Carpenter and Kirkpatrick 1996). However, evidence suggests that some types of support would in fact benefit high-avoidants: Simpson et al. (2007) found that dismissing-avoidant partners were calmed by receiving instrumental (practical) support, and DeFronzo, Panzarella, and Butler (2001) found that avoidant students whose support figures helped to reinterpret a stressful event more positively for them were less depressed or anxious afterward. Therefore, distancing from a partner is not adaptive when times are hard.

IMPLICATIONS AND APPLICATIONS

The theory and research we have discussed show clearly that understanding the nature of attachment working models can help to clarify and predict individual differences in relationship perceptions, behaviors, and functioning. This knowledge should equip psychologists with the tools to design interventions aimed at ameliorating anxious and avoidant people's relationship difficulties via increasing the security of their working models of self and/or other. Three relevant social-psychological interventions have recently been developed (outside of the attachment tradition). First, Marigold, Holmes, and Ross (2007) instructed participants with low self-esteem (i.e., a negative working model of self) to think about compliments they had received from their romantic partner and describe why their partner admired them and what this meant for them and their relationship (the abstract meaning condition). They found that compared to a control condition, those in the abstract meaning condition benefited more from the compliments and reported higher self-esteem and relationship satisfaction over a period of two weeks. Although rather specific, this approach shows that models of self can be overridden. Second, a host of studies have shown that self-affirmation (i.e., focusing on one's values or strengths) allows people to cope better with negative feedback or stress by restoring self-integrity (Sherman and Cohen 2006). Although this technique has had less success buffering against interpersonal rejection, it seems to go some way toward establishing a more coherent and clear model of self rather than focusing only on the valence of self-views. Third, scholars have proposed using regular expressions of gratitude (a "count your blessings" approach) to increase well-being (Wood, Froh, and Geraghty 2010). Given that everyday gratitude in a romantic relationship increases subsequent relationship satisfaction, and an intervention expressing gratitude to a friend increases perceived strength of the relationship (Algoe, Gable, and Maisel 2010; Lambert et al. 2010), this may be a fruitful direction for further relationship interventions to target the working model of the other.

However, the most desirable type of intervention would be one that promotes full security-based self-representations and positive working models of self and other. We know that specific models of self and other can develop in particular relationships, and indeed the development of a secure bond—and corresponding regular activation of secure models—is one mechanism by which therapeutic relationships can be effective (Parish and Eagle 2003). Recent studies have shown that parallel processes can also be induced using experimental priming: subliminally presenting security-related words, using guided imagery, or writing about a secure attachment relationship (Carnelley and Rowe 2010; Mikulincer et al. 2001; Rowe and Carnelley 2003). Security priming activates secure working models and has been shown to increase positive affect, state self-esteem, felt security, empathy, clarity of other-models, and a willingness to self-improve after failure, in ways above and beyond positive mood induction (e.g., Alfasi et al. 2011; Kumashiro and Sedikides 2005; see Carnelley and Rowe 2010, for a review). That is, security priming moves both models of self and other in directions toward security. Promising findings suggest that repeated security priming can have sustained effects over a few days (Carnelley and Rowe 2007; Gillath, Selcuk, and Shaver 2008), supporting its potential to be developed into an intervention. For example, if one or both members of a couple wrote or talked about an episode from their relationship that evoked feelings of security, those partners should be able to engage secure models of self and other in subsequent interactions and thus move their relationship toward security and optimal functioning.

CONCLUSIONS AND FUTURE RESEARCH DIRECTIONS

We have outlined some of the ways in which secure attachment working models of self and other differ from insecure models in terms of their valence, structure, and regulation. The care-giving environments in which individual differences in attachment anxiety and avoidance emerge give rise to models of self and other that can help us to understand and explain the textured differences in secure and insecure people's romantic relationships. In particular, the sources on which self-esteem is based for highly anxious (i.e., constant approval and intimacy) and highly avoidant persons (i.e., maintaining distance and self-reliance) explain many of the different ways in which they experience relationship difficulties. Likewise, the stubbornly negative models of other people held by high-avoidants explain many of the ways that they behave toward potential and current partners. Together, this set of processes underlies the struggles and eventual failure of many insecure people's romantic relationships. However, by identifying the source of these challenges, we have also been able to suggest points at which to intervene and highlight security priming as one likely direction for development of future interventions.

Several areas remain under-investigated and need further research. For example, much of the research we have reviewed (with some commendable exceptions) is limited to short-term or dating relationships and relatively young samples. It is vital that researchers study more committed relationships and samples across the whole lifespan in order to understand if the consequences of working models change over time. Other types of relationship (e.g., friendships) and other sexual orientations (e.g., lesbian, gay, bisexual, and transgender; Carnelley et al. 2011) also involve many of the underlying processes described here and deserve fuller investigation. Methodologically, more studies that include behavioral and psychophysiological observation are needed in order to reduce the problems of self-report biases and shared method variance inherent in many survey studies. And it is crucial to collect data from both members of a couple in order to study interactions between each partner's models of self and other: Feeney (2008) argues that attachment relationships can only be fully understood at the level of the dyad. With additional research of these important (and resource-intensive) types, scholars will gain an increasing understanding of the roles of working models in individual differences in relationship functioning. We will also be even better equipped to observe the smooth, tumultuous, or distant relationships all around us and understand why they function as they do.

REFERENCES

Ainsworth, M. D. S., M. C. Blehar, E. Waters, and S. Wall. 1978. *Patterns of attachment: Assessed in the strange situation and at home.* Hillsdale, NJ: Erlbaum.

Alfasi, Y., R. H. Gramzow, and K. B. Carnelley. 2010. Adult attachment patterns and stability in esteem for romantic partners. *Personality and Individual Differences* 48:607–611.

Alfasi, Y., R. H. Gramzow, K. Carnelley, J. B. Ruscher, and R. A. R. Gurung. 2011. Attachment and significant-other-concept clarity: Individual differences and situational priming. Unpublished manuscript.

Algoe, S. B., S. L. Gable, and N. C. Maisel. 2010. It's the little things: Everyday gratitude as a booster shot for romantic relationships. *Personal Relationships* 17:217–233.

Bartholomew, K., and L. M. Horowitz. 1991. Attachment styles among young adults: A test of a four-category model. *Journal of Personality and Social Psychology* 61:226–244.

Baumeister, R. F. 1998. The self. In *The handbook of social psychology*, 4th ed., edited by D. T. Gilbert, S. T. Fiske, and G. Lindzey, 680–740. New York: McGraw Hill.

Birnbaum, G. E. 2007. Attachment orientation, sexual functioning, and relationship satisfaction in a community sample of women. *Journal of Social and Personal Relationships* 24:21–35.

Birnbaum, G. E., H. T. Reis, M. Mikulincer, O. Gillath, and A. Orpaz. 2006. When sex is more than just sex: Attachment orientations, sexual experience, and relationship quality. *Journal of Personality and Social Psychology* 91:929–943.

Boag, E. M., and K. B. Carnelley. 2011. Attachment and prejudice: The mediating role of empathy. Unpublished manuscript.

Bogaert, A. F., and S. Sadava. 2002. Adult attachment and sexual behavior. *Personal Relationships* 9:191–204.

Bowlby, J. 1969. *Attachment and loss.* Vol. 1, *Attachment.* New York: Basic Books.

Bowlby, J. 1973. *Attachment and loss.* Vol. 2, *Separation: Anxiety and anger.* New York: Basic Books.

Bowlby, J. 1979. *The making and breaking of affectional bonds.* London: Tavistock.

Bowlby, J. 1980. *Attachment and loss.* Vol. 3, *Sadness and depression.* New York: Basic Books.

Brandt, A. C., and R. Vonk. 2005. Safe and sound: Stability and contingency of self-esteem as a function of attachment style. Poster presented at the 6th annual meeting of the Society for Personality and Social Psychology, New Orleans, January.

Brennan, K. A., and K. B. Carnelley. 1999. Using meaning to mend holes in the nomological net of excessive reassurance-seeking and depression. *Psychological Inquiry* 10:282–285.

Brennan, K. A., C. L. Clark, and P. R. Shaver. 1998. Self-report measurement of adult romantic attachment: An integrative overview. In *Attachment theory and close relationships*, edited by J. A. Simpson and W. S. Rholes, 46–76. New York: Guilford.

Brennan, K. A., and K. A. Morris. 1997. Attachment styles, self-esteem, and patterns of seeking feedback from romantic partners. *Personality and Social Psychology Bulletin* 23:23–31.

Butzer, B., and L. Campbell. 2008. Adult attachment, sexual satisfaction, and relationship satisfaction: A study of married couples. *Personal Relationships* 15:141–154.

Campbell, L., J. A. Simpson, J. Boldry, and D. A. Kashy. 2005. Perceptions of conflict and support in romantic relationships: The role of attachment anxiety. *Journal of Personality and Social Psychology* 88:510–531.

Carnelley, K. B., E. G. Hepper, C. Hicks, and W. Turner. 2011. Perceived parental reactions to coming out, attachment, and romantic relationship views. *Attachment and Human Development* 13:217–236.

Carnelley, K. B., S. Israel, and K. A. Brennan. 2007. The role of attachment in influencing reactions to manipulated feedback from romantic partners. *European Journal of Social Psychology* 37:968–986.

Carnelley, K. B., and R. Janoff-Bulman. 1992. Optimism about love relationships: General vs. specific lessons from one's personal experiences. *Journal of Social and Personal Relationships* 9:5–20.

Carnelley, K. B., P. R. Pietromonaco, and K. Jaffe. 1994. Depression, working models of others, and relationship functioning. *Journal of Personality and Social Psychology* 66:127–140.

Carnelley, K. B., P. R. Pietromonaco, and K. Jaffe. 1996. Attachment, caregiving, and relationship functioning in couples: Effects of self and partner. *Personal Relationships* 3:257–277.

Carnelley, K. B., and A. C. Rowe. 2007. Repeated priming of attachment security influences later views of self and relationships. *Personal Relationships* 14:307–320.

Carnelley, K. B., and A. C. Rowe. 2010. Priming a sense of security: What goes through people's minds? *Journal of Social and Personal Relationships* 27:253–261.

Carpenter, E. M., and L. A. Kirkpatrick. 1996. Attachment style and presence of a romantic partner as moderators of psychophysiological responses to a stressful laboratory situation. *Personal Relationships* 3:351–367.

Cohen, S., and T. A. Wills. 1985. Stress, social support, and the buffering hypothesis. *Psychological Bulletin* 98:310–357.

Collins, N. L., and B. C. Feeney. 2004. Working models of attachment shape perceptions of social support: Evidence from experimental and observational studies. *Journal of Personality and Social Psychology* 87:363–383.

Collins, N. L., M. B. Ford, A. C. Guichard, and L. M. Allard. 2006. Working models of attachment and attribution processes in intimate relationships. *Personality and Social Psychology Bulletin* 32:201–219.

Collins, N. L., and S. J. Read. 1990. Adult attachment, working models, and relationship quality in dating couples. *Journal of Personality and Social Psychology* 58:644–663.

Collins, N. L., and S. J. Read. 1994. Cognitive representations of attachment: The structure and function of working models. In *Advances in personal relationships: Attachment processes in adulthood,* vol. 5, edited by K. Bartholomew and D. Perlman, 53–92. London: Jessica Kingsley.

Cooper, M. L., A. W. Albino, H. K. Orcutt, and N. Williams. 2004. Attachment styles and intrapersonal adjustment: A longitudinal study from adolescence into young adulthood. In *Adult attachment: Theory, research, and clinical implications,* edited by W. S. Rholes and J. A. Simpson, 438–466. New York: Guilford Press.

Cooper, M. L., M. Pioli, A. Levitt, A. Talley, L. Micheas, and N. Collins. 2006. Attachment style, sex motives, and sexual behavior: Evidence for gender specific expressions of attachment dynamics. In *Dynamics of romantic love: Attachment, caregiving, and sex,* edited by M. Mikulincer and G. S. Goodman, 243–274. New York: Guilford.

Crocker, J., and C. T. Wolfe. 2001. Contingencies of self-worth. *Psychological Review* 10:593–623.

Davila, J., and R. J. Cobb. 2003. Predicting change in self-reported and interviewer-assessed adult attachment: Tests of the individual difference and life stress models of attachment change. *Personality and Social Psychology Bulletin* 29:859–870.

Davis, D., P. R. Shaver, and M. L. Vernon. 2004. Attachment style and subjective motivations for sex. *Personality and Social Psychology Bulletin* 30:1076–1090.

Deci, E. L., and R. M. Ryan. 1995. Human autonomy: The basis for true self-esteem. In *Efficacy, agency, and self-esteem,* edited by M. Kernis, 31–49. New York: Plenum.

DeFronzo, R., C. Panzarella, and A. C. Butler. 2001. Attachment, support seeking, and adaptive inferential feedback: Implications for psychological health. *Cognitive and Behavioral Practice* 8:48–52.

Feeney, B. C., and N. L. Collins. 2001. Predictors of caregiving in adult intimate relationships: An attachment theoretical perspective. *Journal of Personality and Social Psychology* 80:972–994.

Feeney, J. A. 1999. Issues of closeness and distance in dating relationships: Effects of sex and attachment style. *Journal of Social and Personal Relationships* 16:571–590.

Feeney, J. A. 2002. Attachment, marital interaction, and relationship satisfaction: A diary study. *Personal Relationships* 9:39–55.

Feeney, J. A. 2004. Hurt feelings in couple relationships: Towards integrative models of the negative effects of hurtful events. *Journal of Social and Personal Relationships* 21:487–508.

Feeney, J. A. 2008. Adult romantic attachment: Developments in the study of couple relationships. In *Adult attachment: Theory, research, and clinical applications*, 2nd ed., edited by J. Cassidy and P. R. Shaver, 456–481. London: Guilford.

Feeney, J. A., and P. Noller. 1991. Attachment style and verbal descriptions of romantic partners. *Journal of Social and Personal Relationships* 8:187–215.

Feeney, J. A., C. Peterson, C. Gallois, and D. J. Terry. 2000. Attachment style as a predictor of sexual attitudes and behavior in late adolescence. *Psychology and Health* 14:1105–1122.

Fishtein, J., P. R. Pietromonaco, and L. Feldman Barrett. 1999. The contribution of attachment style and relationship conflict to the complexity of relationship knowledge. *Social Cognition* 17:228–244.

Foster, J. D., M. H. Kernis, and B. M. Goldman. 2007. Linking adult attachment to self-esteem stability. *Self and Identity* 6:64–73.

Fraley, R. C. 2002. Attachment stability from infancy to adulthood: Meta-analysis and dynamic modeling of developmental mechanisms. *Personality and Social Psychology Review* 6:123–151.

Fraley, R. C. n.d. Attachment style. http://www.web-research-design.net/cgi-bin/crq/crq.pl/. Accessed June 6, 2011.

Fraley, R. C., and P. R. Shaver. 1998. Airport separations: A naturalistic study of adult attachment dynamics in separating couples. *Journal of Personality and Social Psychology* 75:1198–1212.

Fraley, R. C., and N. G. Waller. 1998. Adult attachment patterns: A test of the typological model. In *Attachment theory and close relationships*, edited by J. A. Simpson and W. S. Rholes, 77–114. New York: Guilford.

Frei, J. R., and P. R. Shaver. 2002. Respect in close relationships: Prototype definition, self-report assessment, and initial correlates. *Personal Relationships* 9:121–139.

Gillath, O., E. Selcuk, and P. R. Shaver. 2008. Moving towards a secure attachment style: Can repeated security priming help? *Social and Personality Psychology Compass* 2:1–15.

Graham, S. M., and M. S. Clark. 2006. Self-esteem and organization of valenced information about others: The "Jekyll and Hyde"-ing of relationship partners. *Journal of Personality and Social Psychology* 90:652–665.

Griffin, D. W., and K. Bartholomew. 1994. Models of the self and other: Fundamental dimensions underlying measures of adult attachment. *Journal of Personality and Social Psychology* 67:430–445.

Hart, J. J., P. R. Shaver, and J. L. Goldenberg. 2005. Attachment, self-esteem, worldviews, and terror management: Evidence for a tripartite security system. *Journal of Personality and Social Psychology* 88:999–1013.

Hazan, C., and P. R. Shaver. 1987. Romantic love conceptualized as an attachment process. *Journal of Personality and Social Psychology* 52:511–524.

Hepper, E. G., and K. B. Carnelley. 2008. Adult attachment and daily feedback: Lability of self-esteem and relationship evaluations. Paper presented at International Association of Relationship Research Conference, Providence, RI, July.

Hepper, E. G., and K. B. Carnelley. 2010. Adult attachment and feedback-seeking patterns in relationships and work. *European Journal of Social Psychology* 40:448–464.

Hepper, E. G., and K. B. Carnelley. In press. The self-esteem roller coaster: Adult attachment moderates the impact of daily feedback. *Personal Relationships*.

Hepper, E. G., H. A. Hogarth, and K. B. Carnelley. 2006. Attachment orientation as a moderator of the association between sexual behavior and sexual self-views. Poster presented at International Association for Relationship Research conference, Crete, July.

Impett, E. A., and L. A. Peplau. 2002. Why some women consent to unwanted sex with a dating partner: Insights from attachment theory. *Psychology of Women Quarterly* 26:360–370.

Joiner, T. E., G. I. Metalsky, J. Katz, and S. R. H. Beach. 1999. Depression and excessive reassurance seeking. *Psychological Inquiry* 10:269–278.

Joireman, J. A., T. L. Needham, and A. L. Cummings. 2002. Relationships between dimensions of attachment and empathy. *North American Journal of Psychology* 4:63–80.

Kane, H. S., L. M. Jaremka, A. C. Guichard, M. B. Ford, N. L. Collins, and B. C. Feeney. 2007. Feeling supported and feeling satisfied: How one partner's attachment style predicts the other partner's relationship experiences. *Journal of Social and Personal Relationships* 24:535–555.

Kernis, M. H., and B. M. Goldman. 2003. Stability and variability in self-concept and self-esteem. In *Handbook of self and identity*, edited by M. R. Leary and J. P. Tangney, 106–127. New York: Guilford.

Kershaw, T. S., S. Milan, C. Westdahl, J. B. Lewis, S. S. Rising, R. Fletcher, and J. R. Ickovics. 2007. Avoidance, anxiety, and sex: The influence of romantic attachment on HIV-risk among pregnant women. *AIDS and Behavior* 11:299–311.

Kim, Y. 2005. Emotional and cognitive consequences of adult attachment: The mediating effect of the self. *Personality and Individual Differences* 39:913–923.

Kirkpatrick, L. A., and C. Hazan. 1994. Attachment styles and close relationships: A four-year prospective study. *Personal Relationships* 1:123–142.

Knee, C. R., A. Canevello, A. L. Bush, and A. Cook. 2008. Relationship-contingent self-esteem and the ups and downs of romantic relationships. *Journal of Personality and Social Psychology* 95:608–627.

Kumashiro, M., and C. Sedikides. 2005. Taking on board liability-focused information: Close positive relationships as a self-bolstering resource. *Psychological Science* 16:732–739.

Kunce, L. J., and P. R. Shaver. 1994. An attachment-theoretical approach to caregiving in romantic relationships. In *Advances in personal relationships: Attachment processes in adulthood*, vol. 5, edited by K. Bartholomew and D. Perlman, 205–237. London: Jessica Kingsley.

Lambert, N. M., M. S. Clark, J. Durtschi, F. D. Fincham, and S. M. Graham. 2010. Benefits of expressing gratitude: Expressing gratitude to a partner changes one's view of the relationship. *Psychological Science* 21:574–580.

Leary, M. R., E. S. Tambor, S. K. Terdal, and D. L. Downs. 1995. Self-esteem as an interpersonal monitor: The sociometer hypothesis. *Journal of Personality and Social Psychology* 68:518–530.

Leary, M. R., and J. Tangney. 2003. *Handbook of self and identity.* New York: Guilford.

Levy, K. N., S. J. Blatt, and P. R. Shaver. 1998. Attachment styles and parental representations. *Journal of Personality and Social Psychology* 74:407–419.

Levy, M. B., and K. E. Davis. 1988. Love styles and attachment styles compared: Their relations to each other and to various relationship characteristics. *Journal of Social and Personal Relationships* 5:439–471.

Luke, M. A., G. R. Maio, and K. B. Carnelley. 2004. Attachment models of the self and others: Relations with self-esteem, humanity-esteem, and parental treatment. *Personal Relationships* 11:281–303.

Main, M., N. Kaplan, and J. Cassidy. 1985. Security in infancy, childhood, and adulthood: A move to the level of representation. *Monographs of the Society for Research in Child Development* 50:66–104.

Marigold, D. C., J. G. Holmes, and R. Ross. 2007. More than words: Reframing compliments from romantic partners fosters security in low self-esteem individuals. *Journal of Personality and Social Psychology* 92:232–248.

Mikulincer, M. 1995. Attachment style and the mental representation of the self. *Journal of Personality and Social Psychology* 69:1203–1215.

Mikulincer, M. 1998. Adult attachment style and affect regulation: Strategic variations in self-appraisals. *Journal of Personality and Social Psychology* 75:420–435.

Mikulincer, M., V. Florian, P. A. Cowan, and C. P. Cowan. 2002. Attachment security in couple relationships: A systemic model and its implications for family dynamics. *Family Process* 41:405–434.

Mikulincer, M., G. Hirschberger, O. Nachmias, and O. Gillath. 2001. The affective component of the secure base schema: Affective priming with representations of attachment security. *Journal of Personality and Social Psychology* 81:305–321.

Mikulincer, M., and N. Horesh. 1999. Adult attachment style and the perception of others: The role of projective mechanisms. *Journal of Personality and Social Psychology* 76:1022–1034.

Mikulincer, M., I. Orbach, and D. Iavnieli. 1998. Adult attachment style and affect regulation: Strategic variations in subjective self-other similarity. *Journal of Personality and Social Psychology* 75:436–448.

Mikulincer, M., and P. R. Shaver. 2004. Security-based self-representations in adulthood: Contents and processes. In *Adult attachment: Theory, research, and clinical implications,* edited by W. S. Rholes and J. A. Simpson, 159–195. New York: Guilford Press.

Mikulincer, M., and P. R. Shaver. 2007. *Attachment in adulthood: Structure, dynamics, and change.* New York: Guilford.

Mikulincer, M., P. R. Shaver, N. Bar-On, and T. Ein-Dor. 2010. The pushes and pulls of close relationships: Attachment insecurities and relational ambivalence. *Journal of Personality and Social Psychology* 98:450–468.

Mikulincer, M., P. R. Shaver, and D. Pereg. 2003. Attachment theory and affect regulation: The dynamics, development, and cognitive consequences of attachment-related strategies. *Motivation and Emotion* 27:77–102.

Mikulincer, M., P. R. Shaver, and K. Slav. 2006. Attachment, mental representations of others, and gratitude and forgiveness in romantic relationships. In *Dynamics of romantic love: Attachment, caregiving, and sex*, edited by M. Mikulincer and G. S. Goodman, 190–215. New York: Guilford.

Morgan, H. J., and P. R. Shaver. 1999. Attachment processes and commitment to romantic relationships. In *Handbook of interpersonal commitment and relationship stability*, edited by J. M. Adams and W. H. Jones, 109–124. New York: Plenum.

Murray, S. L. 1999. The quest for conviction: Motivated cognition in romantic relationships. *Psychological Inquiry* 10:23–34.

Murray, S. L., J. G. Holmes, and D. W. Griffin. 1996. The benefits of positive illusions: Idealization and the construction of satisfaction in close relationships. *Journal of Personality and Social Psychology* 70:79–98.

Murray, S. L., J. G. Holmes, and D. W. Griffin. 2000. Self-esteem and the quest for felt security: How perceived regard regulates attachment processes. *Journal of Personality and Social Psychology* 78:478–498.

Parish, M., and M. N. Eagle. 2003. Attachment to the therapist. *Psychoanalytic Psychology* 20:271–286.

Park, L. E., J. Crocker, and K. D. Mickelson. 2004. Attachment styles and contingencies of self-worth. *Personality and Social Psychology Bulletin* 30:1243–1254.

Pietromonaco, P. R., and L. Feldman Barrett. 1997. Working models of attachment and daily social interactions. *Journal of Personality and Social Psychology* 73:1409–1423.

Pietromonaco, P. R., and L. Feldman Barrett. 2006. What can you do for me? Attachment style and motives underlying esteem for partners. *Journal of Research in Personality* 40:313–338.

Rholes, W. S., J. A. Simpson, S. Tran, A. M. Martin, and M. Friedman. 2007. Attachment and information seeking in romantic relationships. *Personality and Social Psychology Bulletin* 33:422–438.

Ross, L. R., and B. Spinner. 2001. General and specific attachment representations in adulthood: Is there a relationship? *Journal of Social and Personal Relationships* 18:747–766.

Rowe, A., and K. B. Carnelley. 2003. Attachment style differences in the processing of attachment-relevant information: Primed-style effects on recall, interpersonal expectations, and affect. *Personal Relationships* 10:59–75.

Rowe, A., and K. B. Carnelley. 2005. Preliminary support for the use of a hierarchical mapping technique to examine attachment networks. *Personal Relationships* 12:499–519.

Schachner, D. A., and P. R. Shaver. 2004. Attachment dimensions and sexual motives. *Personal Relationships* 11:179–195.

Schmitt, D. P., and J. Allik. 2005. Simultaneous administration of the Rosenberg Self-Esteem Scale in 53 nations: Exploring the universal and culture-specific features of global self-esteem. *Journal of Personality and Social Psychology* 89:623–642.

Shaver, P. R., and M. Mikulincer. 2002. Attachment-related psychodynamics. *Attachment and Human Development* 4:133–161.

Shaver, P. R., D. A. Schachner, and M. Mikulincer. 2005. Attachment style, excessive reassurance seeking, relationship processes, and depression. *Personality and Social Psychology Bulletin* 31:343–359.

Sherman, D. K., and G. L. Cohen. 2006. The psychology of self-defense: Self-affirmation theory. In *Advances in Experimental Social Psychology*. Vol. 38. San Diego: Academic Press.

Simpson, J. A., W. S. Rholes, and J. S. Nelligan. 1992. Support seeking and support giving within couples in an anxiety-provoking situation: The role of attachment styles. *Journal of Personality and Social Psychology* 62:434–446.

Simpson, J. A., W. S. Rholes, and D. Phillips. 1996. Conflict in close relationships: An attachment perspective. *Journal of Personality and Social Psychology* 71:899–914.

Simpson, J. A., H. A. Winterheld, W. S. Rholes, and M. M. Oriña. 2007. Working models of attachment and reactions to different forms of caregiving from romantic partners. *Journal of Personality and Social Psychology* 93:466–477.

Sroufe, L. A., and E. Waters. 1977. Attachment as an organizational construct. *Child Development* 48:1184–1199.

Steiner-Pappalardo, N. L., and R. A. R. Gurung. 2002. The femininity effect: Relationship quality, sex, gender, and significant-other concepts. *Personal Relationships* 9:313–325.

Stephan, C. W., and G. F. Bachman. 1999. What's sex got to do with it? Attachment, love schemas, and sexuality. *Personal Relationships* 6:111–123.

Waters, E., S. Merrick, D. Treboux, J. Crowell, and L. Albersheim. 2000. Attachment security in infancy and early adulthood: A twenty-year longitudinal study. *Child Development* 71:684–689.

Wei, M., B. Mallinckrodt, L. M. Larson, and R. A. Zakalik. 2005. Adult attachment, depressive symptoms, and validation from self versus others. *Journal of Counseling Psychology* 52:368–377.

Wethington, E., and R. C. Kessler. 1986. Perceived support, received support, and adjustment to stressful life events. *Journal of Health and Social Behavior* 27:78–89.

Wood, A. M., J. J. Froh, and A. W. A. Geraghty. 2010. Gratitude and well-being: A review and theoretical integration. *Clinical Psychology Review* 30:890–905.

Zayas, V., and Y. Shoda. 2005. Do automatic reactions elicited by thoughts of romantic partner, mother, and self relate to adult romantic attachment? *Personality and Social Psychology Bulletin* 31:1011–1025.

Zeifman, D., and C. Hazan. 2008. Pair bonds as attachments: Re-evaluating the evidence. In *Adult attachment: Theory, research, and clinical applications*, 2nd ed., edited by J. Cassidy and P. R. Shaver, 436–455. London: Guilford.

Zuroff, D. C., and D. K. Fitzpatrick. 1995. Depressive personality styles: Implications for adult attachment. *Personality and Individual Differences* 18:253–365.

Chapter 12

Crossing the Line Online:
Racial Preference of Internet Daters

Kathryn A. Sweeney and Anne L. Borden

Popular media has highlighted an increase in interracial unions, implying that people in the United States are embracing greater racial unity (Ataiyero and Rubin 2007; Lobe 2005; Rodriguez 2004). Although national polls find that young people are willing to date outside of their race (Gallagher 2002; Ludwig 2004), this chapter calls into question reports based on survey data to examine the role of technology in relationship formation. It explores the use of Internet dating sites as rich sources for data and examines the willingness of Internet daters to date across racial lines.

Although survey data indicate that young people express a willingness to date outside of their race (Gallagher 2002), both structural and ideological constraints remain and limit preference—and most partnerships—to those within racial groups. These continued impediments to dating are evident from low rates of interracial marriage (U.S. Census Bureau 2002). Interracial unions have increased since the 1967 Supreme Court decision lifting all legal bans on interracial marriages (Aldridge 1973; Kalmijn 1993; Monahan 1976), yet marriage between interracial partners remains a small percentage of marriages in the United States. The total number of recorded interracial marriages increased from just over 1 percent of all married couples in 1980 but remains only about 3 percent of all marriages in 2002 (U.S. Census Bureau 2002). Interracial relationships provide one barometer of race relations in the United States (Aldridge 1978; Foeman and Nance 1999). Singles can now meet partners over the Internet and purposefully choose the characteristics of potential dates. Internet dating is one way in which changes in technology and greater access to the Internet influence family formation. This chapter advances research methods beyond opinion survey research (that must rely on hypothetical situations) to use an Internet dating site to examine preferences of those involved in an actual search for a partner.

OPPORTUNITIES AND CONSTRAINTS IN PARTNER SELECTION

Two prominent complementary arguments explain the continued low rates of interracial relationships: (1) contact or structure and (2) the role of dominant culture and common ideas about race (i.e., racial ideology). Theories of contact posit that the pool of people one meets and comes into contact with is limited by physical boundaries that determine whom someone dates and eventually marries (Blau, Blum, and Schwartz 1982; Sigelman et al. 1996; South and Messner 1986). Racial ideology, on the other hand, focuses on the role of dominant conceptions about race and relationships and the influence of those in one's inner social circle in determining partnerships (Billingsley 1988; Ferber 1998; Marx 1978 [1932]). Together, these theories help to explain how singles choose partners.

STRUCTURAL CONSTRAINTS AND PARTNER SELECTION

Lack of contact due to continued racial residential segregation, occupational segregation, and same-race networks limits whom young men and women consider as potential partners (Blau, Blum, and Schwartz 1982; Collins 2004; South and Messner 1986). If the opportunities are not available for interaction across race lines, then the likelihood of someone dating across them is also limited. Theories of contact are closely aligned with theories of propinquity (for a discussion, see Fujino 1997). Propinquity relies on ratios of one race to another within a given geographical area to explain marriage outside of one's racial group. If there are few people of one's racial/ethnic group in a given area, singles are more likely to date outside of their racial group. The prevalent use of the Internet and Internet dating makes propinquity in one's immediate geographical area and contact in neighborhoods, churches, and schools less relevant by expanding social networks to a greater number of people extending to a larger metropolitan area. Having a larger network increases opportunities for contact outside of one's group (Granovetter 1995), which may also increase opportunities to meet a partner (Kalmijn 1993) and possibly change attitudes and consideration as to who is a potential partner.

Past research indicates that contact with other racial/ethnic groups may lead to an increase in favorable attitudes toward other groups and a greater likelihood of future interactions (Moore 2002). This is one indication of how structure and ideology work together and are difficult to separate in analysis. It is important to note that past research found that theories of propinquity predict greater racial out-marriage among black men and women than is actually evident (Farley 1999), meaning contact and group size alone do not predict interracial unions.

IDEOLOGICAL CONSTRAINTS IN PARTNER CHOICE

It is not only whom singles have the opportunity to meet but also what singles have been taught to think about different groups and overarching societal ideas about race that influence partner preferences. People tend to choose partners of similar race, social class, and education levels (Kalmijn 1991). For race, same-race marriage is the norm dictated by dominant culture and practice. "Throughout United States history, the fear of Black political and economic equality [in particular] has been rearticulated as the fear of interracial sexuality and guarded against with force" (Ferber 1998, 42), and thus dominant culture and social norms shape ability and willingness of singles to date across race lines (Billingsley 1988; Marx 1978 [1932]).

Racial ideology is "the racially based framework used by actors to explain and justify (dominant race) or challenge (subordinate race or races) the racial status quo" (Bonilla-Silva 2003, 9). The framework of the dominant group becomes the overarching framework of society, even as subordinate groups may also hold oppositional views and resist the dominant framework (Bonilla-Silva 2003; Hooks 1984). Social norms and racial ideology are linked to the individuals in one's inner social circle, which in turn affects whom someone is willing to date. Influence and pressure from family and friends affect who is considered "dating material," including if it is considered socially appropriate to date outside of one's race (Hooks 1984; Kennedy 2003; Rosenblatt, Karis, and Powell 1995).

Ideas about race and dating norms and history demonstrate how race is more than a way to categorize identity. Dating norms are not only racialized but also influenced by gender within race. For example, black women's history of sexual exploitation by white men contributes to ideologies today. According to Collins (2004), individual black women who choose white men may be reminders of this oppression. In addition, black men have historically been demonized as sexually aggressive, which has resulted in physical harm through beating and lynching for sexual contact, or suspicion thereof, with white women. This legacy affects the racial ideology and contemporary decisions of whom men and women of different race and ethnicities marry (Kennedy 2003). By making interracial unions taboo, the dominant group maintains power and authority through isolation and exclusion, evident in the long history of legal restriction and social sanctions against interracial marriage (Du Bois 2000 [1935]; Ferber 1998; Hodes 1997, 1999; Lewis, Yancey, and Bletzer 1997).

Dominant ideas about race, pressure from family and friends, social norms, legal sanctions, and the extensive history of oppressive relationships between white people and black people influence decisions about whom to date and marry (Rosenblatt, Karis, and Powell 1995). Within the United States, black and white people have been viewed as being at opposite ends of the racial hierarchy (Bonilla-Silva 2002; Collins 2004; Omi and Winant 1994) and restricted from "mixing," which has led to individuals using racial profiling in partner selection. Racial profiling occurs when people state they want to date only someone of certain races because they prefer characteristics, values, and culture, but these decisions are based on larger assumptions and racial stereotypes (Kennedy 2003). Although both individual and societal racism and discrimination motivate many of these decisions, most daters do not recognize their own unconscious prejudice or how dominant ideas about race influence their choices (Bonilla-Silva 2003; Kennedy 2003).

OVERLAPPING AND INTERSECTION OF STRUCTURAL AND IDEOLOGICAL CONSTRAINTS

Partner selection is further complicated by other classifications, such as class, education, and religion. Position and status based on dominant culture and norms influence how people interact even when they are required to interact due to close proximity. For example, many black women have contact with white men who within the job hierarchy are their managers and superiors (Tomaskovic-Devey 1993). Although they may have sustained contact, their role in the institution is dictated by dominant culture as well as their racial ideology; defined roles may have an effect on the types of interaction and boundaries that are maintained. Interaction is limited by one's own status in relation to others as well as contact through work, school, and neighborhood, common family networks, and voluntary associations (Kalmijn and Flap 2001).

People tend to marry individuals with traits similar to their own (Kalmijn 1991), yet whereas marriage across socioeconomic status and religion has become more common, marriage across race lines remains rare (particularly for black and white men and women). Those who do marry across racial lines tend to have higher formal education and income levels than those in same-race marriages and tend to marry spouses of a similar economic status (Heaton and Albrecht 1996; Lewis, Yancey, and Bletzer 1997). In addition, rates of interracial marriage differ by gender, with about 73 percent of black/white non-Hispanic/Latino marriages between a black male and white female and 27 percent between a white male and black female (U.S. Census Bureau 2000).

Recent research points to propinquity as explaining cross-racial relationships rather than the once-prevalent explanation of status exchange (i.e., one partner trades his or her racial status for the attractiveness or financial status of the partner) (Merton 2000 [1941]; Yancey and Yancey 1998). In this chapter, the continued influence of dominant norms regarding interracial unions is examined as racial preferences for a dating partner. This allows the specific exploration of ideas about race in a context in which networks of contact are expanded.

DATING AND THE INTERNET

The Internet provides new and unique opportunities for daters to extend contact across immediate geographical boundaries and expand typical social networks. Through Internet dating, those seeking a partner are no longer limited to people in their neighborhood, workplace, or social circles. Internet dating provides an ideal opportunity for researchers because it allows observation of what happens when structural constraints are reduced and singles are given an opportunity to choose to date someone of any race. In other words, it allows the authors to examine the effects of dominant ideas about race and social norms regarding dating by eliminating some of the typical constraints of contact.

The dramatic growth of Internet culture (e.g., reliance on e-mail and Internet search engines for daily activities) over the past ten years has made Internet personals a regular part of life for many. Those who use Internet dating sites are able to post "profiles" containing information about themselves (e.g., photos, occupations, interests). Singles search the profiles of others and contact potential mates. Once considered taboo, Internet dating has now become a commonplace way to connect with potential partners (Harmon 2003; Hollander 2004; Orr 2004).

Estimates indicate that Match.com, a popular Internet dating website, has approximately fifty million profiles online (Williams 2004). A *New York Times* article, "Online Dating Sheds Its Stigma as Losers.com," reports that more than forty-five million Americans visited online dating sites during June 2003 (Harmon 2003), and Match.com boasts receiving more than two hundred e-mails a month notifying them of engagements and marriages resulting from their website (Collier 2005). According to the Pew Internet and American Life Project, thirty million Americans claim to know someone who is either in a long-term relationship or a marriage that began online (Madden and Lenhart 2006).

Whereas previous research relied on the use of personal advertisements in newspapers and magazines to examine choices in dating partners (Yancey and Yancey 1998), this analysis adds a new data source, that of Internet dating, which further widens networks and reduces structural barriers that typically prevent contact (e.g., segregated neighborhoods). Internet personals are likely used more often than newspaper personals ever were (Egan 2003), making them a relevant record of partner selection. The few studies that have been done using Internet dating personals and profiles as a source of data have lacked comparison across racial/ethnic groups (Wilson, McIntosh, and Insana 2007) and not dealt with gender within racial groups (Phua and Kaufman 2003). This chapter uses Internet dating profiles and multinomial logistic regression to examine willingness to date across racial lines in the context of expanded contact. Here we address the following overarching question: Are young black and white men and women willing to date a person of another race when limitations of contact and typical social networks are reduced through the use of Internet dating? Variation by gender within race is examined.

RESEARCH DESIGN AND METHODOLOGY

Data Source

Data were gathered from a widely known general public Internet dating site whose name is kept anonymous as one measure of ensuring confidentiality. It is free to browse the site, search for potential dating partners, and create a profile. Daters pay a monthly fee of approximately twenty dollars for services such as the opportunity to contact other daters by instant message or e-mail. After a dater creates an Internet dating profile, it becomes public information available on the website. Other daters search and browse the website looking for potential "matches." Daters are not matched by a computer system. Rather, they choose others to contact through an e-mail system internal to the site. They send one another e-mails with messages that indicate they liked what they saw in a profile and would like to get to know a person better.

The sample was drawn from a general dating site rather than a site geared toward specific groups because one of our goals was to explore the usefulness of online dating sites as a means to examine general partner preferences. In addition, we are not interested in those who are specifically looking for partners of another race per se but a look at what "mainstream" daters prefer. Our research questions are best answered by a large public access site geared to all groups and used by the "average" Internet dater. Unlike specialty sites, the general data site has a large pool of participants, is easy to access, is relatively inexpensive, is well known among Internet users, and provides a sample closer to the general population than would a specialty dating site.

Collecting data from an Internet dating site provides an unobtrusive way to observe the actual preferences of daters. Although it is possible for someone to answer a survey question regarding whether he or she would be willing to date someone of any race in the affirmative, that answer would not have any "real-world" consequences. However, if an Internet dater selects "any race," the single will face consequences in the form of e-mails from other singles of any race. Using the Internet dating site provides data on actual preferences of daters, a measure with potentially more validity than survey opinion data.

Sample

The sample includes men and women between the ages of twenty-one and thirty years seeking a heterosexual partner. This age range reflects the typical age of people seeking marriage partners, with the median age of first marriage for U.S. women being 25.5 (24.9 in Georgia) and for U.S. men being 27.0 (26.4 in Georgia) (U.S. Census Bureau 2005a, 2005b). The sample is limited to metropolitan Atlanta, Georgia, to control for regional variations in racial composition and for current and past race relations related to geographical history. The greater Atlanta area, as a southern metropolis growing from an increase in migrants from across the country and the world and as the capital of a state that was one of the last to allow interracial marriage, provides an interesting site for the study (Aldridge 1973).

There were at least one thousand men seeking women and at least one thousand women seeking men in this age range in the Atlanta metropolitan area who were seeking partners at the time the data for this study were collected. Because the dating site only shows one thousand potential matches at a time and does not publish data on users, there is no way to determine exactly how many registered daters in the age range are on the site. An exploratory sample of four hundred daters from the Atlanta area was constructed by doing searches on the site for a man seeking a woman specifying both age range (twenty-one to thirty years) and geographical area (metropolitan Atlanta). The search was repeated with the same age and geographical constraints for a woman seeking a man. The site lists the most recent advertisements first. To create a random sample, therefore, the time of day and day of the week when the data were entered were varied to avoid biasing the sample toward those who write their advertisement during specific time periods, such as late at night or on weekends. In addition, collection did not always start on the first page of advertisements. Data were entered at two different points in time to further randomize the sample: June to August 2004 and February to May 2005. Each dater was assigned a number, and their demographic information and selections for partner preferences were recorded in a spreadsheet. To protect confidentiality, data that would identify any particular individual were avoided (e.g., screen names and photographs). Data throughout the "Results" section (below) are presented only in aggregate form. The sample was restricted to black and white men and women and excludes other racial/ethnic groups (1) because of the exploratory sample limiting the size of other groups in the sample, and (2) due to the perception that black and white people occupy different ends of the racial composition in the United States (Bonilla-Silva 2002).

Once duplicate entries and entries of daters who identify with a race/ethnicity other than black and white were deleted, a sample of 330 daters remained (table 1). The sample includes a total of 165 men seeking women and 165 women seeking men. One hundred fifty-seven of the total sample are black and 173 are white. According to the American Community Survey (2005), the population of metro Atlanta is 30 percent black and 59 percent white. Although our sample is 47.5 percent black and 52.5 percent white, the more even ratio may be because the sample was limited to young people. Atlanta has a large population of black young adults because of the presence of over forty colleges and universities and because many young people in the South move from rural areas to Atlanta for employment. Thirty-six percent of men living in the Atlanta metropolitan area between the ages of twenty and twenty-nine are black compared with 51 percent who are white. Thirty-one percent of women in this age group are black and 52 percent are white (American Community Survey 2005).

Table 1
Description of sample of individuals seeking dating partners.

	Black women (N = 83)	Black men (N = 74)	White women (N = 82)	White men (N = 91)	Total sample (N = 330)
Age (mean)	25.9	27.4	25.5	26.3	26.3
Education					
High school	7%	6%	11%	3%	7%
Some college	37%	45%	30%	33%	36%
College	40%	34%	43%	42%	40%
Postgraduate	10%	12%	12%	21%	14%
Employed full time	54%	77%	82%	91%	70%
Religious (attends services once or more per week)	65%	64%	71%	51%	62%
Political (identifies as conservative or liberal)	18%	26%	28%	39%	28%

Note: A breakdown of income is not included because 64% of black women, 53% of black men, 54% of white women, and 44% of white men did not answer the question about income.

Variables

There are two primary components of an Internet dating profile: the personal profile and the preferences section. Independent variables stem from the personal profile, where the Internet dater answers questions about him- or herself, including income, education, and race/ethnicity. The dependent variable of racial preference stems from the preferences section, where daters indicate their preferences in a dating partner.

Independent Variables: The Personal Profile

The independent variables for this study include personal characteristics such as demographics and ideology measures. In creating the personal profile, the dater chooses from nine closed-ended options regarding their own race/ethnicity: black, white, Hispanic, Native American, East Indian, Pacific Islander, Middle Eastern, other, and interracial. For each dater, data were recorded on gender, age, race/ethnicity, education, employment status, income, religion, religiosity, and political views. The variable for respondents' race was recoded as a dichotomous variable, with 0 = black and 1 = white. The same is true of gender, with 0 = male and 1 = female.

Those filling out a profile were asked for their education level: some high school, high school graduate, some college, college graduate, or postgraduate. The variable for education level was recoded where a value of 0 = less than high school, high school, or some college and 1 = college educated or greater. Daters also indicated if they worked full time, part time, were a homemaker, retired, self-employed, a student, unemployed, or worked at home. The measure of employment used in the model indicates 0 =unemployed or employed part time and 1 = employed full time or in school. Measures of ideology include religiosity and strength of political views. Daters indicated if they attended religious services more than once a week, weekly, monthly, only on holidays, rarely, or never. The variable for religiousness used in the model has a value of 0 if the person does not attend services regularly and 1 if he or she reports attending religious services once or more per week.

Finally, a measure of political ideology is used. Respondents indicated in their profile if they were very conservative, conservative, middle of the road, liberal, very liberal, or not political. Because of limitations in sample size, the distinction between those who were liberal and those who were conservative among the politically minded was not obtainable. The measure used compares those who are middle of the road and not politically minded (politically minded = 0) with those who identify as politically minded whether conservative or liberal (politically minded = 1). Because of limitations in response to questions about income, income was not included as a variable in the model. However, the inclusion of employment status and education provides some basic indication of socioeconomic status level.

Dependent Variable and Model

Daters indicate their racial preferences in a potential partner from a list with the following options: black = African American, white = Caucasian, Hispanic − Latino, Asian, East Indian, Middle Eastern, Native American, Pacific Islander, other, interracial, and any race. The Internet dating site allows daters to select multiple races from the preferences list. Some daters only choose one race, some choose to select three or four races, and some choose "any race" as an option. This study examines willingness to date someone of another race, specifically the willingness of a white man or woman to date a black woman or man and of a black man or woman to date a white woman or man. Multinomial logistic regression (using SPSS) extends the principles of regression by allowing a multiple-category, noncontinuous dependent variable for the examination of various interaction effects and by providing the probability that an event will occur (Hamilton 1992). The use of logistic regression allows for determination of the likelihood that a white person preferred to date a white or a black person and determination of the likelihood that a black person preferred to date a white or a black person.

Multinomial logistic regression allows for three categories of the noncontinuous dependent variable measuring willingness to date a person of a certain race: (1) choosing black as one of the options for a potential partner, (2) choosing white as one of the partner selection options, and (3) choosing the option of "any race" or checking off options for both black and white indicating willingness to date someone of either race. The model examines the effects of characteristics of the dater—including race (0 = black, 1 = white), gender (0 = male, 1 = female), education level (0 = less than high school, high school, or some college; 1 = college or more), employment (0 = unemployed or employed part time, 1 = employed full time or in school), being religious (0 = does not attend services regularly, 1 = attends religious services once or more per week), and being politically minded (0 = not political or middle of the road, 1 = identifies as conservative or liberal)—on willingness to date a black person, white person, or someone of any race. The logit equivalent R2 for this model (Nagelkerke) equals 0.491, which means that 49 percent of the variance of the dependent variable is explained by the factors included in this model.

Limitations and Concerns

One limitation with the data is that the dating site did not provide an option regarding the type of relationship (e.g., "casual dating" or "serious relationship") which the dater is seeking. This provides a limitation in that the researchers cannot be sure that study participants are seeking a marriage partner. Nonetheless, there are many other dating sites that allow specifically for daters to select that they are interested in very casual relationships or "play." The assumption here is that daters who are not serious in their search for a long-term partner may gravitate toward other dating sites.

There is some concern in Internet research that online daters may not be entirely truthful because they are not in a face-to-face situation. Cornwell and Lundgren (2001) found that in chat rooms there is often dishonesty or misrepresentation. However, others found that representation in Internet dating is likely to be honest and accurate because, unlike those in chat rooms, Internet daters anticipate that the online interaction will eventually result in face-to-face contact (Hardey 2002). Online singles seeking intimate relationships use their Internet identity as a foundation for building trust and establishing real-world relationships rather than constructing false or fantasy selves (Hardey 2002). Indeed, the intention of online dating is real-life interaction, dating, and possible marriage (Hardey 2002). Internet daters, like face-to-face daters, may choose to emphasize or deemphasize certain qualities to make themselves more appealing. However, just like all other forms of social research, this chapter makes the necessary assumption of honest representation from subjects. Internet sources do not differ from surveys or interviews in this way, and therefore the validity is not affected. In fact, one strength of Internet research is its unobtrusive nature that avoids response bias. Another limitation to this study is that these exploratory findings cannot be generalized to all daters. The sample is skewed toward people of higher socioeconomic status, which is a function of those who have regular access to the Internet and those who view Internet dating as a viable action. Most of the men and women in the sample have education levels of some college or a college degree, with similar rates of people in each category by race and gender. Given that there are higher rates of interracial marriage among people with higher socioeconomic status (Heaton and Albrecht 1996), if anything, the findings should show increased willingness to cross racial boundaries.

RESULTS

Ideological Dating Hierarchies: Descriptive Statistics

Twenty-two percent of black singles and 31 percent of white singles chose the particular characteristic preference of "any race" for their potential partners. Although these findings indicate a large percent of respondents choosing the category of any race for their potential partner, most singles specified what races they seek in a partner. According to frequencies alone, more black singles chose white as a potential match than white singles chose black for their potential partner. This data indicates a hierarchy of racial groups considered appropriate for dating. Simple frequencies provide data on each race that daters chose as a possibility for a potential partner. It illustrates that both white and black daters first and foremost chose to date someone of the same race. Most black men and women (71.3%) prefer to date someone black, 32.5 percent Hispanic/Latino, 17 percent white, 14.6 percent Native American, 12.7 percent Pacific Islander, 10.8 percent Asian, 9.6 percent Middle Eastern, and 3.8 percent East Indian. Thirteen percent of black daters chose "other," 8.9 percent chose the category of "interracial," and 24.2 percent stated "any race" was fine. Most white men and women (66.5%) chose white for a potential match, 43.9 percent Hispanic/Latino, 18.5 percent Native American, 18 percent Asian, 14.5 percent Pacific Islander, 9.2 percent Middle Eastern, 5.2 percent East Indian, and only 2.9 percent black. Nearly 10 percent of white daters chose "other," 0.6 percent preferred interracial, and 31 percent stated they would date someone of any race.

The racial hierarchy evident from these frequencies occurred for both black and white singles but was particularly present in the preferences of white singles. Fewer than 3 percent of whites chose black as a potential dating match, but 18 percent would date someone who is Asian and nearly half of the white daters in our sample checked off the box indicating Latino/a as an option.

Strong Effect of Race on Willingness to Partner Across the Color Line

The racial/ethnic hierarchy that emerged from examination of simple descriptive statistics places black and white people at opposite ends of the preference spectrum for white daters but less so for black daters. Although the frequencies noted above refer to respondents choosing each racial category for a potential match, the following indicates frequencies when respondents chose white for a potential match but did not include black on their list of options or when a

Table 2
Logistic regression output for model predicting willingness to date certain races.

	Log odds B (SE)	Exp (B)
Willingness to date a white person compared to willingness to date a black person		
Race (0 = black, 1 = white)	4.720[b]	112.209
	(0.810)	
Gender (0 = male, 1 = female)	−0.097	0.907
	(0.479)	
Race[a] dater gender	0.637	1.891
	(1.332)	
Education (1 = college or more)	−0.103	0.902
	(0.381)	
Employment (1 = full time or student)	−0.519	0.595
	(0.528)	
Religious (1 = attends service once or more per week)	−0.519	0.595
	(0.412)	
Political (1 = identifies as conservative or liberal)	−0.453	0.636
	(0.461)	
Willingness to date a white person compared to willingness to date a black or white person		
Race (0 = black, 1 = white)	1.505[b]	1.524
	(0.458)	
Gender (0 = male, 1 = female)	0.421	4.502
	(0.548)	
Race[a] dater gender	−0.809	0.445
	(0.653)	
Education (1 = college or more)	0.278	1.321
	(0.296)	
Employment (1 = full time or student)	0.548	1.730
	(0.389)	
Religious (1 = attends service once or more per week)	0.142	1.152
	(0.309)	
Political (1 = identifies as conservative or liberal)	−0.222	0.801
	(0.326)	

[a]$p < .05$.
[b]$p < .001$.
Note: Compared to willingness to date a white person.

respondent chose black for a potential date but did not chose white as an option as well. The majority of black respondents chose black for a potential partner match while not choosing white for a potential date (59%). Similarly, most whites chose white for a potential partner but did not check off the option to date a black person (67%). When broken down by gender within race, 70 percent of white men chose white only (meaning no other racial group is chosen from the list), and 63 percent of white women did the same. Fifty-four percent of black men chose black only for their potential partner, with 63 percent of black women doing the same (table 2).

Based on these frequencies, multinomial logistic regression was used, which allows for the comparison of the effects of variables on three categories of the dependent variable, in this case race of a potential partner match. This model compares willingness to date a black partner compared with a white partner and willingness to choose both black and white (or the "any race" option) compared with white for partner preference. This gives the likelihood that someone with the various characteristics (black, white, male, female, etc.) would choose one of these options versus another in their potential match category. The model includes educational attainment, employment, religiosity, and identifying as political, yet the only variable that remains significant is race of the dater. Findings indicate that the effects of race mediated by gender are that black women (B = 4.720 + 0.637 = 5.357) are more likely than white women to choose to date a black potential partner than a white match. The same is true for black men (B = 4.720) compared with white men. Black women are more likely (B = 1.505 – 0.809 = 0.696) than white women to be willing to date a black person and a white person—meaning they choose both black and white as potential matches or chose the "any race" category—than to choose a white dating match. The same is true for black men (1.505) compared with white men. Although other independent variables were not significant, dater race was consistently significant for each value of the dependent variable for both the multinomial logistic coefficient and the correlation. This signifies the importance of race when choosing potential partners, even when gender, education, and other variables are taken into account.

DISCUSSION

The Internet provides an underexplored source of data and an opportunity to study partner selection when structural limitations are reduced and social networks are expanded. It allows us to examine how ideas about race shape partner selection when some of the constraints of contact are reduced. Although we are not measuring racial ideology per se, findings provide an indication of the role of race in partner selection, which is connected to dominant ideas about race or racial ideology. What is unique about this study is that those who use Internet dating are seeking to expand their own networks, whether they are looking for someone with a certain educational background, interests, income, or race. We are thus able to examine the role of race in a situation in which networks are not as limited as they are in daily "live" interaction.

Findings support that increased networks using Internet dating lead to greater opportunities to date someone of another race while also providing evidence that dominant ideology continues to limit preferred racial/ethnic groups for partner selection. Even with the limitations of contact reduced through the Internet, structure and ideology work together to influence partner choices.

The finding that 22 percent of black singles and 31 percent of white singles chose "any race" for their potential partner is surprising given the low rates of intermarriage in the United States. This finding complicates how contact and ideology operate to affect who is willing to date outside of their race. It is possible that this finding is also a representation of the young urban population sampled. The large number of white and black people willing to date outside of their race may support findings that people are more likely to date interracially because they do not view dating as the serious commitment that marriage is (Fujino 1997). Daters may also represent themselves as open to dating any race but then eliminate potential partners at a later stage of contact.

Even though these findings indicate some willingness to date someone of any race, most singles specified which races they seek in a partner, providing evidence that ideology continues to have an impact on dating preferences. Most singles were unwilling to date across the black/white divide, which can be attributed to racial ideology. In general, black people have greater contact with whites in daily lives than most whites tend to have with black people. Increased contact with whites may help explain why more black singles included white in the list of potential partners compared with white singles who included black in their list of potential match characteristics.

The racial hierarchy evident from general frequencies supports previous research regarding dominant racial ideology and the color/status hierarchy wherein whites and lighter-skinned individuals have historically been and continue to be privileged and preferred, or valued, by white daters and dominant society (Bogardus 1929; Bonilla-Silva 2002; Spickard 1989). The racial hierarchy is particularly evident in the preferences of white singles. That whites choose Asian and Latino over black for potential partners corresponds to Bonilla-Silva's (2002) theory of the triracial hierarchy, which categorizes certain groups as more or less acceptable for whites to date. Rank in the hierarchy for whites corresponds to skin color: The lighter the skin color, the more acceptable it is to date someone of another race (Bonilla-Silva 2002).

The Internet reduces structural limitations, yet ideas about race and possible positive and negative previous contact may continue to influence choices to not date across racial lines. Findings imply the possibility of two different types of networks changed through this use of technology, one in which whites expand networks to meet people outside of their race and one in which blacks use dating sites to expand networks and meet partners of the same race. Using the Internet may work to expand networks for those of minority racial/ethnic groups surrounded by whites and give racial minority men and women the opportunity to meet a partner of the same race. This complicates findings and further indicates how structure and ideology intricately operate together.

Sexualized, gendered stereotypes based on a history of oppression (i.e., slavery) also continue to influence ideology and partner choices (Moran 2001). During slavery, laws that determined a child's status according to the mother's status as free or enslaved were enacted (Hodes 1997, 1999). This enabled white men to not only maintain but also enlarge their "property" because children of black women and white men were considered slaves. White men had unsanctioned access to black enslaved women, which led to stereotypes of black women as oversexualized women or "jezebels." The stereotype of the clean, pure, frail white woman stood in direct contrast.

Another stereotype, the "mammy," developed from a strong asexual black woman who worked in the master's home, taking care of the white woman's children. The mammy was considered a "safe" black woman who did not have any needs, including those of the romantic or sexual nature. The law determining racial and slave status of children under slavery also meant that the children of white women and black men threatened the system of slavery because again status was determined by the mother. Sexualized stereotypes of black men developed that labeled black men as sexually promiscuous, hypersexualized, aggressive, and bestial, thus enabling the justification of violent penalties for black men suspected of interacting "inappropriately" with white women. Black men were labeled as dangerous and to be feared in order to keep white women from interacting with them (Hodes 1997, 1999).

More contemporary stereotypes of black women stem from historical perspectives, and may also influence partner choices, including those of the "welfare mother" and "welfare queen" (Collins 2000): "In contrast to the welfare mother who draws upon the moral capital attached to American motherhood, the welfare queen constitutes a highly materialistic, domineering, and manless working-class women" (Collins 2000, 80). These stereotypes place black women at the bottom of male dating hierarchies and may limit available choices for black women. Black women continue to face various stereotypes, including the persistent valuing of white European physical features (Collins 2000). Stereotypes help maintain contrasting images of black and white men and women and thus a constructed divide between them. These images and sexualized stereotypes, which are historically tied to oppression and slavery and more current circumstances in the United States, continue to shape relationship choices and opportunities between black and white men and women today. Each stereotype maintains a boundary across which black and white people do not interact, date, or marry.

The historical legacy of these stereotypes continues to influence and limit contemporary relationships. Yancey (2002) argued the sexual double standard that women face may result in a fear of stigma concerning promiscuity that prevents women from interracially dating. By this argument, a woman who would "date anyone" is judged negatively in our culture. Men, on the other hand, who are not subject to this double standard, may be more willing to move outside of dating norms. This argument is based on whites and is tied to power, history, and the sexualized racial stereotypes discussed earlier. Although there are similar patterns, there may be different processes shaping partner preference for white women and black women. The argument of a double standard proposed by Yancey (2002) may explain why white women are largely interested in only dating white men. However, a different process is likely affecting the choices that black women make.

The large percentage of black women who prefer to only date black men may be explained by racial ideology, which is based on a history that is very different from that of white women. Black women have been oppressed by white men, going back to slavery and Reconstruction, during which laws and social sanctions allowed white men to sexually exploit black women without consequences. According to past research, for many black women, being romantically involved with a white man is a symbol of this oppression, which may explain our findings (Collins 2000). It is also argued that black women reject interracial relationships in favor of same race relationships that will strengthen the black community and perpetuate their culture (Collins 2004). Thus the process likely differs by race within gender.

CONCLUSION

Exploring Internet dating allows for unobtrusive observations of daters in a natural environment with real-life consequences. The use of this form of technology increases the validity of findings compared with research that relies on hypothetical situations and opinion surveys. When dating via the Internet, singles use a service that automatically diminishes structural constraints and expands social networks, yet within this service, dominant ideas about race remain a prevalent factor in partner preference. Even though past contact may still shape current attitudes and ideology (Moore 2002), choices are increased. This study finds evidence that some singles take advantage of open networks of Internet dating. However, the significant role of race in determining willingness to date across racial lines indicates the continued importance of dominant ideas about race dictating same-race relationships, and this analysis provides evidence of a racial/ethnic hierarchy of people who are "acceptable" to date and to partner with and illustrates how this differs by race and particularly applies to whites. The hierarchy is also evident when looking at the multinomial logistic regression results that provide the likelihood of white men and women to be willing to date a black partner. Even when geographical and network constraints are reduced, race continues to shape racial choices in partner selection.

This research provides some support for racial ideology and social pressures differing for race and gender groups. These findings start to fill the gap of how race continues to matter in partner preference. There is a need for more research to tease out the nuanced ways in which structure and ideology work together to influence partner selection and how technology further complicates and enhances family formation processes.

This project opens a door of possibilities with Internet data and Internet dating. Internet dating sites are an unobtrusive way to examine the characteristics people value when searching for a partner. It also allows for the expansion of the concept of contact to include more than neighborhoods, workplaces, and social circles. This project focuses on the importance of interracial unions over other factors, such as age, education, class designation, and religious background. Future research should use this rich source of data to examine additional variables, focusing on the role of religion, regional differences, education, and income, and extend the study to singles seeking same-sex partners to see if there are similar or different processes taking place with these various groups and to examine interethnic dating and interracial dating that does not involve whites. This exploratory study demonstrates the vast data on partner preferences and the role of technology that is available through Internet dating sites. Additional research is needed to determine general use patterns of Internet dating by gender and age within racial/ethnic groups. Future studies should also build on this analysis and follow Internet daters through the process of dating to investigate whom people choose to make contact with through the Internet dating site, whom they actually date, and what types of relationships they develop.

NOTE

This chapter is adapted and reprinted from Kathryn A. Sweeney and Anne L. Borden, "Crossing the Line Online: Racial Preference of Internet Daters," *Marriage and Family Review* 45, no. 6 (January 2009). Reprinted by permission of the publisher, Taylor and Francis, http://www.tandf.co.uk/journals/.

REFERENCES

Aldridge, D. P. 1973. The changing nature of interracial marriage in Georgia: A research note. *Journal of Marriage and the Family* 35:641–642.

Aldridge, D. P. 1978. Interracial marriages: Empirical and theoretical considerations. *Journal of Black Studies* 8(3):355–368.

American Community Survey. 2005. Detailed tables B01001 sex by age total population, B01001A sex by age white alone, B01001B sex by age black or African American alone, S0201 selected population profile black or African American alone, S0201 selected population profile white alone. U.S. Bureau of the Census, http://factfinder .census.gov/servlet/DTSubjectShowTablesServlet?_lang=en&_ts=272975265513/.

Ataiyero, K. T., and B. M. Rubin. 2007. Interracial marriage: A cultural taboo fades. *Chicago Tribune*. Lexis-Nexus database, Racial Preference and Internet Dating 757. Downloaded by Kathryn A. Sweeney, October 21, 2009. Accessed March 6, 2008.

Billingsley, A. 1988. *Black families in white America*. New York: Simon and Schuster.

Blau, P. M., T. C. Blum, and J. E. Schwartz. 1982. Heterogeneity and intermarriage. *American Sociological Review* 47:45–62.

Bogardus, E. S. 1929. Public opinion as a social force: Race reactions. *Social Forces* 8:102–105.

Bonilla-Silva, E. 2002. We are all Americans! The Latin Americanization of racial stratification in the USA. *Race and Society* 5:3–16.

Bonilla-Silva, E. 2003. *Racism without racists: Color-blind racism and the persistence of racial inequality in the United States*. New York: Rowman & Littlefield.

Collier, J. G. 2005. The big easy: No longer a last resort for losers, internet dating is keeping the wedding bells ringing. *Calgary Herald*, E3.

Collins, P. H. 2000. *Black feminist thought* (2nd ed.). New York: Routledge.

Collins, P. H. 2004. *Black sexual politics: African Americans, gender, and the new racism.* New York: Routledge.

Cornwell, B., and D. C. Lundgren. 2001. Love on the internet: Involvement and misrepresentation in romantic relationships in cyberspace vs. real space. *Computers in Human Behavior* 17:197–211.

Du Bois, W. E. B. 2000 [1935]. Miscegenation. In *Against racism: Unpublished essays, papers, addresses 1887–1961*, by W. E. B. Du Bois, edited by Herbert Aptheker. Amherst: University of Massachusetts Press, 1985. In *Interracialism: Black-white intermarriage in American history, literature, and law*, edited by W. Sollers, 461–473. New York: Oxford University Press.

Egan, J. 2003. Love in the time of no time. *New York Times Magazine*, November 23, 66.

Farley, R. 1999. Racial issues: Recent trends in residential patterns and intermarriage. In *Diversity and its discontents: Cultural conflict and common ground in contemporary society*, edited by J. Smelser and J. C. Alexander, 85–128. Princeton: Princeton University Press.

Ferber, A. 1998. *White man falling: Race, gender, and white supremacy.* Lanham, MD: Rowman & Littlefield.

Foeman, A. K., and N. T. Nance. 1999. From miscegenation to multiculturalism: Perceptions and stages of interracial relationship development. *Journal of Black Studies* 29:540–557.

Fujino, D. C. 1997. The rates, patterns and reasons for forming heterosexual interracial dating relationships among Asian Americans. *Journal of Social and Personal Relationships* 14:809–828.

Gallagher, C. 2002. Interracial dating and marriage: Fact, fantasy and the problem of survey data. In *The quality and quantity of contact: African Americans and whites on college campuses*, edited by R. M. Moore, 240–253. Boston: University Press of America.

Granovetter, M. 1995. *Getting a job: A study of contacts and careers.* 2nd ed. Chicago: University of Chicago Press.

Hamilton, L. C. 1992. *Regression with graphics: A second course in applied statistics.* Pacific Grove, CA: Brooks/Cole.

Hardey, M. 2002. Life beyond the screen: Embodiment and identity through the internet. *Sociological Review* 50:570–585.

Harmon, A. 2003. Online dating sheds its stigma as Losers.com. *New York Times*, June 29, 1.

Heaton, T., and S. L. Albrecht. 1996. The changing pattern of interracial marriage. *Social Biology* 43:203–217.

Hodes, M. E. 1997. *White women, black men: Illicit sex in the nineteenth-century south.* New Haven, CT: Yale University Press.

Hodes, M. E., ed. 1999. *Sex, love, race: Crossing boundaries in North American history.* New York: New York University Press.

Hollander, P. 2004. The counterculture of the heart. *Society* 41:59–77.

Hooks, B. 1984. *Feminist theory: From margin to center.* Boston: South End Press.

Kalmijn, M. 1991. Status homogamy in the United States. *American Journal of Sociology* 97:496–523.

Kalmijn, M. 1993. Trends in black/white intermarriage. *Social Forces* 72:119–146.

Kalmijn, M., and H. D. Flap. 2001. Assortative meeting and mating: Unintended consequences of organized settings for partner choices. *Social Forces* 79:1289–1312.

Kennedy, R. 2003. *Interracial intimacies; sex, marriage, identity, and adoption.* New York: Pantheon Books.

Lewis, R., Jr., G. Yancey, and S. S. Bletzer. 1997. Racial and nonracial factors that influence spouse choice in black/white marriages. *Journal of Black Studies* 28:60–78.

Lobe, J. 2005. U.S.: Rise in inter-racial marriages adds color to melting pot. IPS Inter Press Service. Lexis-Nexis database. Accessed March 6, 2008.

Ludwig, J. 2004. Acceptance of interracial marriage at record high. The Gallup poll Tuesday briefing. Lexis-Nexis database. Accessed August 4, 2004.

Madden, M., and A. Lenhart. 2006. Reports: Online activities and pursuits. Pew Internet and American Life Project. http://pewinternet.org/~/media//Files/Reports/2007/PIP_Teens_Social_Media_Final.pdf.pdf/. Accessed October 24, 2011.

Marx, K. 1978 [1932]. The German ideology. In *The Marx-Engels reader*, edited by R. C. Tucker, 146–200. New York: Norton.

Merton, R. K. 2000 [1941]. Intermarriage and the social structure: Fact and theory. In *Interracialism: Black-white intermarriage in American history, literature, and law*, edited by W. Sollors, 473–492. New York: Oxford University Press.

Monahan, T. 1976. An overview of statistics on interracial marriage in the United States, with data on its extent from 1963–1970. *Journal of Marriage and the Family* 38:223–231.

Moore, R. M., III, ed. 2002. *The quality and quantity of contact: African Americans and whites on college campuses.* Boston: University Press of America.

Moran, R. F. 2001. *Interracial intimacy: The regulation of race and romance.* Chicago: University of Chicago Press.

Omi, M., and H. Winant. 1994. *Racial formations in the United States from the 1960s to the 1990s.* 2nd ed. New York: Routledge.

Orr, A. 2004. *Meeting, mating and cheating: Sex, love and the new world of online dating.* Upper Saddle River, NJ: Reuters, Prentice Hall.

Phua, V. C., and G. Kaufman. 2003. The crossroads of race and sexuality. *Journal of Family Issues* 24:981–994.

Rodriguez, Y. 2004. *Love beyond borders: Increasingly Georgians are breaking boundaries of race, culture, faith in seeking a mate.* Atlanta Journal-Constitution, February 11, IF.

Rosenblatt, P. C., T. A. Karis, and R. D. Powell. 1995. *Multiracial couples: Black and white voices.* Thousand Oaks, CA: Sage.

Sigelman, L., T. Bledsoe, S. Welch, and M. W. Combs. 1996. Making contact? Black/white social interaction in an urban setting. *American Journal of Sociology* 101:1306–1332.

South, S. J., and S. M. Messner. 1986. Structural determinants of intergroup association: Interracial marriage and crime. *American Journal of Sociology* 93:659–687.

Spickard, P. R. 1989. *Mixed blood: Intermarriage and ethnic identity in twentieth-century America.* Madison: University of Wisconsin Press.

Tomaskovic-Devey, D. 1993. *Gender and racial inequality at work: The sources and consequences of job segregation.* Ithaca, NY: ILR Press.

U.S. Census Bureau. 2000. Hispanic origin and race of coupled households: 2000. http://www.census.gov/population/cen2000/phc-t19/tab01.pdf/. Accessed March 19, 2008.

U.S. Census Bureau. 2002. Children's living arrangements and characteristics: March 2002 and earlier reports. In *Annual Demographic Supplement to the March 2002 Current Population Survey, Current Population Reports, Series: 20–547.* Washington, DC: Bureau of the Census.

U.S. Census Bureau. 2005a. Table R1204. Median age at first marriage for men: 2005, 2005 American Community Survey. http://factfinder.census.gov/servlet/GRT Table?_bm=y&-_box_head_nbr=R1204&-ds_name=ACS_2005_EST_G00_&-_lang=en&-format=US-3/. Accessed March 18, 2008.

U.S. Census Bureau. 2005b. Table R1205. Median age at first marriage for women: 2005, 2005 American Community Survey. http://factfinder.census.gov/servlet/GRTTable?_bm=y&-geo_id=01000US&-_box_head_nbr=R1205&-ds_name=ACS_2005_EST_G00_&-_lang=en&-redoLog=false&-format=US-30&-mt_name=ACS_2005_EST_G00_R1204_US30&-CONTEXT=grt/. Accessed March 18, 2008.

Williams, A. 2004. E-dating bubble springs a leak. *New York Times,* December 12, 1.

Wilson, S. B., W. B. McIntosh, and S. P. Insana. 2007. Dating across race. *Journal of Black Studies* 37:964–982.

Yancey, G. 2002. Who interracially dates: An examination of the characteristics of those who have interracially dated. *Journal of Comparative Family Studies* 33:179–190.

Yancey, G., and S. Yancey. 1998. Interracial dating: Evidence from personal advertisements. *Journal of Family Issues* 19:334–348.

Chapter 13

Woolf, Le Guin, and Winterson: Androgyny as a Literary Strategy in Twentieth-Century Women's Writing

Cristina Liquori

> For their two bodies, joined together as they were, were merged in one, with one face and form for both. As when one grafts a twig on some tree, he sees the branches grow one, and with common life come to maturity, so were these two bodies knit in close embrace: they were no longer two, nor such as to be called one, woman, and one, man. They seemed neither, and yet both.
>
> Ovid

The concept of androgyny has disrupted hegemonic understandings of sex, gender, and sexuality in literature for over two thousand years. Ovid's account of the ancient myth of Hermaphroditus in book 4 of his *Metamorphoses* is one of the first depictions of androgyny in literature. The fusion of Hermaphroditus and the female nymph in the pool creates a single body in between sexes—a state defined as intersex—also known as a hermaphrodite. Hermaphroditus is destined to an existence somewhere between male and female. By cursing the pool in which he was altered, Hermaphroditus expresses his anger and resentment at this disruptive transformation. Androgyny for him is a weakening punishment because he no longer fits the biologically understood binary; most disconcerting to him is his loss of pure masculinity. He finds nothing empowering about his androgynous state. However, two thousand years later, there is a new purpose in reexamining the meaning and function of androgyny in literature.

Androgyny can be represented in literature biologically, such as the intersex in Ovid's tale, or psychologically—in the mind and behavior of the characters. Whether it is manifested in the body or the psyche, androgyny has great potential to disrupt normative constructions of sexual identity. Rather than the binaries of male/female and masculine/feminine, the mind and body exist in a state of vacillation between the dichotomized categories. Sexual identity becomes a spectrum of signification—a continuum replaces the cultural dichotomy.

Because the normative cultural binaries of sexual identity are patriarchal, disrupting these binaries is in the interest of feminist writers. As opposed to men, who see androgyny as a weakened state tainting their masculinity, there is potential in the androgynous state for women. Disrupting hegemonic ideas of sex, gender, and sexuality is part of the feminist agenda in order to unsettle women's inferior position in the patriarchal system. To this end, three androgynous feminist texts by women writers are examined in this chapter: Virginia Woolf's *Orlando*, Ursula Le Guin's *The Left Hand of Darkness*, and Jeanette Winterson's *The PowerBook*. These texts demonstrate how androgyny can be theorized as a disruptive literary device used strategically by feminist writers to destabilize the heteronormative patriarchal constructions of sexual and gender identity and bring feminism into dialogue with the discourse of queer theory.

WOOLF, *ORLANDO*, AND FEMINISM'S FIRST WAVE

Securely situating *Orlando* within a wave of feminism is a difficult task. Virginia Woolf's relationship with feminism was as equivocal as her personal life. By the time *Orlando* was published in 1928, she had married Leonard Woolf, worked for women's suffrage in the United Kingdom, had three mental breakdowns, and was three years into her love affair with Vita Sackville-West.[1] A year later, in 1929, *A Room of One's Own* was published, which has long been associated with Western feminist issues, as has her later work, *Three Guineas*. Perhaps most striking about Woolf is the influence she has had on feminist theory despite the ambiguity and multiplicity of her ideas. There is a "complexity of Virginia Woolf's feminist positions" and thus no doubt a "flexibility with which she may be read as a feminist."[2] As Hermione Lee points out, "In the dialogue between Woolf and her readers, a great variety of Virginia Woolfs have come into being."[3] Laura Marcus acknowledges that for this reason, Woolf has become the "exemplar for any number of different forms of feminism, although the fixing of Woolf to one position rather than another is wholly counter to her strategies and perspectives."[4] Supporting this is Woolf's continued political ambivalence at a time when she was producing important scholarship on women's issues.

Woolf was educated during the vibrant and active first wave feminist movement in Britain. The main goal of this movement was to challenge officially man-
dated political inequality—hence the fight for suffrage. Woolf began to work with
the suffragists in 1909.[5] She recognized the "wrongness of the present state of
affairs" and "felt action [was] necessary."[6] She was very aware of the inequalities of
the patriarchal system, especially in the field of literature. However, for a woman
fighting for women's rights, Woolf was remarkably unenthusiastic. Laura Marcus
explains that Woolf was reluctant to participate in a political cause she felt "nonetheless impelled to support."[7] Woolf was grudgingly involved with the People's Suffrage Organization for a very brief period of time.

This is not to say Woolf did not have a significant effect on the movement, as
participation numbers reached their peak during Woolf's involvement in 1910.
She withdrew from political activism and the fight for suffrage shortly thereafter,
however, and began writing *The Voyage Out*, published in 1913. By analyzing Alex
Zwerdling's writings, Marcus realizes that "this reluctance was ... entirely consistent with her subsequent withdrawal from feminist activism.... The struggle
for women's right to vote was too narrow a cause."[8] For Woolf, there was a greater
cause for which to fight, and inequalities ran deeper than at the voting polls. Thus
Woolf's concerns about women's experiences extended far beyond the paradigms
of first wave feminism.

Some of Woolf's most important work, which was "rediscovered" by second
wave critics during the 1970s, centered on the inequality of women's expression
of sexuality. She recognized that for women, "telling the truth about sexuality ...
turns out to be still harder to accomplish. For although men have the freedom to
write about sexuality and the passions, this is severely controlled in women and
... internalized."[9] But Woolf blamed this on the patriarchal system as a whole; the
blame rested "no more upon one sex than upon the other."[10] Anyone conscious of
sex difference, including feminists, she believed, had a part in creating the inequalities for women. She goes so far as to say, "Women—but are you not sick to death
of the word?"[11] Far from "sisterly," this quotation points to her disassociation from
the greater feminist cause.

She thus proposed a concept controversial to both sexes: the androgynous
mind. Androgyny became the concept by which Woolf could position herself
between the male writers and polemic feminists of the day. Laurel Thatcher Ulrich
assesses that "Woolf's invocation of androgyny conveyed her ambivalence about
the British women's suffrage movement."[12] Woolf did not see the suffrage movement as relevant to the progress of women's expression of sexual identity, since it
did not earn them economic or social equality. In other words, women were still
not free to determine their own gender roles or habits of sexuality. Woolf saw
androgyny as a tool for addressing these inequalities in fiction and thus avoided
confining herself to the first wave feminist movement.

As Elizabeth Wright expresses, the androgynous mind has been by far the most
contentious of Woolf's ideas for feminist critics.[13] While some, such as Carolyn

Heilbrun, see it as an empowering state of equality, others, such as Julia Kristeva, see it as the loss of subjectivity or womanhood altogether. Kristeva argues that androgyny is the "absorption of the feminine by man," and that by "veiling the feminine in woman, androgyneity settles its accounts with femininity—the androgyne is a phallus disguised as a woman; not knowing the difference, he is the sliest masquerade of a liquidation of femininity."[14] But Woolf was not ignorant of her controversial proposition, nor of the other options and paths for women outside of androgynous empowerment. Woolf explains that "a thousand pens are ready to suggest what you should do and what effect you will have. My own suggestion is a little fantastic, I admit; I prefer, therefore, to put it in the form of fiction."[15] Though she is referring to *A Room of One's Own*, this passage subtly echoes her publication of *Orlando*.

In her attempt to say something truthful about sexual identity and women's issues in this context, Woolf wrote *Orlando* as a biography while utilizing androgyny as a fantastical element. She asserts that the ultimate goal of biography is to achieve a "blend of both the truth and the personality of [the] subject."[16] In creating androgyny, "fact only takes one so far, at which point one must leap into the world of vision. . . . Woolf admits the inadequacy of biographical fact when faced with visionary fantasy."[17] Louise Poresky's feminist reading of *Orlando* parallels this interplay with the shifting between a futile masculinity and a necessary femininity. Poresky observes that "not until Orlando becomes a woman can she permit full expression to her spiritual needs. As a woman, Orlando gradually loses interest in fame and vanity, the issues of the ego, and concentrates on her own integrity and spiritual development."[18] Poresky associates androgyny with the feminine and marks it as an illustrative quality for the strength and virtue found in femininity. This is an important example of how *Orlando* can be read as a feminist novel.

Situating the text within feminist movements can illuminate the previous reading of *Orlando*. Poresky's analysis comes in a publication from 1981, after the second feminist wave embraced Woolf's work. During her lifetime, and for three decades after her death in 1941, Woolf was dismissed as an aesthete.[19] Because she was categorized as a feminist and modernist writer, her fiction was explored superficially: The first feminist movement did not find value in *Orlando*. Historian Blanche Cook analyzes this neglect: "Woolf understood that freedom—personal, economic, and political—to which we aspire connects our work with passion to all our human relations. We were told, on the other hand, that she was a mad, virginal Victorian spinster-wife, precious and elitist. And so we were denied access to the most eloquent creator of a woman-loving socialist feminist vision of the early twentieth century."[20] Only recent scholarship has truly brought about a real understanding of Woolf's life and her fiction. Marcus explains that *Orlando* "has only recently become a central, and even exemplary, text for feminism and postmodernism."[21] This discrepancy can be attributed to the fact that Woolf was indeed ahead of her time and thus has more to offer the critics of today than those in early-twentieth-century England.

It is Woolf's choice to deploy androgyny strategically that separates her from her time period. Not only is she politically ambivalent, but she utilizes an ambiguous, and thus disruptive, literary device. She escapes her strict definition as a modernist and a feminist by utilizing performative identities and a "radical undermining of fixed gender identities."[22] Pamela Caughie explains that Woolf's feminism is actually "an effect of her formal experiments" rather than their cause.[23] In other words, Woolf created her fiction via experimentation with sex and sexuality, and as a result, she found a feminist mode of expression. She did not set out originally with feminist goals in mind. In this sense, Woolf can be read by feminist critics, but she will forever elude the strict definition of "feminist" because of her forays into other schools of thought. Woolf was more interested in experimenting with identity on a grander scale, and she reached far beyond the goals of her contemporary feminist movement, which were limited to political equality. Her use of androgyny in *Orlando* demonstrates not only her awareness of the need for a new empowering theory for women but also her desire to go beyond strictly feminist, women-centered issues.

LE GUIN, *THE LEFT HAND OF DARKNESS*, AND SECOND WAVE FEMINISM

Situating Ursula Le Guin within a feminist context illuminates the feminist readings of *The Left Hand of Darkness*. Le Guin bears a striking resemblance to Woolf in that she was a woman writer in a male-dominated field: science fiction in the 1960s. Le Guin also wrote during a vibrant feminist movement: the second wave in the United States. The movement became a second wave because "in the 1960s, few Americans knew anything any longer about the campaign that had culminated in the passage of the Women's Suffrage Amendment in 1920."[24] For second wave feminism, "the harried housewife" became the image to challenge, and goals focused on personal, social, and economic equality, which winning the vote did not achieve. The movement was "dedicated to raising consciousness about sexism and patriarchy."[25] Like the first wave of feminism in the United Kingdom, much of the second wave centered on empowering women in their own right. This focus on women's identity is reflected by the establishment of the National Organization for Women in 1966.[26] While the first wave sought political equality in order to empower the female identity, the goal for second wave feminists was economic and social equality for the same ends. Thus the second wave of feminism in the United States, like the first wave in the United Kingdom, was focused on sexual difference and the strength of women's identity.

What is important to note about her situation is that Le Guin was detached from the feminist movement at the time of publication for *The Left Hand of Darkness*, much like Woolf in 1928. In fact, Le Guin did not consider herself a feminist in 1969: "This was back in the sixties before I'd read any of the feminists, except for Virginia Woolf. *The Second Sex* was out, but I hadn't read it yet, and the rest of

American feminists were just writing their books. *The Left Hand of Darkness* served as my entry into these issues—issues we proto-feminists seemed to be thinking about at the same time."[27] This statement from Le Guin is striking for a number of reasons. First, we must recognize that Woolf was her only source for scholarship and fiction dealing with women's issues at this time. Le Guin admits to having read *Orlando* at a young age. Second, this passage makes it apparent that Le Guin was not influenced by the major ideas of second wave feminism of this time. She had not yet read Betty Friedan's *Feminine Mystique*, nor had she been exposed to the sexual difference theorists of the second wave movement. Woolf was her one "feminist" experience. For this reason, Le Guin is able to exceed the available paradigms of the time period while creating her androgynous text. In choosing androgyny as a literary device within her text, Le Guin resists sexual difference theory. She admits that she "dissatisf[ies] a lot of [her] feminist friends, because [she doesn't] go as far as they would like."[28] This confession emphasizes Le Guin's overall discord with the second wave feminist movement and sexual difference theorists.

Whether it was because of her reading of Woolf or her unawareness of the importance of sexual difference in feminist theory at the time, Le Guin chose to write an androgynous text. Much like Woolf, Le Guin was not trying to write a fictional manifesto for feminist modes of expression. Rather, Le Guin explained, "one of the things I was trying to do in the book was to get away from stereotyped roles of manhood and womanhood."[29] This desire, though she was not a "feminist" per se, certainly came from growing up in a patriarchal society, where stereotypes restricted her own sex; hence her desire to do away with them in her "thought-experiment."

Though it might not have been her original or sole intention, Le Guin has nonetheless made remarkable contributions to feminism with *The Left Hand of Darkness,* as her strategic androgyny disrupts normative sexual identities. Additional feminist readings of this text are similar to that of *Orlando*. Feminist critics have recognized how the text counters the binary of male and female and advocates for the "acceptance of dualities as complementaries . . . there is some truth in each, but there is no complete truth in only one."[30] This challenge directly disrupts the binary that maintains the patriarchal system, against which second wave feminists were fighting. Feminists recognized Le Guin's "daring subject matter" in *The Left Hand of Darkness* and "its intelligent concern with the psychic and sociocultural consequences of gender."[31]

Ellen Morgan also recognizes Le Guin's choice of science fiction as a powerful tool for the feminist cause itself. She assesses that "fantasy remains the primary vehicle for the depiction of women who successfully breach the barriers of sexual caste in order to achieve authenticity. So fantasies are an important kind of feminist literature."[32] It is vital to have women science fiction writers because the genre also has been used to stereotype women. Morgan advocates for the potential of the "androgynous fantasy" for feminist causes, referencing both *Orlando* and *The Left Hand of Darkness* in her analysis. She sees both of these texts as reflective of a "hunger for images of authentic female liberation."[33] Morgan sees these fantasies not as utopian but as a "rearrangement" showing how "equitable treatment for women may be fostered."[34] Morgan interprets the androgyny in these texts as deployed for purely feminist agendas.

The strength of Le Guin's text is that it is recognized by not only a female audience but also a male readership. Elizabeth Cummins notes that Craig and Diana Barrow have noted Le Guin's contribution as positing "typically biased heterosexual males as her main audience" and creating "a protagonist with whom they can identify and so have their awareness about gender identity sharpened."[35] This is vitally important because Le Guin's androgynous text allows her to reach beyond the feminist audience of her time. Much like Woolf, Le Guin was not as concerned with the current feminist movement as she was with the human sexual existence as a whole in 1969. This concern encouraged her strategic use of androgyny and contributed to her success in reaching beyond purely feminist aims.[36]

WINTERSON, *THE POWERBOOK*, AND FEMINISM'S THIRD WAVE

Situating Jeanette Winterson within third wave feminism complements the feminist readings of not only *The PowerBook* but also *Orlando* and *The Left Hand of Darkness*. Feminism has undergone much change and development over the three decades since the second wave movement in both America and Europe. Winterson began writing in the United Kingdom at the beginning of the third wave movement, publishing her first text in 1984. The third wave feminist movement is difficult to define. This is no accident, as it is deliberately broad in scope and reach. This dispersion stems, for one, from Donna Haraway's "A Manifesto for Cyborgs," in which she criticizes any theory that totalizes or makes human existence "essential."[37] In many ways, this is a direct criticism of second wave feminists who adopted the "essence" of femininity in their theories. Instead of adopting a restrictive definition, third wave feminism depends on its "position in relation to . . . socio-cultural, technological, and political climate."[38] Amber Kinser goes on to say that recent third wave feminists "practice feminism in a schizophrenic cultural milieu."[39] The heterogeneity of ideologies and praxes leads to much "pluralist thinking." This theoretical environment for feminism is the one in which Winterson writes and develops her modes of expression.

Winterson's feminism parallels that of Haraway in her recognition of the importance of technology for disrupting sexual identity. Haraway explains that "late twentieth-century machines have made thoroughly ambiguous the difference between natural and artificial, mind and body . . . and many other distinctions."[40] This technological ambiguity is clearly utilized by Winterson in *The PowerBook*. Haraway explains that new technology facilitates the creation of a "world without gender" and "suggest[s] a way out of the maze of dualism in which we have explained our bodies and our tools to ourselves."[41] Ambiguity of identity challenges patriarchal ideology, which maintains these inhibitory "dualisms" and thus fosters feminist aims of deconstructing them. For this reason, Winterson's androgynous text falls within the paradigms of third wave feminism and can be read as a feminist mode of expression.

Winterson's feminism echoes that of Woolf in many ways as well. Like Woolf, though there is a "pervasive influence of feminism" in her mode of expression, she "expects to be called simply 'a writer,' as male authors usually are."[42] Winterson also exhibits the same "reluctance to be [termed] feminist."[43] She wishes to avoid the label of "feminist writer," though she addresses many issues pertinent to the third wave of the Western feminist movement. Additionally, although she employs experimental metafiction[44] and elements of fantasy, she also evades being labeled as a "postmodernist writer."[45] Winterson successfully aligns with the paradigms of third wave feminism precisely because she refuses to be categorized. Unlike Woolf and Le Guin, Winterson fits in the wave of which she is a product. Her avoidance of categorization, evident in Woolf and Le Guin as well, is why each of their texts appeals to third wave feminist critics. For this reason, critics have read *The Power-Book* as a feminist text, despite the slippery definitions of the author.

Lucie Armitt offers an explanation of how *The PowerBook* is situated within the paradigms of third wave feminism. She acknowledges that the freedom of sexual identity in *The PowerBook*, created by strategic androgyny, correlates to the third feminist wave. Armitt asserts that "freedom is surely the watchword of feminism, but the freedom in question here is freedom *from* responsibility. In terms of feminist theory, it is Third Wave feminism that shares most common ground with this novel."[46] She follows this assessment with an analysis of the narrator's offer of "freedom just for one night" and the blurring of sexual identity from the start of the novel. In many ways, this freedom stems from the fantastical components of the novel, just as in *Orlando* and *The Left Hand of Darkness*. *The PowerBook* explores what this freedom means for the lives of women. Because of this exploration, Armitt argues that Winterson plays a "crucial role in the shaping of contemporary literary feminism."[47]

We can read *The PowerBook* via third wave feminism by examining Winterson's use of mapping and location within the text. Gavin Keulks sees these maps as a way to outline the "margins of meaning and identity."[48] For the character Ali, the locations or "web of coordinates" provides places of reference from which she then defines herself. This parallels the paradigms of third wave feminism since, as Kinser explains, identity is defined in relation to climate. In other words, identity is created in relationship to your position in the world. The narrator explains, "I cannot give my position accurately. The coordinates shift. I cannot say, 'Where,' I can only say, 'Here,' and hope to describe it to you, atom and dream."[49] This aligns with third wave feminism's belief in both freedom—an arbitrary "where"—and then individually defining the "here," or rather, her personal identity.

Situating these androgynous texts within their feminist context allows the reader to understand why androgyny is useful for women writers in particular.

Much is to be said for the power of androgyny to disrupt patriarchal ideas of sex and gender. The novels' context further reveals that these women are interested in disrupting patriarchy because of the inequalities patriarchy fosters. Women pursue this freedom by disrupting ideas of sex and gender because, as Monique Wittig argues, "difference and gender mark women only."[50] Thus strategic androgyny becomes an effective tool for literary exploration of feminist modes of expression. Cheri Register provides the best synopsis of why androgyny in literature benefits the feminist movement in particular. She explains that "once literature begins to serve as a forum, illuminating female experience, it can assist in humanizing and equilibrating the culture's value system, which has historically served predominantly male interests."[51] She believes that androgyny in literature can work to bring about "cultural androgyny." Most important, she believes, along with other feminist critics, that there must be a "female impulse in literature" in order to achieve it. In other words, women writers are the key component in achieving "cultural androgyny." This means that disruptions of sexual identity in literature can translate into the cultural world and serve for the betterment of women's situation in the patriarchal system, an idea paralleling Winterson's belief that the purpose of literature is "to open up spaces in a closed world."[52] Feminists fight against a world that has been closed to them as women. Thus we can conclude that androgyny is a device fit to "open up" new possibilities of the woman's sexual experience. The opening up of possibilities leading to fluidity of categorization is, in fact, the very aim of third wave feminism. Woolf, Le Guin, and Winterson all achieve this aim in their androgynous texts, and thus we can situate all three women authors within the paradigms of third wave feminism.

What also unites Winterson, Woolf, and Le Guin is their choice of androgyny, which suggests a broader scope of their fiction than simply "feminist writing." Just as Woolf evaded political involvement with the first wave, and Le Guin was unaware of greater feminist theory in 1969, Winterson rejects the sole label of "feminist writer." This avoidance of categorization, too, parallels third wave ideology. These running parallels with third wave feminism do not coincidentally involve a choice to write androgynous texts. However, each of these authors expresses greater interests than simply feminist modes of expression. Though it is clear that the context of each novel illuminates how it challenged patriarchy, it cannot be ignored that the deconstruction of sexual identity questions *hetero*patriarchy as well. Strategic androgyny becomes the perfect literary device at the intersection of the goals of feminism and queer theory. Each text's androgyny then illustrates the desire of each of the authors to incorporate queer theory in her feminist mode of expression.

THE QUEERNESS OF ANDROGYNOUS TEXTS

Now that each text is situated within the paradigms of third wave feminism because of their use of strategic androgyny, it is vital to explore another mode of expression that androgyny fosters: queer fiction. Because Woolf, Le Guin, and Winterson avoid being labeled as solely "feminist writers," an analysis of their texts regarding androgyny and sexual identity would not be complete without addressing the texts' inherent queerness. Queer theory can be difficult to define concisely, but in general, it is a "way to signify something strange" and "to denote one's difference, one's 'strangeness,' positively."[53] More specifically, queer theory aims to understand the significance of sexuality and gender and their impact on everyday life.[54] Nikki Sullivan explains that to "queer" something is "to make strange, to frustrate, to counteract, to delegitimize."[55]

Androgyny does indeed make strange the ideas of sex and gender. The embodied androgynous mind frustrates common conceptions of sexual identity. And androgynous texts counteract and delegitimize patriarchal literature and culture. The disruptive effects of androgyny, as illustrated earlier, parallel the exact purposes of queer theory. Lois Tyson illuminates this relationship: "Building on deconstruction's insights into human subjectivity (selfhood) as a fluid, fragmented, dynamic collectivity of possible 'selves,' queer theory defines individual sexuality as fluid, fragmented, dynamic collectivity of possible sexualities."[56]

For Tyson, queer theory recognizes the "continuum of sexual possibilities."[57] In other words, queer theory cannot be understood through the stereotypical binaries of sexual identity. This assessment most clearly draws the inherent parallel between androgyny and queerness. Androgyny becomes the ideal strategy for destroying the binary and creating a continuum of definition. To more thoroughly exhibit this correlation, it is prudent to specifically examine queer elements of each androgynous text, keeping in mind that queer theory has its roots in gay and lesbian studies. Just as feminism challenges the dominant patriarchal society, queer theory works to disrupt elements of heteronormative culture.

REREADING ORLANDO

Virginia Woolf's affair with Vita Sackville-West, to whom she dedicated *Orlando*, is a clear indication that the novel necessitates a queer reading. Additionally, elements of *A Room of One's Own* suggest Woolf's interest in queer issues. Michèle Barrett explains: "By examining *A Room of One's Own* more closely, one can also discover a hope to examine homosexual identity as well, as it has been suggested that it contains 'homoerotic' undertones. Woolf herself even suggested that for this work, she would be called a feminist and a Sapphist."[58] The passage above suggests that she intended to address the problems not only of women's sexuality and identity but also of homosexuality. Woolf was the first woman writer of the twentieth century to recognize and utilize the power of androgyny strategically in literature to incorporate elements of both issues.

Orlando perfectly exemplifies the power of androgyny to queer a text. It is most clearly illustrated soon after Orlando has undergone his/her change in sex. The narrator explains his/her feelings of previous and current love: "And as all Orlando's love had been women, now, through the culpable laggardry of the human frame to adapt itself to convention, though she herself was a woman, it was still a woman she loved; and if the consciousness of being of the same sex had any effect at all, it was to quicken and deepen those feelings which she had had as man."[59] A close reading of this passage reveals Woolf's suggestion of the relationship between androgyny and homosexuality. The passage obviously reveals the physical reality of a woman loving a woman, but the narrator suggests that neither Orlando nor the beloved has any real "consciousness" of it as a homosexual relationship. Even if they did, the narrator is implying that the queerness of the relationship only makes it more intense and poignant. Louise Poresky acknowledges that Orlando "can love another woman much better as a woman herself than as a man."[60] In many ways, this implies that Woolf saw queerness as empowering.

Poresky argues that it is not in fact the specific sexual identity of Orlando or Sasha that queers the text but, rather, their androgyny. Their homosexuality exists because of "the point of similarity between Orlando and Sasha . . . in the suggestion of seeming androgyny."[61] She believes that "as an androgyne she can love a woman without any impediment."[62] Rather than a homosexual woman being associated with masculinity, she is androgynous. This leaves the categorization of her sexuality open-ended. Woolf's androgyny, then, becomes strategic in that she queers the text, while leaving it open to interpretation, never solidifying a definite heterosexual or homosexual identity for either of these two characters.

Orlando demonstrates the power of androgyny to queer a text through not only women's sexual attraction, but men's as well. The relationship between Archduke Harry and Orlando becomes queer as the text progresses. Eventually, "the Archduchess (but she must in future be known as the Archduke) told his story—that he was a man and always had been one; that he had seen a portrait of Orlando and fallen hopelessly in love with him."[63] This passage illustrates a male homosexual attraction, both created and queered by androgyny. At this point, Orlando is now a "woman," but he/she was a man when the Archduke fell in love with him. The androgyny creates the queerness because of the potential for both Orlando and the Archduke/duchess to be either a man or woman but vacillating somewhere in between. Therefore, the definition of sexuality is just as fluid and irresolute as the sex and gender of the characters. Fluidity queers hegemonic ideas of sexuality as a binary between homosexuality and heterosexuality and even disrupts the belief that a designated sexuality must indeed exist.

Along with her reluctance to identify with the feminist movement, Woolf was ambivalent about her own sexual identity. This ambiguity is manifested in the androgyny of *Orlando*. What should also be mentioned is Woolf's desire and yet hesitation to identify as a homosexual. Her ideal "integrity" in fiction was inhibited by her reluctance to explicitly express a homosexual identity. Though ambivalence and contradiction constantly surrounded Woolf's own sexual identity, androgyny can be seen as an attempt to move toward a queer "integrity." Throughout her life she grew "less flirtatious and seductive in her writing about women."[64] Although she had the Bloomsbury Group,[65] known for pushing the boundaries of conventional sexuality, Woolf did not have a vast queer literary movement with which to identify. But just as Woolf can be read via the paradigms of third wave feminism, her fiction can now be read and enhanced by contemporary queer theory. Whether Woolf intended it or not, her text demonstrates how the theory of strategic androgyny functions for queer modes of expression.

ANOTHER LAYER OF *THE LEFT HAND OF DARKNESS*

Though she does not associate with a gay or lesbian community, Ursula Le Guin demonstrates how androgyny functions to queer science fiction. Because of her lack of awareness of the majority of feminist ideologies at the time of publication, Le Guin fearlessly addresses sexuality questions outside of women's issues. In not having to identify as a "feminist writer," "lesbian feminist" or "queer writer," Le Guin is able to manifest her ideas on gender in a fictional text that serves multiple purposes. Like Woolf, Le Guin is able to subtly question both patriarchy and heteronormative ideology. Beyond the previous feminist readings of *The Left Hand of Darkness*, an obvious queer element needs to be recognized in the analysis of the text's androgyny and construction of sexual identity.

As in *Orlando*, the characters are androgynes in *The Left Hand of Darkness*. Not only is their sex ambiguous, but that ambiguity translates into fluid sexuality as well. The androgyny in *The Left Hand of Darkness* queers the normative idea of sexual attraction. First, the concept of "kemmering" queers normal sexual practice because of its cyclic nature of latency and attraction. Kemmering disrupts the hegemonic idea that sexuality is a solid, constant element of the human existence. Instead, sexuality is not a part of sexual identity because it does not manifest in behavior or practice for the majority of one's existence. This "practical" explanation of androgyny, then, not only works to disrupt sex and gender as before but also queers the idea of sexuality in the text.

Another way Le Guin queers the text is through the creation of androgynes who feel love and affection for each other. Because of this, Gethenians all appear to be similar sexually, and their relationships suggest homosexuality. There are moments between characters that demonstrate this ambiguity. The narrator describes an encounter between Arek of Estre and Estraven: "He put out his hand and touched Estraven's hand, as if he were making certain that the frost was driven out. At the touch, though Estraven was a day or two from his kemmer, he felt the fire waken in himself. So for a while both held still, their hands touching."[66] This passage becomes resonant of homosexuality because of the pronoun use. Though they are androgynes, the use of "he" for both of these characters implies their sameness. Additionally, the fire conveys their attraction to each other. And so readers must ponder an ambiguous state of sexuality on top of the fluid state of sex and lack of gender on Gethen. The added element of homosexuality queers a text that already frustrates and makes strange all understanding of sexual identity.

Another relationship that queers the text is that between Genly Ai and Estraven. Genly Ai is the only biological male in the story, although he grows psychologically androgynous. Genly Ai also describes Estraven with some feminine characteristics, but readers know that Estraven is an androgyne. Though they never have an explicit sexual interaction, the love they feel for each other is made clear as time progresses. They make sacrifices for each other and care and work for each other, and Genly Ai feels the pain of loss when Estraven dies. Genly Ai admits that "a profound love between two people involves, after all, the power and chance of doing profound hurt. It would never have occurred to me before that night that I could hurt Estraven."[67] This passage is an important indication of the existence of passion between the two characters. It queers normative ideas of sexuality because of Estraven's androgyny and Genly Ai's biological reality. If the reader perceives Estraven as a male because of the use of the pronoun "he," the relationship could be read as homosexual. If both are seen as androgynous, the instability of sex fluidizes the conception of sexuality.

Elizabeth Cummins recognizes the love between Estraven and Genly Ai, and illustrates how androgyny queers Genly Ai's perspective on sexuality. Because Genly Ai's perception is most similar to that of human readers, their interpretation is queered as well. Cummins observes that their relationship "consists of sharing many intimacies but not that of sex."[68] Most important, she argues that Genly Ai, "in loving the androgyne, has lost the perception of his race as the 'proper' human form."[69] This assessment is important because Genly Ai's conception of humanity is queered by androgyny in the same way as the reader's perspective on sexuality.

In an interview with Jonathan White in 1994, Le Guin admitted to wishing she had explored the topic of homosexuality more in *The Left Hand of Darkness*. She admitted that "the insistence that sexual partners must be of opposite sex is naïve. It never occurred to me to explore their homosexual practices, and I regret the implication that sexuality has to be heterosexuality."[70] Though this admission might lead some people away from a queer reading of the novel, readers must give Le Guin more credit than she gives herself. If she can address feminist issues successfully and powerfully through androgyny without a true background in feminist scholarship, she can also find queer modes of expression without consciously intending to. As illustrated earlier, there are numerous ways of queering her text, and she does indeed explore the possibility of homosexuality. And so although the exact point of sexual contact between Gethenians involves the sexual organs of one male and one female, the overall androgyny of the text still works to queer the understanding of sex and sexuality.

THE POWERBOOK AND ITS OBVIOUS QUEERNESS

The queer elements in Jeanette Winterson's androgynous text are more apparent than in Woolf's or Le Guin's. But one must remember that Winterson is the only one of the three writing during the queer theory movement of the 1990s.

Winterson is also the only one of the three to produce fiction after the emergence of Judith Butler and others who contributed to queer theory. Woolf wrote in a time when homosexuality was buried, repressed, and termed "perverse" by Freud. Le Guin was writing on the cusp of homosexuality's political emergence but relatively soon after Betty Friedan's publication of *The Feminine Mystique,* which insisted on excluding lesbians from the feminist movement. As the first president of NOW, Friedan "argued that lesbian rights were not pertinent to NOW and that they would discredit the organization and movement."[71] Friedan feared that homosexuality would put the organization in "jeopardy," a view that had much to do with the cultural atmosphere in 1969. But Winterson has the advantage of writing during a period of strong queer tendencies in literature and a less suppressive environment for homosexuals. This environment, however, is obviously still not ideal, and thus Winterson still searches for new queer, as well as feminist, modes of expression.

For as much as Winterson does not wish to identify as a "feminist writer," she also avoids definition as "lesbian feminist" or "queer writer."[72] This best explains her choice of androgyny because it destabilizes heteropatriarchal ideas of sex, gender, and sexuality without assigning a sexual identity to the text's characters or, indeed, author. The fluidity of androgyny, instead, facilitates the development of multidimensional characters who serve both feminist and queer modes of expression, multiplying Winterson's categorization as a writer. Like Woolf and Le Guin, Winterson pushes the boundaries of classification that most women writers typically face. She expands the reach of her fiction via the androgynous text and integrates queer expression with feminist illustration.

Especially for the purposes of *The PowerBook,* it is important to distinguish lesbian feminism from queer theory. Sonya Andermahr makes this separation clear: "lesbian-feminist critics place the emphasis on the critique of heteropatriarchy and the privileging of lesbian bonds. . . . Critics informed by postmodern and queer theory foreground, rather, the *range* and *deconstructive potential* of sexual identities treated in Winterson's work."[73] This explains why queer theory is more applicable to these androgynous texts than lesbian feminism. The reality is that androgyny, while it can foster a critique of heteropatriarchy, primarily functions on its own "deconstructive potential of sexual identities."

Once again, *The PowerBook* exemplifies the power of androgyny to queer a text because the concepts of fluid sex and gender lead to a destabilized notion of sexuality. Again, we return to the story of Ali and the princess. The sexual encounter between them clouds any sense of a normative sexual experience; because of the androgyny involved, readers cannot label their interaction as either heterosexual or homosexual. The reader and Ali believe she is a biological girl, and the princess believes she is a man. Throughout the course of the text, Ali develops as an androgynous character. And so how do we account for his/her sexuality? Is Ali a homosexual because she "kissed her" and "it wasn't so bad"?[74] Is she straight because the princess believes it is a man making love to her? Is this even sex because it is really the tulip stem "making a bridge from [Ali's] body to hers"?[75] Winterson's goal in this scene is not to categorize either Ali or the princess, nor to limit or classify their sexuality. Rather, the scene queers the reader's conception of sexual identity altogether. The process of determining a single sexuality is frustrated, and the binary system of homosexual and heterosexual is delegitimized.

Winterson queers sexuality within the text by making ambiguous scenes of heterosexual and homosexual love. At points in the text, the reader could forget to whom the narrator is referring, and often, the reader could confuse the identity of the narrator. This queers sexuality within the text, as the elusive narrator and beloved become androgynous: They could be any sex or gender, and thus their sexual encounter could be either heterosexual or homosexual. In the story of Lancelot and Guinevere, Lancelot says, "You were unaware of me. You were sitting on a low stone beach with your hands in front of you, palms up, as though you were a book you were straining to read. Though you were all in black and I could not see your face, the arch of your back, your shoulders, your neck, made a curve I know from loving you."[76]

This passage frustrates the categorization of sexuality, for although it is a knight speaking to a princess, it is also the narrator speaking to her beloved. Readers need to remember that these stories are being produced and sent over the Internet from the narrator to the lover. In many ways, the stories become representations of their love and sexual experiences. Because the unidentifiable narrator and receiver are androgynous, as explained above, the narration queers the sexuality of the passage because its categorization is unknowable. Again, the binary categories of sexuality are delegitimized.

Jeanette Winterson is notorious for self-representation in her novels. This is another reason one cannot ignore the queer aspect of *The PowerBook*: Jeanette Winterson herself is a lesbian. But again, this is not her only concern. Just as feminism is not her only mode of expression because she is a woman, queer theory is not her only fictional paradigm. Because of this range of concerns, androgyny becomes the perfect choice of literary device. Winterson is able to not only serve feminist purposes but also queer the sexuality of her text, further pushing the destabilizing effect of androgyny on sexual identity.

STRATEGIC ANDROGYNY: CREATING A COMMON SPACE

This chapter so far has demonstrated how strategic androgyny in *Orlando*, *The Left Hand of Darkness*, and *The PowerBook* serves the needs for both feminist and queer expression of three women authors. Similarly, the chapter has explicated how androgyny became these authors' device of choice, disallowing their categorization as solely "feminists" or "queer writers." In avoiding these categorizations for themselves as women, these three writers construct a new discourse between feminism and queer theory. Above all else, their choice of androgyny both reveals and creates this integration. In many ways, the fluidity of androgyny parallels that of third wave feminism. Thus strategic androgyny becomes a new tool for creating a queer dialogue within contemporary feminist ideology.

The queer aspects of each text suggest that Woolf, Le Guin, and Winterson aimed to represent a more holistic human sexual identity, which means they all reached beyond feminist modes of expression. They wished to portray the human existence—not just the feminine existence or the queer existence, but the experience of an entire whole. Androgyny becomes the strategy for illustrating this whole. As Louise Poresky explains, "With Marmaduke, Orlando finds an ideal in human relationships because both share in an androgynous nature. Being androgynous within, neither of them suffers from the obscurity and falsity that, according to Orlando, typically separate the sexes."[77] This passage exhibits how androgyny leads to a fluid sexual identity, which then facilitates "ideal" human relationships. By incorporating both feminist and queer modes of expression via strategic androgyny, Woolf, Le Guin, and Winterson are able to represent this human ideal.

In many ways, Winterson's work is the culmination of what Woolf and Le Guin did before her. Andermahr recognizes that "while Winterson utilizes and reworks many features of the lesbian romance genre, she ultimately strives to write beyond gender *and* genre to inscribe a new discourse of sexual love capable of speaking to and about all human lovers."[78] All three of these women writers aim for a place beyond gender, and they get there by utilizing strategic androgyny. This place beyond gender allows for a text to reveal issues of both feminist and queer theory. The combination of these two movements enables the texts to represent all sexual identities that are somehow repressed or oppressed by patriarchal society, and thus these texts are able to speak of "all human lovers" and represent their experiences.

One might ask why all texts that are feminist modes of expression can not facilitate this common ground between feminism and queer theory.[79] In other words, why have other feminist texts had so little contact with queer theory? The answer relates to the theories of Luce Irigaray, Julia Kristeva, and Hélène Cixous. The triad of French feminists was particularly aware of sexual difference, as were their worldly predecessors, Betty Friedan, Simone de Beauvoir, and so on. Judith Butler observes that feminist ideas aligned with these theories do not incorporate queer theory. She explains that "those very terms, masculine and feminine, are destabilized in part through their very reappropriation in lesbian sexuality. I take it that this is one reason why sexual difference theorists resist queer theory."[80] For these "cultural feminists," Kathy Rudy notes, "queer theory prods us to question our attachment to the stable categories of men and women; from this perspective, feminism misses the mark when it relies on the very bifurcation it is trying to correct."[81] Thus one must use a new technique in order to reconcile feminism with queer theory. In order to integrate queer theory within a feminist mode of expression, the feminist author must destroy the patriarchal binary of sexual difference or, rather, expand on it. And so the theory of strategic androgyny becomes a successful method of incorporating queer textual aspects with the expression of feminist issues.

CONCLUSION

This chapter has illustrated what androgyny is, shown how it is deployed in literature, and theorized why it is a successful literary strategy in twentieth-century women's writing. It has mapped the societal understanding of androgyny from the early twentieth century, to the 1970s and Luce Irigaray, and, finally, to Judith Butler in the 1990s. It has exemplified how Woolf, as well as Ursula Le Guin and Jeanette Winterson, utilize androgyny to disrupt the hegemonic understanding of sexual and gender identity in their novels. It has demonstrated that strategic androgyny not only facilitates feminist readings of *Orlando*, *The Left Hand of Darkness*, and *The PowerBook* but also incorporates an inherent queerness that is productive of a new discourse between feminist and queer theory.

From these similarities, it becomes clear why androgyny functions as a strategy for each mode of expression, reconciling them in literary texts. Instead of reading a text via feminism *or* queer theory, androgyny justifies a queer rereading of feminist texts. Androgyny facilitates the very disruption that both feminists and queer theorists are looking for while also providing the ability to shape the individual. Strategic androgyny destabilizes the binaries without destroying a sense of identity all together. This is important to both feminists and queer theorists, as each emphasizes the necessity for identity in their political movement. But instead of binary categorization, androgyny allows identity to exist somewhere between masculine and feminine, heterosexual and homosexual. This is the freedom that third wave feminists pursue and the frustration that queer theorists celebrate.

So why does this relationship matter? What is produced by this new dialogue? What does it mean for literary theory in the future? First, this relationship facilitates a rereading of pivotal feminist texts, as reconciling queer theory with feminist texts allows for new insight along the lines of sexual identity. Because both feminism and queer theory are concerned with issues of sex, gender, and sexuality, reading a text with two lenses fully reveals the text's relevant implications. By rereading *Orlando*, *The Left Hand of Darkness*, and *The PowerBook*, we demonstrate that feminist readings of the text do not uncover all that is said about sexual identity. Rather, the inherent queerness of androgyny necessitates a queer rereading of these texts. Only then is a more holistic commentary on sexual identity within the texts created. In reconciling the two schools of thought, a more thorough analysis of each text is conducted.

Second, this relationship facilitates the creation of new value in old texts. Though the analysis was conducted chronologically, each text can be considered contemporary and relevant. *Orlando* once again enters modern discourse, as its fluidity aligns with many of the paradigms of the third wave. *The Left Hand of Darkness* can be also read as a third wave feminist text, as it too promotes freedom from totalizing sexual identity. And *The PowerBook* is very much the epitome of the third wave in which it was written. Additionally, each of these texts can be reread for their queerness. What this does is reconcile old texts with new criticism and erases the distance between the texts and theories that chronology seems to create.

And finally, this relationship creates a new sense of the value of androgyny. Its ability to create dialogue between two theories that are concerned with sexual identity validates its use as a literary device. Recognizing the power of androgyny to more fully illustrate the human sexual existence allows readers to reevaluate androgynous texts of the past while creating possibilities for androgynous works in the future. Rereading texts of the past assures that previous feminist and queer work is not lost in the progression forward and not limited by their context. The creation of new androgynous works will further push the possibilities of how hegemonic patriarchal ideas and heteronormative binaries can be disrupted in literature. The potential of strategic androgyny to become a widely used literary device is great, especially for those looking to further reconcile feminist and queer theory.

Of course, there are still a number of questions to pose at the conclusion of this chapter. How can this be practically applied to the real world? Is Cheri Register's proposition of "cultural androgyny" possible? My answer is that though Western culture is steeped in operating via binary oppositions, androgynous literature can contribute to the awareness of unstable sex, gender, and sexuality categories. Literature deploying strategic androgyny can make readers question their conventional assumptions about sexual identity and how they construct it for themselves and others. Awareness is the first step for change. And so, although total "cultural androgyny" may not be an immediate possibility, greater awareness of the instability of sexual identity can foster productive and beneficial questions of the traditional conventions of sex and sexuality.

The last questions I will pose are not so easily answered. Who will write the next monumental androgynous texts? Where will androgyny take feminism and queer theory? Or, maybe, where will feminism and queer theory take androgyny? Will this dialogue between the two theories continue? What can this discourse do to create a greater concern with sexual identity? What other cultural effects will stem from strategic androgyny in literature? What other texts can be reread via strategic androgyny? Can more relationships between contemporary and past texts be fostered via androgyny? These are questions that only future research and the progression of time will answer.

NOTES

1. Sue Roe and Susan Sellers, Chronology, in *The Cambridge companion to Virginia Woolf*, ed. Sue Roe and Susan Sellers (Cambridge: Cambridge University Press, 2000), xx–xxii.

2. Sue Roe and Susan Sellers, preface to *The Cambridge companion to Virginia Woolf*, ed. Sue Roe and Susan Sellers (Cambridge: Cambridge University Press, 2000), xv.

3. Hermione Lee, Virginia Woolf's essays, in *The Cambridge companion to Virginia Woolf*, ed. Sue Roe and Susan Sellers (Cambridge: Cambridge University Press, 2000), 91.

4. Laura Marcus, *Virginia Woolf* (London: Northcote House Publishers, 2004), 239.

5. Roe and Sellers, Chronology, xx.

6. Marcus, *Virginia Woolf,* 211.

7. Ibid.

8. Ibid.

9. Michèle Barrett, *Virginia Woolf: Women and writing*, comp., ed., and introduced by Michèle Barrett (New York: Harcourt Brace Jovanovitch, 1979), xvi.

10. Ibid., 93.

11. Ibid., 100.

12. Laurel Thatcher Ulrich, *Well-behaved women seldom make history* (New York: Random House Digital, 2008), 33.

13. Elizabeth Wright, Re-evaluating Woolf's androgynous mind.

14. Julia Kristeva, *Tales of love*, trans. Leon S. Roudiez (New York: Columbia University Press, 1987), 71.

15. Virginia Woolf, *Orlando: A biography* (New York: Mariner Books, 1973), 102.

16. Louise A. Poresky, *The elusive self psyche and spirit in Virginia Woolf's novels* (London: Associated University Press, 1981), 154.

17. Ibid., 155.

18. Ibid., 159.

19. Roe and Sellers, preface, xiv.

20. Ulrich, *Well-behaved women,* 217.

21. Marcus, *Virginia Woolf,* 239–240.

22. Ibid., 240.

23. Ibid.

24. Ulrich, *Well-behaved women,* 191.

25. Inderpal Grewal, *Transnational America: Feminisms, diasporas, neoliberalisms* (Durham, NC: Duke University Press, 1987), 248.

26. Ibid., 195.

27. Larry McCaffery and Sinda Gregory, An interview with Ursula Le Guin, in *Conversations with Ursula K. Le Guin*, ed. Carl Freedman (Jackson: University of Mississippi Press, 2008), 40.

28. Ibid.

29. Irv Broughton, Interview, in *Conversations with Ursula K. Le Guin*, ed. Carl Freedman (Jackson: University of Mississippi Press, 2008), 49.

30. Elizabeth Cummins, *Understanding Ursula K. Le Guin* (Columbia: South Carolina University Press, 1990), 82.

31. Carl Freedman, introduction to *Conversations with Ursula K. Le Guin*, ed. Carl Freedman (Jackson: University of Mississippi Press, 2008), ix–xxi, xiii.

32. Ellen Morgan, The feminist novel of androgynous fantasy, *Frontiers: A Journal of Women Studies* 2, no. 3 (1977); *JSTOR*, Web, October 16, 2009.

33. Morgan, Feminist novel, 3.

34. Ibid.

35. Cummins, *Understanding Ursula K. Le Guin*, 78.

36. It is worth noting that Le Guin's feminist ideas and scholarship developed over time, much like Woolf's. Anne Aronson explores their similarities and differences in her

article Composing in a material world: Women writing in space and time, *Rhetoric Review* 17 (1999).

37. Donna Haraway, A manifesto for cyborgs, in *The Norton anthology: Theory and criticism*, ed. Vincent B. Leitch (New York: Norton, 2001), 2269–2299.

38. Amber E. Kinser, Negotiating spaces for/through third-wave feminism, *NWSA Journal* 16, no. 3 (2004): 124–153; *JSTOR*, Web, February 7, 2010.

39. Kinser, Negotiating spaces, 133.

40. Haraway, "Manifesto for cyborgs," 2272.

41. Ibid., 2299.

42. Susana Onega, *Jeanette Winterson* (Manchester: Manchester University Press, 2006), 2–3.

43. Ibid., 110.

44. Onega recognizes the postmodern obsession with "writing about writing."

45. Onega defines postmodernism because of the "self-referentiality characteristic of metafiction and the pleasure in the equivocal truths and epistemological hesitation characteristic of the fantastic with an apparently contradictory realism enhancing interest in history and in the traditional storytelling aspect of fiction" (2).

46. Lucie Armitt, *Contemporary women's fiction and the fantastic* (London: Palgrave Macmillan, 2000), 22.

47. Ibid., 25.

48. Gavin Keulks, Winterson's recent work: Navigating realism and postmodernism, in *Jeanette Winterson: A contemporary critical guide*, ed. S. Andermahr (New York: Continuum, 2007), 148.

49. Jeanette Winterson, *The powerbook* (New York: Vintage, 2001), 247.

50. Alexandra Harris, *Virginia Woolf* (London: Thames & Hudson, 2011), 145.

51. Cheri Register, American feminist literary criticism: A bibliographical introduction, in *Feminist literary theory: A reader*, ed. Mary Eagleton (Malden, MA: Blackwell, 2000), 236–241.

52. Margaret Reynolds, Interview with Jeanette Winterson, in *Jeanette Winterson: The essential guide to contemporary literature*, by Margaret Reynolds and Jonathan Noakes (London: Vintage, 2003), 11.

53. Nikki Sullivan, preface to *A critical introduction to queer theory* (New York: New York University Press, 2003), 81–97.

54. Ibid., vi.

55. Ibid.

56. Lois Tyson, Lesbian, gay, and queer criticism, in *Critical theory today* (New York: Routledge, 2006), 317–358, 335.

57. Ibid.

58. Barrett, *Virginia Woolf*, xxiii.

59. Woolf, *Orlando*, 161.

60. Poresky, *Elusive self psyche*, 173.

61. Ibid., 163.

62. Ibid., 173.

63. Woolf, *Orlando*, 179.

64. Barrett, *Virginia Woolf*, xxiv.

65. The Bloomsbury Group was a group of writers in London in the early twentieth century. The group included Woolf, John Maynard Keynes, and E. M. Forster. They all

expressed freedom from conventional ideas of sex and sexuality and were all seeped in homosexual rumors.

66. Ursula Le Guin, *The left hand of darkness*, 40th anniversary ed. (London: Little
Brown UK, 2009), 87.

67. Ibid., 174.

68. Cummins, *Understanding Ursula K. Le Guin*, 84.

69. Ibid., 87.

70. Jonathan White, Coming back from the silence, in *Conversations with Ursula K. Le
Guin*, ed. Carl Freedman (Jackson: University of Mississippi Press, 2008), 92–103, 100.

71. Megan K. Murphy, "The fire will not consume us": Exploring the link between ho-
mophobia and sexism in U.S. feminism, *Journal of Gender Studies* 15, no. 3 (2006): 209–221.

72. See Margaret Reynolds's critical overview in Margaret Reynolds and Jonathan Noakes, *Jeanette Winterson: The essential guide to contemporary literature* (London: Vintage,
2003), 157.

73. Sonya Andermahr, Introduction: Winterson and her critics, in *Jeanette Winterson: A
contemporary critical guide*, ed. Sonya Andermahr (London: Continuum International,
2007), 1–13.

74. Winterson, *The powerbook*, 23.

75. Ibid., 25.

76. Ibid., 83.

77. Poresky, *Elusive self psyche*, 177.

78. Andermahr, Introduction, 9.

79. Heather Love's article, Feminist criticism and queer theory, in *A history of feminist
literary criticism*, ed. G. Plain and S. Sellers (Cambridge: Cambridge University Press, 2007),
expands upon the contentious roots and overlapping ideologies of each school of thought.

80. Rosi Braidotti and Judith Butler, Feminism by any other name, *Differences: A Journal
of Feminist Cultural Studies* 6, no. 2 (1994): 27–61; *JSTOR*, Web, January 16, 2010.

81. Kathy Rudy, Queer theory and feminism, *Women's Studies* 29, no. 2 (2000): 195–216;
JSTOR, Web, October 17, 2009.

Appendix:
List of Feminist Books Dealing with
Relationships for Young Readers and Teens

Michele A. Paludi

The following list of revisionist fairy tales and books for children and adolescents helps to challenge stereotypical portrayals of girls and women in relationships. This is not an exhaustive list. For additional recommendations, consult the following resources:

Amelia Bloomer Book List, http://libr.org/ftf/bloomer.html/.
Ms. Blog, http://msmagazine.com/blog/blog/2010/12/24/feminist-fairy-tales-
    for-last-minute-xmas-gifts/.
Charming Children's Books with a Feminist Message, http://www.amazon.com/
    Charming-childrens-books-feminist-message/lm/2ECG4WQCZFDAL/.

FAIRY TALES RETOLD

Title: *Cinder Edna*
Author: Ellen Jackson
Brief description: Cinder Edna is the next-door neighbor of Cinderella. She too
    lives with wicked stepsisters and a stepmother. Cinder Edna, however, meets
    a prince who shares her interests and values her for herself, not for the size
    of her feet.

Title: *Kate and the Beanstalk*
Author: Mary Pope Osborne
Brief description: Kate, not Jack, is the one who climbs the beanstalk, outwits the giant, and consequently brings home riches to her mother.

Title: *Rumpelstiltskin's Daughter*
Author: Diane Stanley
Brief description: Hope, the miller's daughter, wishes to not marry the king, who forced her to spin straw into gold. Rather, she proposes to Rumpelstiltskin, who had helped her. Hope foils the plan of the king to make her spin more gold and eventually is appointed prime minister by her public.

Title: *The Sisters Grimm: The Fairy Tale Detectives*
Author: Michael Buckley
Brief description: Two sisters discover they have descended from the Brothers Grimm. They learn that the fairy tale characters the Brothers Grimm described were real and still exist. The Sisters Grimm need to help these characters.

Title: *The Runaway Princess*
Author: Kate Coombs
Brief description: Princess Meg is fifteen years old. She is locked up in a tower because she objects to her father's plan to marry her to any prince who can accomplish three goals: defeat the kingdom's dragon, a witch, and roving bandits. Meg wants to protect the dragon, who is a baby; protect the witch, who is sympathetic; and protect the bandits, who steal from the rich to give to the poor. Meg is self-reliant and fends for herself.

Title: *Dealing with Dragons*
Author: Patricia Werde
Brief description: Cimorene is a princess who chooses not to drop all the hobbies she loves in order to be schooled to be a "proper" young lady. Cimorene seeks to be captured by a dragon, and she tries to convince the prince not to rescue her.

FICTION

TITLE	AUTHOR
Abiah Rose	Diane Browning
Girls and Not Chicks	Jacinta Brunnell and Julie Novak
Pemba Sherpa	Olga Cossi
Princess Pigtoria and the Pea	Pamela Duncan Edwards

Summer Birds: The Butterflies of Maria Merian	Margarita Engle
Stagecoach Sal	Deborah Hopkinson
Mary's Penny	Tanya Landman
The Runaway Dragon	Kate Coombs
Hawksmaid: The Untold Story of Robin Hood and Maid Marian	Kathryn Lasky
A Golden Web	Barbara Quick
Ninth Ward	Jewell Parker Rhodes
The Paper Bag Princess	Robert N. Munsch
Sleeping Ugly	Diane Stanley
Do Princesses Wear Hiking Boots?	Carmela LaVigna Coyle
Princess Smartypants	Babette Cole
Claydon Was a Clingy Child	Cressida Cowell
Too Many Princes	Valerie Sekula
Tough Princess	Martin Waddell
Clever Katya: A Fairy Tale from Old Russia	Mary Hoffman
The Princess Knight	Cornelia Funke
The Brave Little Seamstress	Mary Pope Osborne
Skateboard Mom	Barbara Odanaka
Girls Are Not Chicks Coloring Book	Jacinta Bunnell and Julie Novak
Girls Think of Everything: Stories of Ingenious Inventions by Women	Catherine Thimmesh
Call Me Madame President	Sue Pyatt

NONFICTION

She Sang Promise: The Story of Betty Mae Jumper, Seminole Tribal Leader	Jan Godown Annino
Soar, Elinor!	Tami Lewis Brown
Emma's Poem	Linda Glaser
Seeds of Change	Jen Cullerton Johnson
Mama Miti	Donna Jo Napoli
Sojourner Truth's Stem-Stomp-Stride	Andrea Davis Pinkney and Brian Pinkney
Fearless: The True Story of Racing Legend Louise Smith	Barbara Rosenstock
She Loved Baseball: The Effa Manley Story	Audrey Vernick
Sonia Sotomayor: A Judge Grows in Brooklyn	Johan Winter
Fearless Female Journalists	Joy Crysdale
The Cowgirl: Hats Off to American Women of the West	Holly George-Warren

Clara Barton: Civil War Hero and American Red Cross Founder	Susan E. Hamen
Lest We Forget: A Salute to the Women Who Entered Corporate America Without a Road Map	Louise Rothery
Curveball: The Remarkable Story of Toni Stone, the First Woman to Play Professional Baseball in the Negro League	Martha Ackmann
Women Aviators: From Amelia Earhart to Sally Ride, Making History in Air and Space	Bernard Marck

About the Editor and Contributors

EDITOR

MICHELE A. PALUDI, PhD, is the series editor for Women's Psychology and for Women and Careers in Management for Praeger. She is the author/editor of 37 college textbooks and more than 170 scholarly articles and conference presentations on sexual harassment, campus violence, psychology of women, gender, and discrimination. Her book *Ivory Power: Sexual Harassment on Campus* (1990, SUNY Press) received the 1992 Myers Center Award for Outstanding Book on Human Rights in the United States. Paludi served as Chair of the U.S. Department of Education's Subpanel on the Prevention of Violence, Sexual Harassment, and Alcohol and Other Drug Problems in Higher Education. She was one of six scholars in the United States to be selected for this subpanel. She also was a consultant to and a member of former New York governor Mario Cuomo's Task Force on Sexual Harassment.

Paludi serves as an expert witness for court proceedings and administrative hearings on sexual harassment. She has had extensive experience in conducting training programs and investigations of sexual harassment and other Equal Employment Opportunity issues for businesses and educational institutions. In addition, she has held faculty positions at Franklin and Marshall College, Kent State University, Hunter College, Union College, and Union Graduate College, where she directs the human resource management certificate program. She is on the faculty in the School of Management. She was recently named "Woman of the Year" by the Business and Professional Women in Schenectady, New York. For the 2011–12 academic year, Dr. Paludi was the Elihu Root Peace Fund Visiting Professor in Women's Studies at Hamilton College.

CONTRIBUTORS

APRIL BLESKE-RECHEK, PhD (2001), completed her doctoral training at the University of Texas at Austin in the area of individual differences and evolutionary psychology. She then spent two years as a research associate for the Study of Mathematically Precocious Youth at Vanderbilt University. Currently she is Associate Professor of Psychology at the University of Wisconsin–Eau Claire, where she recently received the university's coveted Excellence in Teaching award. In addition to teaching courses in research methods, Dr. Bleske-Rechek leads courses in personality, behavioral genetics, and evolutionary psychology. Her research focuses on individual differences, human mating strategies, and friendship. Bleske-Rechek's research has been published in several scholarly journals, including *Psychological Science, Human Nature,* and *Personal Relationships.*

ANNE L. BORDEN is Assistant Professor of Sociology at Morehouse College. She earned her PhD in Sociology at Emory University, her MA in Sociology at the University of New Hampshire, and her BA in Anthropology/Sociology at Rhodes College. She teaches introduction to sociology, research methods, culture and society, social problems, and social media. Her research interests focus on social media, culture, religious material culture and organizations.

KATHERINE B. CARNELLEY received her BA from the University of California–Los Angeles in 1984 and her PhD in Social-Personality Psychology from the University of Massachusetts in Amherst in 1991, supervised by Paula Pietromonaco. From there she trained as a Postdoctoral Fellow at the Institute for Social Research at the University of Michigan–Ann Arbor for three years until she moved to the United Kingdom to work as a Lecturer at Cardiff University. Since the new millennium, she has been at the University of Southampton in England, where she is currently a Senior Lecturer researching close relationships. Her research interests include attachment theory and how attachment models influence the way individuals feel, think, and act in their personal relationships.

MAN CHEUNG CHUNG earned his BA in Psychology and Sociology at the University of Guelph, Canada, his PhD in Psychology at the University of Sheffield, England, and his PhD in Philosophy at the University of Durham, England. He is Professor of Psychology in the Department of Natural Science and Public Health at Zayed University in the United Arab Emirates. His main research is on posttraumatic stress disorder. He is also interested in teasing out philosophical issues in psychopathology and psychotherapy.

KATHLEEN HOLTZ DEAL, PhD, MSW, is an Associate Professor and Co-Chair of the clinical concentration at the University of Maryland–Baltimore School of Social Work. She received her MSW and PhD degrees from the Catholic University of America National Catholic School of Social Service. She teaches courses in clinical practice (MSW) and the theory and practice of social work teaching

(PhD) and develops supervisory training. For the past three years she has taught a doctoral course on clinical supervision at the Smith College School for Social Work. Her years of clinical experience consisted of conducting short- and long-term therapy with individuals, couples, and groups.

Dr. Deal has conducted longitudinal studies of MSW student development and outcome studies of the effectiveness of supervisory training models. Her most recent supervisory study tested the effects of a supervisory training program on student competencies, the relationship between students and their supervisors, and whether these factors were influenced by students' attachment styles. She is currently collaborating with Geoffrey Greif on a book that uses mixed methods to explore the nature of couples' friendships with other couples.

JACKI FITZPATRICK is an Associate Professor in the Human Development and Family Studies Department at Texas Tech University. She has been a faculty member at this university for approximately fifteen years. Fitzpatrick teaches a variety of undergraduate and graduate courses that focus on close-relationship issues. Her areas of research include romance/early marriage, social support/interference, and social experiences of undergraduate students. Fitzpatrick's prior research has been published in a variety of journals, including *Journal of Social and Personal Relationships*, *Family Relations*, *Journal of Family Communication*, *Personal Relationships*, and *Journal of Comparative Family Studies*.

WIND GOODFRIEND earned her PhD in Social Psychology from Purdue University and is now Associate Professor of Psychology at Buena Vista University. She is also the Principal Investigator for the Institute for the Prevention of Relationship Violence, an organization devoted to education and prevention of all forms of relationship abuse. Dr. Goodfriend has won several research and teaching awards, including Psychology Graduate Student of the Year at Purdue in 2003 and Faculty of the Year at BVU in 2008. Her research focuses on commitment and investments in romantic relationships, violence and abuse, gender stereotypes, heterosexism, sexual orientation, and the intersection of psychology and pop culture.

GEOFFREY L. GREIF is a Professor at the University of Maryland School of Social Work, where he has worked since 1984. He was Associate Dean from 1996 to 2007. He received his MSW from the University of Pennsylvania and his DSW from the Columbia University School of Social Work. He is the author of more than one hundred journal articles and book chapters and eleven books, including three coedited volumes. These include *When Parents Kidnap* (coauthored with Rebecca Hegar); *Single Fathers*; *Beating the Odds: Raising Academically Successful African American Males* (written with Freeman Hrabowski and Ken Maton); *Overcoming the Odds: Raising Academically Successful African American Young Women* (written with Hrabowski, Maton, and Monica Greene); and *Group Work with Populations at Risk* (coedited with Paul Ephross). *Buddy System: Understanding Male Friendships* was recently published.

Greif and Kathleen Holtz Deal are currently writing a book on couples and their friendships with other couples. In 2001, Greif chaired Governor Parris Glendening's commission to study sexual orientation discrimination in Maryland. He is a member of various community-based boards, including WYPR, the Baltimore National Public Radio station, the Open Society Institute Leadership Council, and the Board of Social Work Examiners in Maryland. His current research, teaching, and practice interests include child abduction, family therapy, parenting issues, and adult friendships. In 2007, he received the Educator of the Year award from the Maryland chapter of NASW (National Association of Social Workers), and he received the Board of Regents' Excellence in Teaching Award in 2010. He is the father of two and is married to Maureen Lefton-Greif, PhD, Associate Professor at Johns Hopkins University School of Medicine.

ERICA G. HEPPER is a postdoctoral Research and Teaching Fellow at the Centre for Research on Self and Identity, University of Southampton, England, where she obtained her PhD in 2007. Her research focuses on the interplay among the individual self, the relational self, and relationship partners from a social and personality psychology perspective. For example, she studies the way individual differences in attachment style moderate the regulation of the self and interpersonal distance. She also examines self-related emotions and motivation, including the social and relational contexts in which they operate and the individual differences that moderate them. She has published research on attachment, close relationships, and self motives in international social psychological journals.

BJARNE M. HOLMES is Program Director for Psychology and an Associate Professor at Champlain College in Burlington, Vermont. Prior to this he was Director of the Family and Personal Relationships Lab at Heriot-Watt University in Edinburgh, Scotland. He has a PhD in social psychology from the University of Massachusetts Amherst and did further postdoctoral training in developmental psychology at Harvard University. His primary scholarship focuses on understanding how the beliefs we hold about relationships both bias how we interpret social information and influence our behavior. He studies this both within the context of parent/child relationships and within adult romantic relationships. Holmes is an Associate Editor for the *Journal of Social and Personal Relationships* and creator and producer of *Relationship Matters*, the journal's podcast series.

JENNIFER F. HSIA received her bachelor's degree in Biological Sciences from the University of California at Irvine and a master's degree in Biological Sciences from the University of Notre Dame. She is currently a graduate student in the Clinical Psychology Training Program at the University of South Dakota, where she studies relations, coping, and cultural values in farm families.

LAURA J. HUNT received her PhD in Clinical Psychology from the University of Plymouth, England, in 2010. With previous training in forensic psychology and counseling, she is a clinical psychologist currently working in a medium-secure forensic service for the Devon Partnership NHS Trust.

KIMBERLY R. JOHNSON completed her BSc in Applied Psychology in 2007 at Heriot-Watt University, where she is currently working toward her PhD. Her studies focus on adult attachment, social comparison, and subjective well-being, but other research interests include media effects and viewer romantic relationship cognitions, media uses and gratifications, and mood management.

NIELI LANGER received her master's degree in Gerontology from the College of New Rochelle in New York (1985) and PhD in Social Welfare (gerontology concentration) from Fordham University in New York (1989). From 1989 to 1994, she taught social work and gerontology at Our Lady of the Lake University in Texas and then chaired the Division of Gerontology at the University of the Incarnate Word (1995–99) in San Antonio. Since her return to New York, Langer has mentored in the doctoral program of Walden University, has been Adjunct Professor at Fordham University, and has taught in the graduate division of CNR since 2001. Langer has authored three books in adult education and gerontology and more than fifty peer-reviewed and invited articles and chapters. She is a tenured full Professor at the College of New Rochelle.

CRISTINA LIQUORI graduated from Union College in Schenectady, New York, where she completed a dual degree in English and Spanish, focusing on women in literature. She was also a member of the varsity volleyball team at Union for four years. Currently, Liquori is pursuing an MBA at Union Graduate College, where she is specializing in marketing.

WILLIAM E. SCHWEINLE received his doctorate in 2002 from the University of Texas at Arlington, majoring in Social and Quantitative Psychology. He received postdoctoral training in quantitative psychology at the University of Missouri–Columbia. Schweinle has studied men's maltreatment of women for fourteen years and has published several articles and book chapters on the subject of abusive men's social cognition. He is currently Assistant Professor of Biostatistics in the University of South Dakota School of Health Sciences.

STEPHEN SHAROT is Professor of Sociology in the Department of Sociology and Anthropology, Ben-Gurion University of the Negev. He is the author of five books and numerous articles in the sociology of religion, especially Judaism. His most recent book is *Comparative Perspectives on Judaisms and Jewish Identities* (Wayne University Press, 2011). In recent years he has researched the representations of class with particular emphasis on cross-class romances in American films. He has published two articles in this area: "Class Rise as a Reward for Disinterested Love: Cross-class Romance Films, 1915–1928," *Journal of Popular Culture* 43 (2010): 583–599, and "The 'New Woman,' Star Personas, and Cross-class Romance Films in 1920s America," *Journal of Gender Studies* 19 (2010): 73–86.

KATHRYN A. SWEENEY received her PhD in Sociology from Emory University. She is currently Assistant Professor of Sociology in the Behavioral Sciences Department at Purdue University Calumet. Her research looks at how societal inequities of race, class, and gender are perpetuated and challenged in relationships and institutions. Past publications focus on the nuances of white racial ideology, power and decision making in marriages, racialized responses to Hurricane Katrina, and how ideas about race shape arguments used in the anti–affirmative action movement (with Belisa González). Sweeney's current projects examine the role of race in adoptive parent choices and racialized themes in children's books on adoption.

BENITA ZAHN is co-anchor at *NewsChannel 13 Live at 5 and 6* on television station WNYT. She is also the station's health reporter, covering issues including wellness, treatment breakthroughs, aging, nutrition, and the latest health-care trends. In addition, she co-produces and hosts *Health LINK*. Zahn's work has garnered her numerous awards, including being named one of the "100 Women of the Century" by the Albany-Colonie Chamber of Commerce, three Emmy nominations, a Gold Medal in the 1995 New York Festival's International Television competition for "Baby Your Baby," the Distinguished Communicator Award from American Women in Radio and Television, 1997 YMCA Citizen of the Year, the New York State Health Education Week Award, and media awards from the American Cancer Society, the American Lung Association, and the American Heart Association. Zahn has also covered numerous national political conventions, the inauguration of President Barack Obama, the aftermath of 9/11, Hurricane Katrina, and the Unabomber trial. In 2009, Zahn was awarded an MS in Bioethics at Albany Medical College.

Index

Abelman, R., 94, 101
Afifi, W. A., 36, 39
Agnew, C. R., 22, 31, 77, 81, 84, 86
Ahmetoglu, G., 17
Ainsworth, M. D. S., 135, 147
Andermahr, Sonya, 188, 190
androgyny, 175–176, 191–192
   "cultural androgyny," 183, 192
   fluidity of, 188, 190
   power of androgyny to queer a text,
      184–185
   and queer fiction, 183–184
   strategic androgyny, 189–191
   usefulness and power of androgyny,
      182–183
   in the work of Jeanette Winterson,
      181–183
   in the work of Ursula Le Guin,
      180–181
   in the work of Virginia Woolf, 177–179
Ansfield, M., 83, 85
anxiety
   and attachment differences in the self
      system, 138–139
   consequences for romantic relationships,
      140–141
Asada, K., 84, 86

attachment, and romantic relationships,
   133–154
   attachment differences in views of
      others, 142–144
   consequences for romantic relationships,
      144–145
attachment theory, 134–136
Aust, C. F., 97, 100
avoidance
   avoidance and attachment differences in
      the self system, 139–140
   conclusions and future research direc-
      tions, 147
   consequences for romantic relationship,
      141–142
   implications and applications for,
      145–146
   model of others, 142
   model of self, 137
   security and attachment differences in
      the self system, 138

Babchuk, N., 21, 31
Baran, S. J., 94, 99
Barrett, L. Feldman, 141, 153
Barrett, Michèle, 184
Barrow, Craig, 181

Barrow, Diana, 181
Bem, S. L., 69, 70
Bercovici, J., 79
Berry, S. H., 92, 103
Blair, K., 75, 84
Blehar, M. C., 135, 147
Bloomsbury Group, 186, 194–195n65
Boden, J., 83, 85
Boldry, J., 140, 141, 148
Borzumato-Gainey, C., 30, 31
Bowlby, J., 134, 148
Brown, E., 80, 84
Busselle, R. W., 95, 101
Butler, A. C.,145, 150
Butler, Judith, 188, 190

Campbell, L., 140, 141, 148
Carnelley, K. B., 142, 151
Caughie, Pamela, 179
Chang, I. C., 91, 103
Cixous, Hélène, 190
Collins, R. L., 92, 103
Cook, Blanche, 178
Copeland, A., 77, 85
cross-class romance films (1915–1939),
    and disinterested love, 43–58
    Baby Face (1933), 53
    Bed of Roses (1933), 48, 54
    Bought (1931), 48
    characteristics of, 44
    Child of Manhattan (1933), 50
    and class upgrades through marriage, 56
    conclusions concerning, 55–57
    A Coney Island Princess (1916), 49
    consumerism and romance in, 47–48
    disinterested love in, 44–46
    The Duchess of Doubt (1917), 51
    The Easiest Way (1931), 53
    estimate of the numbers of, 43
Cummins, Elizabeth, 181, 187

D'Alessio, D., 94, 95, 100, 101
Davis, K., 75, 85
de Beauvoir, Simone, 190
Deci, E. L., 138, 149
DeFronzo, R., 145, 150

Degges-White, S., 30, 31
DePaulo, B., 83, 85
deVries, B., 22, 32
Drigotas, S. M., 22, 31, 77, 84
Driscoll, R., 75, 85
Dworkin, S. L., 68, 69, 70

Eggermont, S., 93, 100
Eidelson, R. J., 93, 96, 100
Elliott, M., 92, 103
Ellis, Havelock, 59–60, 69
Ellison, C. G., 22, 31
Ellison, C. V., 22, 31
Epstein, N., 93, 96, 100

Farrow, S., 68, 70
Faulkner, S. L., 36, 39
Feeney, J. A., 142, 150
Felmlee, D., 75, 87
The Feminine Mystique (Friedan), 180,
    188
femininity, 181
feminism
    and dualisms, 181–82
    first-wave, 179
    and queer theory, 189–191
    second-wave, 179, 181
    third-wave, 181, 182, 183, 191–192
Ferris, A. L., 95, 100
Fifth Avenue Girl (1939), 55
Finn, S., 96, 100
Friedan, Betty, 180, 188, 190

Gagnon, J., 60
Gambling Lady (1934), 50
The Gay Deception (1935), 51
    gender inequality and ability in, 46–47
Gerbner, G., 90, 100
Gibson, R., 97, 100
The Gilded Lady (1935), 48
The Girl Who Wouldn't Work (1925), 49
Girls About Town (1931), 54
Gold Diggers of 1933 (1933), 54
Gore, M. B., 96, 100
Granello, D. H., 93, 101
The Greeks Had a Word for Them (1932), 54

Greenberg, B. S., 94, 95, 100, 101
Gross, L., 90, 100

Haddock, S. A., 96, 104
Hammond, D., 12, 14
Hands Across the Table (1935), 48
Hansen, C. H., 92, 101
Hansen, R. D., 92, 101
Haraway, Donna, 181
Hard to Get (1938), 51
Hazan, C., 135, 151, 134, 135
Hebrew Home for the Aged, Riverdale,
    New York, 13
Heilbrun, Carolyn, 177–178
Heintz-Knowles, K. E., 95, 101
Hepper, E. G., 142, 151
Her Social Value (1921), 49
Hermaphroditus, 175–176
Hogarth, H. A., 142, 151
Holmberg, D., 75, 84
Holmes, B. M., 93, 94, 96, 101, 102
Holmes, J. G., 146, 152
Home (1919), 48
Honor Among Lovers (1931), 48
The Hot Heiress (1931), 49
Hughes, M., 84, 86
Human Sexualities (Gagnon), 60
Hunt-Carter, E., 94, 103, 105

If You Could Only Cook (1936), 51
Impett, E. A., 141, 151
Irigaray, Luce, 190

Jacobs, L., 53, 55, 57
Johnson, K. R., 93, 94, 96, 101, 102

Kanouse, D. E., 92, 103
Kao G., 80, 87
Kaplan, D. L., 36, 40
Kashy, D. A., 140, 141, 148
Katz, J., 68, 70
Kept Husbands (1931), 49
Keulks, Gavin, 182
Keys, C. B., 36, 40
Kim, J., 98, 102
Kinsey, Alfred, 66

Kirby, M., 94, 102
Kirkendol, S., 83, 85
Knobloch, S., 97, 98, 102
Kristeva, Julia, 190
Kroger, L., 91, 93, 94, 104

Ladies of Leisure (1930), 50
Lansford, J. E., 22, 32
Laws, J. L., 61, 67, 70
Le Guin, Ursula, 176, 183, 188, 190, 191
    as a feminist, 179–180
    resemblance to Woolf as a writer in a
        male-dominated field, 179
    use of science fiction and fantasy by in
        the feminist cause, 180–181
The Left Hand of Darkness (Le Guin), 176,
    182, 189, 191–192
    as an androgynous text, 180–181, 186
    and the queering of science fiction,
        186–187
Lehmiller, J., 81, 86
Lewandowski, L., 94, 103, 105
Liebler, C. A., 22, 32
Lipetz, M., 83, 85
A Little Sister of Everybody (1918), 50
Love, G., 94, 102
love, 1–2
    eight types of, 16
Love in the Time of Cholera (Márquez), 6
Loving, T. J., 22, 31, 77, 84
Lowry, D. T., 94, 102, 103
Luckiest Girl in the World, The (1936), 51
Lund, L. A., 96, 104
Lynch, T. J., 94, 103, 105

Maharaj, A., 80, 84
The Maid's Night Out (1938), 51, 52
male/female and masculine/feminine
    binaries, 176
A Man of Sentiment (1933), 51
"A Manifesto for Cyborgs" (Haraway),
    181
Marcus, Laura, 178
Marigold, D. C., 146, 152
Martino, S. C., R. L. Collins, 92, 103
May, Lary, 43, 58

McCarthy, B., 8–9, 14
McCarthy, E., 8–9, 14
media and relationships, 89–105
  content analysis, 94–96
  cultivation theory, 90, 91
  dysfunctional relationship beliefs, 93
  genre-specific viewing, 93
  intentions and, 92
  learning and, 91
  media effects, 89–91
  mood management, 96–98
  music, 97–98
  priming theory, 90
  relationships and the media, 92–94
  romantic relationship ideas, 93–94,
    95–96
  sexual expectations, 91–92
  sexual media and relationship presenta-
    tions, 91–92
  soap opera programming, 95
  social comparison, 94
  use and gratification, 96–97
Metamorphoses (Ovid), 175
Miss Nobody (1926), 51
moral ambivalence, 53
Morrison, C., 94, 193
Morrison, K., 84, 86
Morgan, Ellen, 180–181
Morgan, M., 90, 100
motifs in cross-class romance films,
  48–52
My Best Girl (1927), 49

Nabi, R. L., 93, 104
National Organization for Women (NOW),
  179
National Social Life, Health and Aging
  Project (NSHAP), 7
Neuendorf, K., 94, 101
nontraditional sexual paths, 59–71
  conclusions concerning, 69
  ethnic variations alternative, 65–66
  gay men, 68
  gender variations alternative, 68–69
  identity transformation, 61–64
  lesbians, 67

orientation variations alternative, 66–68
  response scale for questions related to
    sexual paths, 62 (table 1)
  stereotypical scripts, 65–66
  survey of sexual paths, 61–64
  traditional sexual script, 60–61
  views on possible sexual paths (men and
    women), 63–64 (table 2)
Norell, S., 77, 85

older adults, and sexuality
  awareness of, 3
  Baby Boomers and, 7–8
  conclusions concerning, 13
  definition of terms, 3–5
  double standard in, 6
  intimacy in the community and in long-
    term care, 11–12
  marriage and late-life sexuality, 8–9
  multiple relational dilemmas, 6
  myths concerning, 5
  physical attractiveness, 6
  religion and, 6–7
  remarriage and dating, 10–11
  sexual interaction, 5
  study results of, 7
  widowhood, 9–10
Oliver, M. B., 97, 98, 102
Olsen, B., 92, 103
O'Meara, J. D., 35, 40
Onega, Susana, 194nn44–45
opposite-sex friendships, 35–40
  potential implications of attraction in,
    38–39
  prevalence and intensity of attraction in,
    35–37
  theoretical explanations for attraction in,
    37–38
Orbuch, T., 80, 84
Orchids and Ermine (1927), 51
Orlando (Woolf), 176–179, 180, 182, 189,
  191
  as a biography, 178
  feminist readings of, 178–179
  use of androgyny in, 178–179, 184–186
O'Sullivan, L., 68, 69, 70

Oswald, R., 80, 86
Ovid, 175

Pamela or Virtue Rewarded (Richardson), 44
Panzarella, C., 145, 150
Peplau, L. A., 141, 151
Perse, E. M., 93, 103
Pietromonaco, P. R., 141, 153
platonic couple love, 19–33
    conclusion concerning, 30–31
    discussion and clinical implications, 28–30
    findings concerning, 26–28
    how couples view close couple friends, 19–20
    literature review of, 20–23
    methods of study, 23–25
    sample, 25–26
Poresky, Louise, 178, 190
Possessed (1931), 50
postmodernism, 178, 194n45
Potter, W. J., 91, 103
The PowerBook (Winterson), 176, 191
    as a feminist text, 182
    freedom of sexual identity in, 182
    queer elements in, 187–189
    technological ambiguity and the ambiguity of identity in, 181–182
    use of mapping and location in, 182
Premuzic, Chamorro T., 17
psychological definitions of love, 15–17
    Hazan and Shaver's attachment styles theory (1987), 16, 17
    Lee's styles theory (1977), 15–16, 17
    Sternberg's triangular theory (1986), 16, 17

queer theory, 184

racial preference of Internet daters, 155–174
Red Headed Woman (1932), 53
redemption, of gold diggers, 52–55
Reeder, H. M., 36, 40
Register, Cheri, 183, 192
relationship dissolution, impact on psychological distress, 107–131

attachment, impact on distress following dissolution of a romantic relationship, 118–119 (table 4)
attachment styles, 116–120
cognitive factors, 120–122
cognitive factors, impact on distress following dissolution of a romantic relationship, 121 (table 5)
coping, 123–124
coping, impact on distress following dissolution of a romantic relationship, 124 (table 7)
demographic variables, 108–111
demographic variables, impact on distress following dissolution of a romantic relationship, 109–110 (table 1)
general comments on, 124–125
initiator status, 114–116
initiator status, impact on distress following the dissolution of a romantic relationship, 115–116 (table 3)
an integrative model, 126–128
methodological issues, 125–126
personality factors, 122–123
personality factors, impact on distress following dissolution of a romantic relationship, 122 (table 6)
relationship variables, 111–114
relationship variables, impact on distress following dissolution of a romantic relationship, 112–113 (table 2)
review, 108
Rich Man, Poor Girl (1938), 49
romantic love, 1–2
A Room of One's Own, (Woolf), 176, 178, 184
Ross, R., 146, 152
Rudy, Kathy, 190
Ryan, R. M., 138, 149

Sackville-West, Vita, 176, 184
Sally in Our Alley (1916), 49
Sandefur, G. D., 22, 32
Sapolsky, B. (1982), 95, 104
Sarason, B., 75, 87
Sarason, I., 75, 87

Schnarc, D., 4, 14
Schoepflin, T., 80, 87
Schwartz, P., 61, 67, 70
Segrin, C., 93, 104
sex defined, 4
sexual aggressiveness, 57
Sexual Behavior of the Human Female
    (Kinsey), 7, 66
Sexual Behavior in the Human Male
    (Kinsey), 7, 66
sexual drive defined, 4
sexual identity, 182, 183, 188, 190, 192
sexuality defined, 4
Shapiro, J., 91, 93, 94, 104
sharing, 1
Shaver, P. R., 135, 151
Sherman, A. M., 22, 32
Signorielli, N., 90, 93, 100, 104
Silverman, L., 95, 104
Simpson. J. A., 140, 141, 148
Slatcher, R. B., 21, 32
Smith, S. L., 95, 100
Smith, S. W., 95, 100
Sprafkin, J., 95, 104
Sprecher, S., 75, 87
Stella Dallas (1937), 54
Studies in the Psychology of Sex (Havelock),
    59
support and interference from social net-
    work members, 73–88
  apathy and, 81–82
  approval, 77–78
  concluding comments, 82–84
  dimensions of social interference, 78–81
  dimensions of social support, 75–78
  dimensions of valence and degree of
      effort required for network members
      (family/friends), 82 (table 1)
  disapproval, 80–81
  disruption, 78–79
  facilitation, 76–77
  hindrance, 79–80
  promotion, 75–76
  romantic relationships, social context of,
      73–74

social support and social interference,
    74–75
Subway Susie (1926), 50
Swami, V., 17

Tamborini, R., 97, 104
Tanner, L. R., 96, 104
technology, and the disruption of sexual
    identity, 181–182
Ten Cents a Dance (1931), 48
Three Guineas (Woolf), 176
Towles, D. E., 94, 103
trust, 2
Tyson, Lois, 184

Ulrich, Laurel Thatcher, 177

Vaquera, E., 80, 87
Vial, V., 97, 104
The Voyage Out (Woolf), 177

Wakshlag, J., 97, 104
Wall, S., 135, 147
Ward, L. M., 95, 104
Waters, E., 135, 147
Westman, A. S., 94, 103, 105
Wildermuth, S., 80, 88
Winterson, Jeanette, 176, 181–183, 190, 191
  feminism of, 182, 188
  self-representation in her novels, 189
Wittig, Monique, 183
Woman's Suffrage Amendment (1920), 179
Woolf, Virginia, 176–179, 180, 181, 182,
    183, 190, 191
  affair with Vita Sackville-West, 176, 184
  ambivalence to her own sexual identity,
      185–186
  use of androgyny in her work, 177–179
Working Girls (1931), 45
Wright, Elizabeth, 177

Zeifman, D., 134, 154
Zillman, D., 92, 97, 98, 100, 105
Zimmerman, T. S., 96, 104
Zwerdling, Alex, 177